A Christian Family Guide *to the* Chronicles of Narnia

ROAR!

by Heather Kopp *with* David Kopp

Illustrations *by* Martin French

Multnomah® Publishers
Sisters, Oregon

ROAR!

published by Multnomah Publishers, Inc.

© 2005 by Heather Kopp

International Standard Book Number: 1-59052-5361

Cover and interior art by Martin French
Cover and interior design by Gearbox
Interior typeset by Katherine Lloyd, The DESK

Multnomah is a trademark of Multnomah Publishers, Inc.,
and is registered in the U.S. Patent and Trademark Office.
The colophon is a trademark of Multnomah Publishers, Inc.

Printed in the United States of America

For information:
MULTNOMAH PUBLISHERS, INC.
601 N. LARCH ⟩ SISTERS, OREGON 97759

05 06 07 08 09 10—10 9 8 7 6 5 4 3 2 1 0

DEDICATION

For Kristen Johnson Ingram

TABLE *of* CONTENTS

PART I: TELL ME MORE ABOUT *ROAR!*

PART 2: LET'S TALK ABOUT THE CHRONICLES

Book One: *The Magician's Nephew*

Part 4: Leading the Way into Narnia
Help & Inspiration for Parents

Riding the Light   372
Can a fairy tale ring so perfectly true that it prepares us to meet the Truth in person?
By Kristen Johnson Ingram

PART 5: ROAR! FACT FILES

PART ONE

Tell Me More About *Roar!*

WELCOME TO ROAR!

What looks like a book just might be a door to an extraordinary world for you and the ones you love most!

What you're holding is a celebration for Christian families of all that's magical, memorable, and enduring in the pages of C. S. Lewis's classic, *The Chronicles of Narnia*. Sure, *Roar!* looks and feels like a book, but we hope it's something more.

More, for example, like that painting of a ship in Aunt Alberta's back bedroom.

Or the train station platform in the English countryside, schoolchildren quietly waiting.

Or a door to a wardrobe.

We hope, in other words, that you'll discover *Roar!* to be a portal to Lewis's imaginary world that you and your family will want to return to countless times—and step through.

If this is your first trip to Narnia, you're about to enter one of literature's most beloved lands. *Narnia*—let the wide-eyed child inside you say it, think it, feel it. *Narnia*—a time and place apart, a world where animals talk, myths come to life, schoolkids rule as kings and queens (and do a jolly good job, mind you), and the Great Lion Aslan is Lord over all.

If you've already been to Narnia, it's never too soon or too late to return. Did you read *The Lion, the Witch and the Wardrobe* as a child and can still recall what it felt like to follow Lucy into the snowy woods? Have you stayed up late with college friends musing on metaphors like the Stone Table or Deep Magic? Then now's the perfect time to revisit the books and invite the next generation of readers along.

That's one of the great wonders of the Chronicles. For decades, people from five to ninety-five have fallen under their spell. And since it's literature that adults can enjoy as much as kids, Narnia has long been a favorite for families who love to read together.

That's where *Roar!* comes in. It's a book for the Narniac in your house (Narniac, as in—"Earthling who can't get enough of Narnia"). It's a book for grown-ups and kids who want to travel deeper into every Chronicle; who want more out of each character, story, and spiritual allusion; who like best to talk, laugh, and imagine higher up and further in…together.

We think that's what Professor Lewis would have wanted.

What You'll Find Inside

In *Part 1* you'll meet him through a kid-friendly account of his life called, "A Boy Named Jack." (Jack was the name Lewis preferred to go by among friends and family; for visiting children, it was "Uncle Jack.") Also here in *Part 1* you'll find a diagnostic profile and a creed for the terminal-and-happy-about-it Narniac.

Part 2 takes you to the heart of *Roar!*—a chapter-by-chapter family guide to all seven books called, "Let's Talk About the Chronicles." Each entry starts with a quick summary of the chapter, then follows with helpful conversation starters, "Grown-up Thoughts," quizzes, fasci-nating facts, "Wisdom for Narniacs," and occasional fun or activity features like, "'Bl-*aw*-st and Both-*uh*-ration!': How to talk—really tooowk—like a proper British schoolboy" and "Oh, I Wish I Were a Dufflepud!"

Part 3 tests your knowledge, your pride, and your patience with a ten-part Narniac Final Exam. Covering all seven books, the exam is made up of hard questions, fun riddles, and taxing brainteasers. Younger readers and lap listeners can match wits with their own version, the Final Exam for Little Ones.

In *Part 4*, parents will find a series of feature articles from various contributors that are intended to help you understand and talk about issues the stories might raise—violence, magic, and myth, for example. You'll also find inspiring essays from lifelong Narniacs who have been impacted emotionally and spiritually by the Chronicles.

Finally, *Part 5* collects files you'll come back to again and again: a glossary of difficult words; indexes of creatures, places, and Bible parallels; and a helpful chart showing what happened when in Narnia.

Use *Roar!* after your family has read the Chronicle chapter for the night. Or before. Read *Roar!* front to back, or by the time-honored "wandering but not lost" method. Read it to know where you're going, or to remember where you've been. Keep *Roar!* next to your Chronicle of the moment, or take it with you in the car. After all, in Narnia everything is permitted, and the perfect beginning is just the place you happen to be starting from now.

HOW TO READ THE CHRONICLES

Scholars and fans alike have cheerfully debated how to read the Chronicles for years. Take the issue of sequence. Fact is, most people don't start at the beginning of Narnia. Even Lewis didn't. He wrote *Lion* first, in 1950. From there, the series was published (although not written) in this order:

- *Prince Caspian*, 1951
- *The Voyage of the Dawn Treader*, 1952
- *The Silver Chair*, 1953
- *The Horse and His Boy*, 1954
- *The Magician's Nephew*, 1955
- *The Last Battle*, 1956

In 1994, the Chronicles were reissued in a new order that matched the internal chronology of the stories:

- *The Magician's Nephew*
- *The Lion, the Witch and the Wardrobe*
- *The Horse and His Boy*
- *Prince Caspian*
- *The Voyage of the* Dawn Treader
- *The Silver Chair*
- *The Last Battle*

Does the order matter? Lewis didn't feel as strongly about the issue as some of his fans, but in a 1957 letter to an American boy, he wrote: "I think I agree with your order [chronological] for reading the books more than with your mother's. The series was not planned beforehand as she thinks. When I wrote *The Lion* I did not know I was going to write any more. Then I wrote *P. Caspian* as a sequel and still didn't think there would be any more, and when I had done *The Voyage* I felt quite sure it would be the last. But I found as I was wrong. So perhaps it does not matter very much in which order anyone reads them."

But for you as storyteller and parent, how you process the stories is more important than what order you read them in. For that reason, we encourage you to use *Roar!* with these tips in mind:

1. *Keep the Story First.* Lewis wanted his fantasies read and enjoyed first as stories. Only after the literature had awakened a reader's imagination and emotions, he believed, could meaningful interpretation happen. So don't let any resource, *Roar!* included, get in the way of your family reading experience. Then use what works from the "Let's Talk About It" spreads, and forget the rest. The "What if...?" and "I wonder why...?" questions are especially

important—they encourage imaginations to wander in and out of the story, looking at it from different perspectives.

2. *Celebrate the Christian Message.* Probably about the time they're getting tucked in for the night, your children will be ready to talk about the larger meanings, biblical parallels, and life lessons inherent in the story. And as long as we respect the literary experience, Christian parents don't have to apologize for wanting to make the most of the Chronicles' gospel message. Lewis was unapologetically evangelistic in his intentions for Narnia. He wrote the stories in part because he was trying to correct a lack he'd experienced as a boy. "I thought I saw how stories of this kind could steal past a certain inhibition which had paralyzed much of my own religion in childhood," he wrote. "By casting all these things into an imaginary world, stripping them of their stained-glass and Sunday school associations, one could make them for the first time appear in their real potency."

3. *Trust That God Is at Work.* Unless you want your kids to dread story time or mistake it for Sunday school, resist the urge to moralize or press home every spiritual lesson that occurs to you. Better to invite the Holy Spirit to be on the couch or curled up in bed with you and your child as you read. Your role is to encourage, invite, facilitate what God is already accomplishing in your family. What comes into your child's spirit as a picture, as an unforgettable story, as that still small voice will by His sovereign power grow into something mightily more.

Have you heard that voice in your life? On the pages of the Chronicles? Then you know its power. And therein lies a story…

How *Roar!* Got Its Name

If you don't know this already, you'll soon find out: When Aslan roars, watch out! Things change.

In *Lion,* when he roars in anger, the White Witch runs for her life.

In *Last Battle,* Aslan's roar rouses the giant Father Time from his sleep and a timeless eternity begins.

In *Prince Caspian,* when he roars out a battle cry, well, let's see, a *lot* happens! The whole earth shakes, trees come to life and worship him, mothers press babies close to their breasts, a spontaneous romp erupts among his followers…

There's plenty more roaring in the Chronicles! But our favorite is found in *The Lion, the Witch and the Wardrobe.* It's right after Aslan's resurrection. The great Lion has been playing with Lucy and Susan, "such a romp as no one has ever had except in Narnia." After their joyful leap and tumble together, Aslan announces it's time to get down to business. "I feel I am going to roar," he warns the girls. "You had better put your fingers in your ears."

And when it came, what a roar it was! Unable to look at Aslan, the girls turn and see "all the trees in front of him bend before the blast of his roaring as grass bends in a meadow before the wind."

Aslan's roar is mighty, awe inspiring, even frightening. Those who do not love him must flee. Those who do bow. It reminds us of the exuberant, sovereign voice of God in our families—a voice that *will* find His children and bring them to Himself. Yes, He is fierce, but He is fierce on our behalf.

Do you remember what happens right after Aslan's roar in the story? The Lion turns to the girls. "We have a long journey to go," he tells them. "You must ride on me."

And he crouched down and the children climbed onto his warm, golden back, and Susan sat first, holding on tightly to his mane and Lucy sat behind holding on tightly to Susan. And with a great heave he rose underneath them and then shot off, faster than any horse could go, down hill and into the thick forest. That ride was perhaps the most wonderful thing that happened to them in Narnia.

May the Lord bless the stories of C. S. Lewis in your life as He has for so many. And may *Roar! A Christian Family Guide to the Chronicles of Narnia* be a welcome and urgent personal invitation to you and your children to climb onto the golden Lion named Jesus and hold on for the ride of your lives.

We have a long journey to go.

Heather & David Kopp

You Know You're a

25 Ways to Face the Truth

1. Someone says Lucy, you think Edmund or Susan, *not* Charlie or Snoopy.

2. You've tried at least once to plant a coin or a piece of candy…
   and come back to check your crop.

3. You don't go to the zoo to see the animals. You go to eavesdrop.

4. You knock on the front of every wardrobe—and knock on the back of them, too.

5. You've stared at paintings of sailing ships so long you've gotten seasick.

6. Upon departure, when your friends say, "Gotta go" or "See you later," you respond with, "To Narnia and the North!"

7. You've dreamed about getting tossed by a huge lion, and it was a very good dream.

8. You still jump in puddles, looking for the right one.

9. You'd never trust an ape with needle and thread.

Narniac When...

10. You can tell just by looking at them that donkeys are *genuinely* sorry.

11. You know there's no such thing as a good education that's weak on dragons.

12. You fret that one night you'll go to sleep with dragonish thoughts in your heart.

13. You practice archery, fencing, swimming, and riding...just in case.

14. You're careful to look away if a squirrel seems about to bury a nut.

15. You actually know how much a firkin of wine is.

16. On cold winter days, your thoughts turn to a hot cup of tea with Mr. Tumnus.

17. You're instinctively attracted to people with unfortunate names.

18. You know that beeches and birches are girls, and maples and oaks are boys.

19. After a warm rain, you search wet grass for circles of sleeping Dufflepuds.

20. You know how many stomachs centaurs have, and what they like to digest.

21. You have fantasized about going for a Sunday sail...underground.

22. When you're feeling down, you find that gloomy Wiggle-isms (like "Of course, every bad day comes to a worse end") cheer you up immediately.

23. You believe that all Creation resounds with a mysterious music, if people could only hear it, and the best way to describe it would be "a lion singing."

24. You're deeply reassured by the knowledge that "Wrong will be right, when Aslan comes in sight."

25. You love stories, and know that the best page of the best story is still to come.

A Boy Named Jack

How an Irish Schoolboy Grew Up to Write the Stories We Love

Once upon a time, a young boy with a very unfortunate name grew up in a big drafty house in Belfast, Northern Ireland. Clive Staples Lewis didn't like girls or cats, loved dogs and spent too much time reading under the covers at night.

One day when he was about four, Clive Staples decided to fix his unfortunate name. He suddenly announced to his family that his name was now "Jacksie." From that day on, he refused to answer when anyone called him Clive or Clive Staples or anything else.

Well, that's not quite true. His big brother, Warren, sometimes called him Smallpiggiebotham, or SPB, and Jacksie called Warren Archpiggiebotham, or APB, and it was all in fun. Jacksie and Warren were best friends.

Their mum was smart and pretty and came from a long line of preachers, debaters, and seafaring folk. Their dad was a lawyer with plenty of money but he always worried that his family was heading for the poorhouse. Still, he could tell stories like nobody's business.

The Boy Who Invented Other Worlds

Jacksie began writing before he even started school. He liked rabbits and mice and invented a make-believe world when he was five called Animal Land. Warren, at age eight, was more grown up and wrote about India and sailing ships and trains. Sometimes the brothers combined their stories and had the mice sailing ships while rabbits ruled India. For pets, the

The boarding school was shut down, and not long afterward, "Oldie" was declared insane.

boys had a dog named Tim, a white mouse named Tommy, and a canary named Peter.

Warren had to go away to school when he was ten—a horrible, cruel boarding school in England—and Jacksie missed him terribly. But he did have the run of the house now, and what a house the family lived in! It had rooms upon rooms and hallways that went everywhere and nowhere. The family employed gardeners and cooks, and Jacksie's deaf grandfather lived with them. Jacksie found a space where he could be alone by climbing high in the house and stepping rafter by rafter across the attic. He decorated with bits of old packing cases and the seats of broken kitchen chairs. There, he kept a cash box containing various treasures, a story he was writing, and usually a few apples.

Much too soon, his mother became very ill. Jacksie's house was filled with strange people rushing all about, and the smell of disinfectant was always in the air. Whenever Jacksie was taken to see his mum she lay pale and still but always smiled reassuringly. Once Jacksie had a fever and a toothache and desperately wanted his mother to comfort him, but instead, his dad came into his bedroom with some dreadful news—his mum had died.

SAILING AWAY FROM HOME

It was a terrible blow. And not long after, another one hit. His dad told Jacksie he was sending him to boarding school too. On the sailing boat heading for England, Jacksie changed his name to Jack. He was all grown up now, he announced. He was nine years old.

Boarding school for Jack meant a lot of starchy uniforms and algebra lessons and a horrible headmaster named "Oldie" who had a ghastly habit of beating students. Jack and Warren slept on springless beds and washed in cold water even in winter. To cheer themselves up, the boys made up stories about faraway places.

After a couple of years, things suddenly changed. Jack became sick and went home to have his adenoids out. The boarding school was shut down, and not long afterward, "Oldie" was declared insane. Hooray! Jack and Warren were sent to new schools—better ones this time, and closer to home.

For fun, Jack rode a bike, jogged, swam, read books, and tramped about the countryside. But most of all, he wrote. Short stories, poems, and books poured out of him. Even as a boy he knew his future must lie somewhere in the world of writing.

At fifteen, Jack went to a different school where this time bullies ran rampant. As a

Sometimes the bullies made him late for class and got him into trouble with his teachers.

younger student, Jack was forced to clean up after the older boys. Sometimes the bullies made him late for class and got him in trouble with his teachers. To escape, Jack took as many long walks as he could. A kindly teacher nicknamed "Smewgy" noticed that Jack was a good writer and encouraged him to study classic literature. Jack became good friends with a boy named Arthur Greeves who read widely, played piano, and loved the outdoors. They stayed friends their whole lives.

Jack finished high school out in the countryside with a private tutor, an old friend of his father's named Professor Kirkpatrick. The Professor was logical and brilliant and insisted Jack never talk unless he had something worth saying—an idea that Jack loved, for he hated chitchat, dancing, and social events, and much preferred to study Greek and read classic books by himself. His father wanted Jack to become a lawyer or military man, but Professor Kirk wrote the father in a letter: "Your son will either be a writer or a tutor. Don't try to make him anything else."

A World at War

World War I broke out and Warren joined the service as a British officer, but Jack wasn't old enough yet. He entered Oxford University a week before his eighteenth birthday. He began studies in winter and there was no fuel for heating because of the war. Students attended classes wearing overcoats, scarves, and gloves. Part of the college was turned into a military hospital, and student enrollment fell because so many young men were away at war.

When Jack became old enough for the army he enlisted. He trained in the freezing cold and muddy fields, and every spare moment he wrote poetry to console himself. Then he was sent to the front lines in France. On his nineteenth birthday, he fought in the Battle of the Somme. It was an awful scene. Men shot at each other day and night from muddy trenches. Cold, slimy mud seeped into boots and clothing. Enemy fire streaked in from all around. Before long, thousands of wounded and dying men covered the battlefield, and many of Jack's friends were killed.

A few months later, an exploding mortar shell wounded Jack in the arm and chest, and he was taken to a military hospital to recover.

Finally, the war ended, and Jack went back to being a student at Oxford, where he studied philosophy, literature, and ancient history. While Jack was a student, a poem of his called "Death in Battle" was published in a military magazine—his first writing ever in print.

About a month later, Jack published his first book, *Spirits in Bondage.*

One Evening, in His Study…

Jack had attended church when he was a child, but strayed from his upbringing as a teenager and young man. He said he was an atheist. Mostly, he was angry with God because his mother had died. But he loved reading and discovered that many of his favorite authors were Christians, such as John Donne, George MacDonald, and John Milton. Warren had a motorcycle then, and the brothers often zoomed around the countryside while talking about politics, faith, and God.

Jack graduated from college and became an English professor at Oxford, a position he held for the next twenty-nine years. One of the men he worked with was J. R. R. Tolkien, who later wrote the *Lord of the Rings* trilogy and other books. Jack began work on a science fiction trilogy called *Perelandra* and later a book called *The Screwtape Letters.* He formed a writing group that met every Thursday evening, the Inklings.

Jack and Warren's dad died, and when the brothers tidied up the family house to sell it, they came across a large trunk of all their childhood toys and drawings. They couldn't bear to give or throw it away, so they decided to bury all their old treasures in the family garden. A few weeks later, Jack was working in his study one evening when he became suddenly aware that God was close. He got down on his knees and prayed to accept Christ as his Savior. He was thirty-one.

Jack used his share of the money from his dad's home to buy a home in the English countryside, which he named the Kilns. It had tennis courts and a swimming pool and was surrounded by woods. He lived with a ginger cat named Tom and two dogs. For a time, Jack took care of a girl and an older woman who had lost her son in the war. The son had been a good friend of Jack's and he cared for the woman like his own mother. When Warren retired from the army at age thirty-seven, he too came to live with Jack.

Famous Author Falls in Love

Jack continued to tutor at Oxford while writing books and speaking on the radio. People loved his books and radio talks, and he became famous in England and America. When World War II broke out, the city of London was bombed, and some families decided to send their children to safe homes out in the countryside. Jack and Warren took in three children. To entertain them, Jack made up stories, which turned into *The Lion, the Witch and the Wardrobe* and, later, the Narnia series.

As an older man, Jack left Oxford to be a professor at Cambridge University and wrote several books about his life and faith, including *Surprised by Joy* and *Mere Christianity*. The books did very well, and requests to lecture poured in from all over the world.

One letter came from an American named Joy Gresham whom Jack had met several years earlier while traveling. She was also a writer, and the two became fast friends. Joy had two sons from a previous marriage, David and Douglas, and they all moved to England where Joy and Jack eventually fell in love and got married.

The couple experienced several happy months together, but soon Joy was diagnosed with cancer. She experienced ups and downs in her health, but felt pretty good for about two years. The couple even traveled to Greece for a holiday. This was one of the happiest times for Jack. But soon Joy's health declined again and she died.

Right away, Jack adopted Joy's two sons, and he and Warren raised the boys at the Kilns. But Jack missed his wife Joy terribly. He even wrote a book about his sorrow. It was called *A Grief Observed*.

Later, as his two adopted sons grew up, Jack's health began to fail too. He contracted a bone disease, grew frail, and retired from teaching. C. S. Lewis died quietly one evening while at home, a week before his sixty-fifth birthday. The date was November 22, 1963, the same day president John F. Kennedy and another famous writer, Aldous Huxley, died.

THE BEST STORY EVER

Since C. S. Lewis's death, many books have been written about "Uncle Jack." His own books and writings have become famous and are often quoted around the world. Perhaps the most famous are the seven books about Narnia that he wrote for children.

Have you read them yet?

You absolutely must if you haven't already done so. You'll find stories about a boy with an unfortunate name, sailing ships, bullies, a talking mouse, a big house in the country, and a Professor Kirk. You'll also meet a Being so wonderful you'll want to know Him forever and ever.

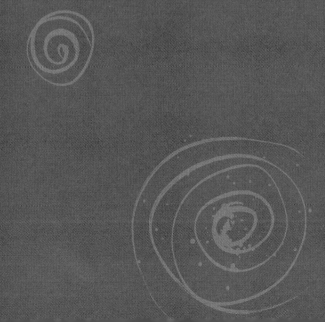

PART TWO

Let's Talk About the Chronicles

The NARNIAC'S CREED

I believe in a lion named Aslan
Who died and rose again
For a greedy child like me.

He is good but not safe,
And the more I grow,
The bigger he becomes.

At Aslan's roar, even the trees bow down.
Yet he comes to romp and play
With any who will join him.

He has another name in our world.
And by knowing him a little in Narnia,
I know him better here.

He's not a tame lion, it's true.
But when I am thirsty,
There is no other stream.

So I will take the adventure that Aslan sends,
And whether I live or die,
he will be my good lord,

Until further up and further in
I finally reach his true country
And leave the Shadowlands behind.

YOUNG NEIGHBORS Digory and Polly fall victim to a foolish uncle's experiments with magic. They're swept out of London into other worlds—first a ruined city ruled by evil Queen Jadis, and then to a dark, lifeless place. Here they watch the great Lion, Aslan, sing a new, perfect world into existence. This is enchanted Narnia, yet already sin has entered to threaten its future.

BOOK ONE

The MAGICIAN'S NEPHEW

CHAPTER 1

> *"It's all rot to say a
> house would be
> empty all those
> years unless there
> was some mystery."*
> *—Digory*

The WRONG DOOR

The Story It's a cold, wet London afternoon when Polly and Digory decide to explore the attics above their row houses. The children stumble unexpectedly into a secret study. Who greets them but Digory's very strange Uncle Andrew! He offers Polly a pretty yellow ring, and when she touches it, she disappears.

Bastables
*Children in books by
Edith Nesbit*

Blub
Cry

Buffer
A foolish old man

Cistern
A hot water tank

Coiner
*Someone who makes
counterfeit (fake) coins*

Grown-up Thoughts
Right off the bat, Lewis delivers strong opinions about grown-ups. And not very flattering ones, either. Adults are predictable, he says, not very curious, and they "come up with uninteresting explanations." It's all in fun, of course, and the author's way of siding with his readers. In this chapter, watch for themes like curiosity versus caution, trust, and the power of mystery—all great subjects to get your kids talking!

*God has chosen to make known to
[His people] the glorious riches of that
mystery…Christ is in you!*
C
OLOSSIANS 1:27,
NIRV

Scary Thoughts

Seems like the children really *want* to believe there's a creepy mystery about Uncle Andrew and the empty house. Are you ever like that?

———————

Curious and Curious-er

Would you have opened the attic door? Reached for the strange yellow ring?

———————

My Secret Place

Where is a secret place you like to hide? Describe what you feel when you're alone there.

———————

"B-b-but it's dark in here!"

Have you explored a tunnel or other dark place—or wished you could? Are you afraid of the dark?

———————

Who You Gonna Trust?

Why did Polly and Digory have a bad feeling about Uncle Andrew? How do you decide who to trust?

———————

LET'S
TALK
ABOUT
IT

WISDOM
for
NARNIACS

———

Be careful of kind uncles with mean eyes.

The Meaning of Everything

"It's a Mad World"

Digory and Polly refer to Uncle Andrew many times as "mad." In Lewis's time, "mad" didn't mean angry. It described anyone who usually behaved strangely (other words: odd, weird, crazy). Today, we'd probably describe that person as mentally ill. Of course, Uncle Andrew probably wasn't really mentally ill. Just very odd—and maybe very evil, too.

Kid Test

What's a Mystery to You?

A mystery is an interesting question or place that you'd love to know more about. Are these mysteries to you?

> *What's under my bed.*
> *What my dog is thinking right now.*
> *Why the stars disappear during the day.*
> *Jesus in my heart.*
> *What it will feel like when I'm grown up.*

CHAPTER 2

"He thinks he can do anything he likes to get anything he wants."
—Digory

DIGORY and HIS UNCLE

The Story Uncle Andrew explains to Digory how the mysterious rings work: yellow takes you out of this world, green brings you back—hopefully! Of course, Uncle Andrew can't possibly take the risk himself because he's too important. He talks Digory into it though. The boy pockets two green rings—so both children can return—and touches the yellow ring. Poof!

Charwoman
A cleaning lady

Chivalry
Ideal qualities such as bravery, courtesy, honor, and gallantry toward women

Jawing
A lot of talking

Showing the white feather
Slang for acting like a coward

Grown-up Thoughts

Children's literature is full of evil characters who pretend to care for kids but actually prey on them. "Nice" Uncle Andrew is definitely one. He's supposed to be Digory's caretaker, someone Digory can trust. Instead he manipulates and uses the children for selfish, evil purposes. What's the good of bad guys? Well-drawn evil characters in literature help kids understand what evil looks like and how to respond in real life.

Those who do wrong speak only twisted words.
PROVERBS 10:32, NIRV

LET'S TALK ABOUT IT

"Rules? What Rules?"

Uncle Andrew thinks he's much too special to have to follow rules. What's it like to be around people like that?

———————

Magic Test

In Narnia, some magic is good, some isn't. Which is Uncle's, and how do you know?

———————

My Favorite Meanies

Name some evil characters in stories you like, and what you remember about them. Did any of them turn out to be good in the end?

———————

The Case of the Disappearing Polly

How did you feel when Digory was trying to decide whether he should touch the yellow ring? Did he do the right thing?

———————

FAST FACT

———

Lewis's original title for this book was, "Polly and Digory."

The Meaning of Everything

Magic Dust

Magic in kid's stories is a special power that comes from outside a person. Lewis creates two kinds of magic at war with each other: bad magic brings evil and suffering, good magic brings joy and healing. In real life, magic is nothing to play with because its source can be the devil, never God (2 Chronicles 33:6, Galatians 5:20). For more on magic, see page 337.

Kid Test

Four Good Ways to Tell Who's Bad [They're R.A.T.S.]

1. **R**ebellious. They think r_____ apply only to other people. (How dumb is that?)

2. **A**rrogant. They're certain they're b_____ than ordinary folks. (But they're not.)

3. **T**ricky. They manipulate others and twist the f_____ to get what they w_____. (Watch out!)

4. **S**elfish (& cruel). They think only about themselves, so they don't care if they h_____ others, even a_____. (Guinea pigs unite! Down with R.A.T.S.!)

Answers on page 431

It was the quietest wood you could possibly imagine.... You could almost feel the trees drinking the water up with their roots. This wood was very much alive.

The WOOD
BETWEEN THE WORLDS

The Story ❀ Digory surfaces from a clear pool to meet up with Polly in the dreamy Wood between the Worlds. They're surrounded by other pools that seem to promise more worlds. After a practice plunge (to make sure they can get back to London), the two kids pick a new pool…and jump!

Gassing
Talking too much

Pluck
Courage and determination

Grown-up Thoughts

The Wood between the Worlds is a sort of spiritual wayside that allows the children to exercise free will. From here on out, they are not victims of Uncle Andrew but brave adventurers by choice. The Wood itself feels a little like being in the quiet presence of God—"He leads me beside quiet waters, he restores my soul" (Psalm 23:2–3). Yet we sense that we're not meant to stay in this safe, dreamy place forever. Great adventures and important accomplishments await.

LORD, you will give perfect peace to anyone who commits himself to be faithful to you. That's because he trusts in you.

ISAIAH 26:3,
NIRV

Meeting Halfway

Polly and Digory argued about what to do next in the Wood. How did they make a compromise?

_____

ZZZZzzz

What was Polly afraid would happen if they stayed in the Wood too long? Do you think she was right?

_____

Don't Forget the Bread Crumbs

What big mistake did Digory almost make?

_____

Your Turn

If you found yourself in that same Wood, what would you do? What would your best friend want to do?

_____

"Now I Remember!"

What caused the children to suddenly remember who they were and where they came from?

_____

WISDOM
for
NARNIACS

———

Explore new worlds, but don't forget the way home.

LET'S
TALK
ABOUT
IT

Narniac Attack | No. 1

[Test your knowledge on Chapters 1–3]

1. Who was still living on Baker Street in London when the story opens?

a) King Arthur
b) Obi Wan
c) Sherlock Holmes

2. What sound do the rings make in Uncle Andrew's study? They…

a) whistle like a teakettle.
b) hum like a vacuum cleaner far away.
c) ring like a bell.

3. The rings only work if they're actually touching your…

a) sister.
b) underwear.
c) skin.

4. Who gave Uncle Andrew the secret box?

a) His sister Letty
b) His fairy godmother
c) Sherlock Holmes

5. What is Uncle Andrew's last name?

a) Ketterley
b) Plummer
c) Kirke

EVERYBODY knows real Brits talk prim, proper, and precise—and most kids from North America don't!

But then again, perhaps you are an American Narniac with *pluck*. You really *do* want to sound like Digory or Polly. In that case, you should make yourself a cup of tea, purse your lips, raise your eyebrows, look *dreadfully* proper…and give it a shot.

In all of the Chronicles except *The Horse and His Boy,* English schoolchildren are central characters. And C. S. Lewis does a *splendid* job of just letting them talk (*tooowk*, actually). Lucy, Eustace, and friends use the Brit-speak common on school grounds in the 1950s. Many of the expressions are still in use today. The language of Digory and Polly in *The Magician's Nephew* (set in London, 1900) is a little more dated, but plenty of fun to imitate.

So, what do we hear when the Chronicles kids start talking?

HOW TO TALK—REALLY TOOOWK—LIKE A
PROPER BRITISH SCHOOLBOY

"Bl-*aw*-st and Both-*uh*-ration!"

Slang words

For example:

Blub. It means cry.

Jaw or *gas.* They mean talk.

Keen means *cool* as in *smart.*

Brick means a *jolly good bloke…* as long as *jolly* means very, and *bloke* means guy or girl.

Exclamations

Kids in Narnia don't ever say "Wow!" or "Dude!" They prefer genuine British outbursts like:

By gum!

Blast!

Bother!

And don't forget *Rot!*

"Turbo" words

Well, you don't want your words to just sit there like cold toast, do you? Neither do the kids in the Chronicles. So they add "turbo" words—adjectives and adverbs for extra punch. For example, if something (say, a test at school) is surprisingly difficult:

Digory might call it *most* unfair. Polly would probably call it *simply* awful, or even *frightfully horrid!* Eustace would go with *jolly rotten.*

Rawth-uh Say It Right

Of course, to talk like a British schoolkid, you need more than words. You need the right sound. Are you ready to polish your British accent?

Oh, let's! Do let's!

Here are three simple rules for instant success:

1. The "A" Rule—

"a" changes to "ah" or "aw."

Examples: Bath or half (where the "a" sounds like "at" or "cat") becomes b*aw*th or h*aw*lf.

2. The "Aw" Rule—

"aw" changes to "woow."

Examples: Walk, talk, or chalk (where "a" sounds like "ah") becomes woowlk, toowlk, or choowlk. Water becomes woowt…

But wait! Water needs Rule 3, too!

3. The "Er" Rule—

"er" changes to "uh."

Examples: Patter, matter (where "er" sounds like "urr" in "gurr") becomes patt-uh and matt-uh. R*aw*ther becomes rawth-uh.

And water? Water becomes woow-tuh!

Put It All Together

Good accent fakers know they can only sound good on a few words. They just use them over and over. So write down a few favorites, and practice getting the right *accents* and the right **emphasis** in the right places.

Like:

"Oh **both**-*uh*! This **butt**-*uh* is simply ***aww***-ful!"

"**Do** be a **decent** chap or I might very well **blub**!"

Or try these from the Chronicles:

"Why, you goose! It's just an ordinary wardrobe. Look! There's the back of it!" [Susan, *Lion*]

"If you don't know how to take a joke, I shan't bother my head about you." [Eustace, *Voyage*]

Finally, don't forget to sprinkle your sentences with proper fillers like: "Rawther!" "Quite!" "Re-aw-lly?" and, "Yes, of cooowrse!"

Got it?

Splendid! Well, then… *Cheerio!*

"We can't get out of it now. We shall always be wondering what else would have happened if we had struck the bell."
–Digory

The BELL AND THE HAMMER

The Story ❋ Digory and Polly explore a dark, ruined world. No one's lived there for centuries, they decide. In a great, silent hall they find statues dressed like kings and queens. How strange! Then, ignoring warnings, Digory strikes a golden bell with a hammer. What will happen next?

Dotty
Mentally unbalanced; crazy

Pound
British unit of money

Grown-up Thoughts

One big idea in this chapter—and often in the Chronicles—is temptation. Why is it, when we're told we shouldn't do something appealing, that that something suddenly gets *more appealing* than ever? (Notice that for this temptation story, Lewis switches gender roles: this time, it's the male, not the female, who can't resist.) Lewis thought deeply on the topic of temptation—his book *The Screwtape Letters* is a classic.

When you are tempted, you shouldn't say, "God is tempting me." ... He doesn't tempt anyone.
JAMES 1:13, NIRV

Dead as Stone

Describe how you would have felt walking through those ruins and looking into the faces of those lifeless people.

———

Just One Bite

Do you know the story of the temptation of Adam and Eve? (Find it in Genesis 3.) How does it remind you of Digory and Polly?

———

"Don't Touch!"

Have you ever wanted to do something just because you were told *not* to? What happened?

———

Ding Dong

Was Digory foolish to ring the golden bell? What would you have done?

———

Oh No! Now What?

What do you think is going to happen next in the story?

———

LET'S TALK ABOUT IT

EAR EXAM

———

They took off the green rings and put them into which pocket?

Answer on page 431

The Meaning of Everything

Is It Boys Against Girls?

Digory says girls "never want to know anything but gossip and rot about people getting engaged." But then, doesn't Digory act "just like a boy" when he twists Polly's arm? At the time in which this book is set (1900, England), boys and girls were treated very differently. Girls were expected to like things like dolls, tea parties, and fancy dresses. For boys it was sports, battles, and adventure. Lewis treats his boys and girls evenly when it comes to courage, leadership, and flaws. But he draws some traditional lines, too—no girls in hand-to-hand combat, for example.

Try This at Home

Making Faces

Polly and Digory could tell a lot about the beautifully dressed people in the great hall just by looking at their faces. Try these looks (can you hold them for ten seconds?):

sad	hungry
frightened	cruel
loving	

Can your family guess from your expression what you're feeling?

"I was the Queen. They were all my people. What else were they there for but to do my will?"
—Jadis

The DEPLORABLE WORD

The Story ❋ Beautiful but frightening Queen Jadis has been awakened by the bell. She takes the kids on a forced tour of the ruined city of Charn, which she destroyed by speaking the "Deplorable Word." But when she tells the children to take her to their world, they make a grab for their green rings.

Incantations
Words with magical power

Minions
Lowly and powerless followers

Reasons of State
Politics

Grown-up Thoughts

What do we know so far about Queen Jadis?

She chooses "victory" at any cost.
She thinks others exist only to be used by her.
She is proud and self-obsessed—"Has your uncle power like mine?"
She blindly shifts blame to her sister.

Sound like Uncle Andrew? Here's the difference: Uncle Andrew is a human who dabbles in witchcraft. Jadis, as you'll see in future chapters, is a Witch and Satan figure.

Keep your tongue from evil and your lips from speaking lies.

Psalm 34:13

Bad Vibes

How can you tell that Jadis is an evil queen?

———

Worth the Win?

Queen Jadis killed off her sister and a whole world just so she could claim "victory." Have you ever won an argument or contest only to discover that winning wasn't worth it? Talk about it.

———

Royal Flub

The Queen thinks Uncle Andrew is a powerful king. Hmmm! What do you think she'll do when she meets him face-to-face?

———

Deplorable What?

Lewis never says what the Deplorable Word is. Any guesses? Some people think the Deplorable Word stands for the Atom Bomb. One family decided it was "take."

———

Powerful Words

Read James 3:3–5. What three things does James compare the power of the tongue to?

———

Uncle Andrew was bowing and rubbing his hands and look-ing…extremely frightened. He seemed a little shrimp of a creature beside the Witch.

The BEGINNING OF UNCLE ANDREW'S TROUBLES

The Story ❧ Queen Jadis follows the children all the way back to Uncle Andrew's study. "Tomorrow I will begin the conquest of the world," she announces. When she storms out of the room, the children get a breather, but things are about to get *most* upsetting for Uncle!

Deucedly
Devilishly, crazily

Frock-coat
A man's dress coat with knee-length skirts

Hansom
A horse-drawn carriage

Pax
Slang for calling a truce or making peace

Grown-up Thoughts

In this chapter it becomes clear that Uncle Andrew is going to pay a high price for his bad choices. Now instead of abusing others, he will get abused by Jadis. It's a fun reversal:

His "experiment" with the rings, as he called it, was turning out more successful than he liked: for though he had dabbled in Magic for years he had always left all the dangers (as far as one can) to other people.

Stories are superb for teaching consequences, even if they're delayed (like real life).

He who digs a hole and scoops it out falls into the pit he has made.

PSALM 7:15

Vanity

Uncle Andrew is described as "vain as a peacock; that was why he had become a Magician." What could that mean?

———

Something in the Air?

Why do you suppose Jadis began to lose her beauty and strength while in the Wood between the Worlds?

———

"So Sorry..."

Digory apologized to Polly because he'd treated her badly. Why do apologies make a difference anyway?

———

Silly Man

Why is Uncle Andrew being foolish when he dresses up for the Queen?

———

You're Not Going to Believe This!

If you were Polly, what's the first thing you'd tell your family when you got back home?

———

LET'S
TALK
ABOUT
IT

WISDOM
for
NARNIACS

———

Sometimes the silliest kind of silliness happens in grown-ups.

The Meaning of Everything

Those Dem Words

Some of the words in *Magican's Nephew* aren't too nice! You might be wondering, "Does 'dem' mean 'damn'?" Yes—it's just a milder form of the word, like "darn." Then there's Polly telling Digory not to be a donkey. Well, something like that! Today, the word "ass" is derogatory in more ways than one. If your family is reading aloud, you might want to skip words you don't want repeated. (And watch as Polly and Digory learn to treat each other better in the chapters ahead.)

Kid Test

"I am your magical power. I am invisible, but at your command, I can do all these things":

Put out a fire—Proverbs 26:20

Give other people strength
—1 Thessalonians 5:11

Separate close friends
—Proverbs 16:28

Cut like a sword—Proverbs 12:18

Bring healing—Proverbs 12:18

"I belong to you. WHAT AM I?"

CHAPTER 7

*"Jiminy!" he said.
"She's loose in London.
And with Uncle
Andrew. I wonder
what on earth is going
to happen now."*
—Digory

WHAT HAPPENED *at the*
FRONT DOOR

The Story ◈ Get ready! Here comes…a flying aunt (Letty), a rampaging Witch (Jadis), an angry mob (or are they just curious?), a stampeding horse (Strawberry), a wrecked carriage (it's stolen), an old man talking through his hat (Uncle Andrew), and a boy who's trying to save London *and* his dying mother (Digory). Whew!

Bow-window
A curved bay window

Cove
British slang for man

Mutton
*The flesh of fully
grown sheep*

Tram
Streetcar

Twopence
*A British coin
worth two pennies*

Grown-up Thoughts
While Queen Jadis wreaks havoc, Lewis helps us to laugh. The Witch, stripped of her powers but still behaving as if she has them, becomes a comic figure. And the humor is reassuring. In the big view of things, followers of Christ *do* have the last laugh. Look at how Paul described Christ's crucifixion: "Having disarmed the powers and authorities, he made a public spectacle of them, triumphing over them by the cross" (Colossians 2:15).

*Be strong and
take heart,
all you who hope
in the* LORD.
PSALM 31:24

Silly, But Not Scary

In the world of London, the Witch doesn't seem so scary anymore, does she? Why is that?

————————

Giggle Meter

What was the funniest thing that happened in this chapter?

————————

Worried About Mom

Digory is very worried about his mother. Have you ever felt worried about someone you loved who was very ill? What happened?

————————

A Witch in Wichita?

What do you think would happen if Jadis showed up at your house? At your school?

————————

Second Thoughts

Do you think Uncle Andrew will ever play with magic again?

————————

EAR EXAM

————

What did Jadis shoplift?

Did You Know? #1

Mum Is Very Ill

Lewis understood the sadness Digory felt about his mother's illness. When Lewis was nine years old, his mother got cancer. He prayed for her to be healed, but she died. Lewis grieved her loss the rest of his life.

Did You Know? #2

London, A.D. 1900

At the turn of the twentieth century (when *The Magician's Nephew* takes place), London was the most important city in the world. Horse-drawn carriages filled the streets, although a few motorcars had been spotted. Beneath the streets ran the world's first subway system—the London Underground. And Queen Victoria had one more year to go on a *very* long reign (1837–1901).

Kid Test

How to Speak Cabby

The Cabby speaks a strange language! Mostly, he seems to have trouble with one letter: *'ere, 'orse, 'im, 'ome,* and *'ave.* What's the missing letter?

"Here Comes *It!*"

On the mysteries of how children play in a story, and—listening to its long rhythms—
know first when Aslan is near.

Who remembers when we were boys, when we were little girls, and someone read us Narnia? I close my eyes and lean into the memory of how my mother read, of the times we had together, and a certain game we played without her knowing.

A schoolteacher and adept at slipping children into books for keeping, she could do all the voices. From page one she made a very scary Witch, and her harrumphing Uncle Andrew was the perfect duffer. (I can still hear her Uncle Andrew with her mouth held in an *O* and her lowest tones quavering sillily!)

And her act! Her act was itself a fascination, so outrageous! She was the maestro, a marvel of poise and varied animations, switching character and keeping her place through so many small-boy interruptions.

Happiness, happiness then seriousness, seriousness then happy and serious at once, that was Aslan coming.

But slumped together with my brothers beside her, us in our Mickey Mouse pajamers and with toothpaste on our breath, would you believe we were *almost* perfectly impervious? She would surely have slipped us into Narnia, sealed us with that forehead kiss, and mailed us off to bed if it hadn't been for the game we'd started playing early on.

Really, Mom had started it herself when she told us at the first about the lion who would come. The cover had the lion, and somehow we started waiting, watching for him. Listening, but mainly listening for the Aslan parts.

We had trained ourselves to hear mostly the vulnerable moments. For these moments always led to Aslan coming in. (The first was when the rings kept being fumbled and the witch accidentally came along with Polly and Digory to the dark place, remember? My neck burns even as I remember the sense of dread, and then—oh, Lord!—that Voice began his singing!)

We came to wait for the long rhythms of the story to resign themselves, always, to the Voice, to a lion who spoke like a man. And even when I was especially tired, I could hear when his part was coming up. It went: happiness, happiness then seriousness, seriousness then happy and serious at once, that was Aslan coming.

Oh, our bedtime game was delicious growing up because he was so easy to hope for! And now that I'm reading the Chronicles to my kids, I've sometimes wondered if they are playing something like it, as they are never so absorbed as I might like them. Elliot and Emmae seem always just ahead of me, scouting maybe, and Cambria is never far behind them, which is still ahead of where I'm reading. (I find myself starting to read mechanically when I suspect they're only sifting for that lion anyway. Something my mom would never have done!)

But just as I begin to feel as though I'm rowing a thick sea of words with no Aslan in sight and my shipmates growing listless, tired of being concerned, I'll see them straighten up together. Or Elliot will hunch down suddenly and spread his hands out in front of him and say intensely, "Okay, okay! Guys! Now just, just listen!" Emmae watches his hands and stops twisting the hem of her pajama bottoms, and Cam takes the cue and grins eagerly and says, "Ohhhhh yeeaaahh! Here comes it!"

I love to watch them, to see them at just the moment when they spot that dab of brightest gold on our horizon. Aslan!

Aslan's come out to play the game again.

—Brian Thomasson

There were no words. There was hardly even a tune. But it was, beyond comparison, the most beautiful noise he had ever heard.

CHAPTER 8

THE FIGHT *at the* LAMP-POST

The Story ❖ After a terrible brawl, the yellow ring does its magic again. Polly and Digory—plus Queen Jadis, Uncle, the Cabby, and his horse—arrive in the Wood. But soon they're swept into a world of dark, lifeless Nothing. Then a Lion—"huge, shaggy, and bright"—begins to sing.

Brick
A helpful, reliable person

Impertinent
Bold, without good manners

Pretty kettle of fish
An awkward or alarming situation

Spirits
An alcoholic beverage, especially distilled liquor

Grown-up Thoughts

We get our first glimpse of Aslan, but only after a Voice begins to sing a world into being. Notice how the listeners responded. When Uncle Andrew saw the Lion, he wished he had a gun. The Witch understood the song better than anyone, and "hated it." But the others were spellbound. How we respond to God depends on our hearts. Jesus said, "Everyone who does evil hates the light, and will not come into the light for fear that his deeds will be exposed" (John 3:20).

"The LORD your God is with you, he is mighty to save. He will take great delight in you, he will quiet you with his love, he will rejoice over you with singing."

ZEPHANIAH 3:17

Temper, Temper

The Witch hurts others when she flies into a rage (can you give examples?). Does losing your temper help when you're angry?

_____

Listen to That Sound

Why do you suppose the Witch and Uncle both hated the Voice of the Lion? Would you have liked it?

_____

The Best Sound

What is the most beautiful sound you've ever heard?

_____

Nothing Doing

Imagine you find yourself in a world of *nothing*—no sound, no light. What would that be like? What would you do?

_____

Call a Cabby

What kind of person do you think the Cabby is?

_____

LET'S
TALK
ABOUT
IT

FAST FACT

_____

Lewis once owned a car but he never learned to drive.

Narniac Attack | No. 2

[Test your knowledge on chapters 4–8]

1. Why did Digory ring the bell with the hammer?

a) Because Polly didn't want to do it herself
b) Because he wanted to see what would happen
c) Because he hoped to wake the room of statues

2. Why did Queen Jadis speak the Deplorable Word?

a) Her sister wouldn't yield her the throne.
b) She didn't think it would really work.
c) She believed it would give her eternal life.

3. Lewis notes that witches are not interested in things or people unless they:

a) are beautiful beyond reason.
b) can be used or manipulated.
c) have red hair and freckles.

4. What happened to Polly when she came home with wet shoes?

a) She was sent to bed without any dinner.
b) She had to apologize to Digory's aunt for getting her carpet wet.
c) She had dinner without the good parts and was sent to bed for two hours.

5. Who started singing a hymn in the dark?

a) Digory
b) The Cabby
c) Strawberry

CHAPTER 9

*"Narnia, Narnia,
Narnia, awake.
Love. Think. Speak.
Be walking trees.
Be talking beasts.
Be divine waters."*
—Aslan

The FOUNDING OF NARNIA

The Story ❋ The Lion song covers Narnia with every kind of growing plant, then—bubbling out of the earth—animals! When the Witch (who isn't Queen of anything anymore) realizes she's powerless, she flees. But the new creatures of Narnia gather around the Lion to receive his touch, his breath.

"Guns be blowed"
An expression of surprise

"Stow it, Guv'nor"
Slang for "Shut up, fellow!"

Yeomanry
A cavalry force that became part of the British Territorial Army

Grown-up Thoughts

The creation of Narnia loosely follows the Genesis story. As with God, the Lion creates from nothing. "All the things were coming...'out of the Lion's head,'" Polly says. Lewis's account gives us a deeper appreciation for the wonders of creation and celebrates the Creator. "Through him all things were made; without him nothing was made that has been made. In him was life, and that life was the light of men" (John 1:3–4). See Bible parallels on page 419 for many other echoes.

God saw all that he had made, and it was very good....

Genesis 1:31

Lion Bashing

The Witch lost her temper and threw a piece of iron bar at the Lion. But he didn't seem to notice. Why, do you think?

_____

Creation Day

How is this story a lot like the Bible account about how God made our earth?

_____

Narnia Dreamin'

When he saw Narnian magic at work, Digory longed for a dream to come true. What was it? What dreams began to dance in Uncle Andrew's head?

_____

Nose Kisses

Why do you think the Lion touched the animals two at a time on the nose?

_____

Growth Spurt

What happened to the size of the animals who were chosen by the Lion? Why do you think he did this?

_____

LET'S
TALK
ABOUT
IT

The trouble about trying to make yourself stupider than you really are is that you very often succeed. Uncle Andrew did. He soon did hear nothing but roaring in Aslan's song.

CHAPTER 10

The FIRST JOKE *and* OTHER MATTERS

The Story ❋ "Hail, Aslan. We hear and obey," say the creatures (finally we know the Lion by name). Laughter and fun follow. Then Aslan takes aside a council to plan for Narnia's protection. While Digory tries to get closer to Aslan, curious animals try to do the same to Uncle Andrew!

Jackdaw
A bird in the crow family

Naiads
Water-nymphs, offspring of the god who arose from Narnia's river; AKA the well-women

"Strike me pink"
An exclamation of great surprise

"Tally-ho! Tantivy!"
Slang for "Let's go!"

Grown-up Thoughts

This chapter is brimming with fun and big ideas. We enjoy watching the animals discover jokes. We hear what people look like to rabbits ("a kind of large lettuce"), and what it might be like if our pets could talk. But there's nothing light about what is happening to Uncle Andrew. He "tried to make himself believe that he could hear nothing but roaring.... He soon did hear nothing but roaring." For Paul's description of a similar miserable state, see Romans 1:16–25.

Humor Is Divine

Aslan loves good jokes.
Do you think Jesus did?
What would make Him laugh?

———————

House Calls

Why do you think Digory
believes Aslan can help
his mother?

———————

Tattle Tails

If your pet could suddenly talk,
what stories do you think it
would tell about you and how
you care for it?

———————

"Terrors!"

Why do you suppose Uncle
Andrew thought the animals
were so scary?

———————

Five Hours Old

Aslan says that evil has already
come to Narnia. What do you
suppose he's talking about?

———————

Ticklers

What part of this chapter
made you laugh?

———————

LET'S
TALK
ABOUT
IT

WISDOM
for
NARNIACS

———

"What you see
and hear depend a
good deal on where
you're standing."

The Meaning of Everything

Myths and Misses

All through the Chronicles, Lewis loves to mix up real and pretend worlds. In this chapter, imaginary beings show up from Greek and Roman mythology: fauns, satyrs, dwarfs, wild people, gods and goddesses, nymphs and naiads. Wow! Lewis believed that mythological stories conveyed important wisdom from ancient times. Of course, myths aren't true (most of the time), but they can show us a truth we might have "mythed." For more on mythology, see page 335.

Uncle Jack Says

"There are two kinds of people: those who say to God, 'Thy will be done,' and those to whom God says, 'All right, then, have it your way.'"

"This is the Boy," said Aslan, looking, not at Digory, but at his councillors. "This is the Boy who did it."

DIGORY AND HIS UNCLE
ARE BOTH IN TROUBLE

The Story ❧ The animals don't know what to make of the unconscious Uncle Andrew. Which end is which? Is he animal or vegetable? Uncle ends up planted and watered! Meanwhile, Aslan hears Digory's confession about his part in bringing the Witch to Narnia, then names the Cabby and his wife King and Queen.

Chap
A man or boy

Cockney
A person from London's East End

Square
Fair and just

Tapir
A chiefly nocturnal mammal with a heavy body, short legs, and a long, fleshy, flexible upper lip

Grown-up Thoughts

Already Narnia is marred by evil, but Aslan pledges to take the worst on himself. "Evil will come of that evil," he says, referring to Digory's rebellion at the bell that brought Queen Jadis to life. "But it is still a long way off, and I will see to it that the worst falls upon myself." In Aslan's pledge, you might hear echoes of Isaiah's prophecy about Jesus Christ—"the punishment that bought us peace was upon him" (Isaiah 53:5).

Plant That Uncle!

Why is it so much fun to laugh at Uncle Andrew now?

———————

Watch Him...Grow?

But wait! Since it's Narnia, do you think Uncle *will* start to grow?

———————

Do You Hear It?

Polly feels sure that anyone who hears Aslan's call will want to come to him, and would be able to. Do you think it's the same way when God calls to us?

———————

No Excuse

At first, Digory didn't want to admit the truth about hitting the bell and waking the Witch. Did you feel sorry for him? Can you think of a time when you decided to tell the truth, even though it was hard?

———————

I'll Pay for That!

Aslan said that he would take the worst consequences of Digory's mistake on himself. Remind you of anyone?

———————

LET'S
TALK
ABOUT
IT

Fast Fact

———

The English bulldog is a symbol of courage and determination for Britons. It was bred eight hundred years ago to fight bulls and bears.

Look It Up

Aslan says he has known the Cabby and the Cabby knows him. But they've only just met! What could Aslan possibly mean? Read Psalm 139:15–16 to find out.

Kid Test

Now Taking Applications for King & Queen

Aslan tells the Cabby and his wife seven ways to be good leaders. Can you think of what they were?

1. Rule your subjects k_____dly.
2. Do j_____ among them.
3. Don't have f_____!
4. Remember, your subjects are not your s_____.
5. Protect them from e_____.
6. In battle, be first in the charge, last in the _____.
7. Bring up your _____ and grand_____ to do the same.

The Lion drew a deep breath, stooped its head even lower and gave him a Lion's kiss. And at once Digory felt that strength and courage had gone into him.

STRAWBERRY'S ADVENTURE

The Story ◈ "It is my wish to plant in Narnia a tree," Aslan tells Digory. It will be a tree of protection. But Digory must travel outside of Narnia to bring back an apple (and its seed). Aslan gives Strawberry wings, and the two children take off on a spectacular ride.

A rumgo

A surprising event

Curvet

A light leap by a horse, in which both hind legs leave the ground just before the forelegs are set down

Grown-up Thoughts

In this chapter we learn important things about Aslan:

> *He is not one you can bargain with.*
> *He feels Digory's grief deeply.*
> *His touch gives strength and courage.*
> *He blesses those he sends on a mission.*
> *He says of his missions that there "will always be a way through."*
> *He "likes to be asked," even if he knows what is needed.*

Any of these traits will make wonderful conversation starters about Jesus with your child.

> *But those who hope in the LORD will renew their strength. They will soar on wings like eagles.*
>
> ISAIAH 40:31

Lion-Sized Tears

Digory was surprised to see Aslan shedding tears about his mother's illness. What does this tell you about the Lion? What made Jesus cry? (See John 11:32–36.)

_____

Lion-Sized Kisses

When Aslan kissed Digory, the boy suddenly felt new strength and courage. When you are afraid, what makes you feel braver?

_____

Just Ask

Aslan "likes to be asked" even if he already knows what is needed. Why, do you think?

_____

Jolly Decent

How can you tell that Digory and Polly are getting along much better now?

_____

Candy Tree?

So, do you think the toffee Digory planted *will* grow?

_____

A Sound in the Night

What do you suppose made that noise in the dark as Fledge and the children were trying to go to sleep? Or do you think the three were just imagining it?

_____

LET'S **TALK** ABOUT **IT**

After all, he thought, the notice on the gate might not have been exactly an order; it might have been only a piece of advice—and who cares about advice?

An UNEXPECTED MEETING

The Story ◈ Digory, Polly, and Fledge arrive at the garden Aslan described, but Digory enters alone. Inside, Digory spots the tree with silver apples. Could it be wrong to taste one, maybe take one for his mother? Then the Witch shows up, looking stronger than ever.

Cataract
A great downpour or waterfall

Forbear
To hold back or resist

Pelt
To move at a rapid pace

Grown-up Thoughts

You could call this chapter, "Digory's Redemption." Unlike Eve's response in the Garden, Digory does *not* take the fruit and seek the knowledge the Witch promises. And unlike what happened at the bell and hammer, he resists the desire to know "what would happen." Given a second chance, Digory obeys Aslan, resists temptation, and preserves happiness for all of Narnia for many years to come. Digory's story might also remind you of Peter, who, after failing Jesus miserably, was forgiven, then recommissioned to serve Him.

Submit yourselves, then, to God. Resist the devil, and he will flee from you.

JAMES 4:7

Big Bird

When Digory saw a big beautiful bird in the trees, he felt watched. Who do you think the bird was?

_____

Rotten Apple

One of the Witch's suggestions was so mean, Digory suddenly realized how evil she was. What did the Witch say?

_____

Just Our Secret

The Witch told Digory that no one would ever know if he took the apple for himself. Do you think that was true?

_____

On and On and On

Digory declared that he didn't want to live forever. What might be fun—or *not* fun—about living forever on earth?

_____

The Right Thing

On the way back to Narnia, Digory was still confused and sad. But remembering something helped him feel sure that he had done the right thing. What was it?

_____

LET'S TALK ABOUT IT

EAR EXAM

_____

Who had been near Fledge and the children in the dark the night before?

Answers on page 43

Kid Test

Temptation Station

Can you remember a time when someone put a lot of pressure on you to do something you knew was wrong? Which of these lies did you hear?

> *You won't get caught.*
> *No one will know.*
> *It will be so much more fun!*
> *You're going to miss out if you don't.*
> *Think about it a little longer…you want it, don't you!*
> *Why should you listen to [your parents, God, your teacher, the Bible]? They don't care about you.*
> *Well, it's not hurting anybody!*

Did you believe any of these lies? Pick one and come up with a good answer for the next time you hear it.

Uncle Jack Says

"Failures are finger posts on the road to achievement."

"Son of Adam," said Aslan, "you have sown well. And you, Narnians, let it be your first care to guard this Tree, for it is your Shield."

The PLANTING of the TREE

The Story ❀ The new King and Queen of Narnia get crowned while old Uncle Andrew gets beaned by nuts and worms (then mercifully put to sleep). Digory receives Aslan's earth-shaking, "Well done!" and then something more—an apple from the Tree of protection. He can't *wait* to take it home.

Half-sovereign, half-crown
Coins formerly used in Great Britain

Bellows
A device that blows air onto a fire to make it burn more fiercely

Smith-craft
The art of forging metals into a desired shape

Grown-up Thoughts

Finally, the outcomes! Cabby and wife are rewarded with leadership and honor. Digory hears Aslan's, "Well done.… You have sown well." Uncle Andrew? Well, that's another story! After years of abusing animals, he's caged by kindhearted animals who just can't figure out how to make him happy. (Best line: "They were really getting quite fond of their strange pet and hoped that Aslan would allow them to keep it.")

Great literature shows us the truths of sowing and reaping. "Do not be deceived," Paul wrote, "God cannot be mocked. A man reaps what he sows" (Galatians 6:7).

A man reaps what he sows. The one who sows to please his sinful nature, from that nature will reap destruction; the one who sows to please the Spirit, from the Spirit will reap eternal life.

GALATIANS 6:7–8

Different Look

This time Digory found he could look straight into the Lion's _____. Why?

_____

King Cab

Why do you suppose Aslan chose a humble Cabby to be king of Narnia? What kind of people did Jesus choose for disciples, and why, do you think?

_____

The Horse Whisperer

What did it sound like in Polly's ear when Fledge whispered to her?

_____

Animal's Pet

The animals cage Uncle, throw food at him, and hope to keep him as a pet forever. Why is this experience such a perfect lesson for Uncle?

_____

Wrong Time, Wrong Way

The Witch picked the fruit "at the wrong time and in the wrong way." Can you think of good things that might turn into wrong things because of *when* or *how* you do them?

_____

WISDOM
for
NARNIACS

_____

Length of days

with an evil heart

is only length

of misery.

LET'S TALK ABOUT IT

'OLD YOUR NOISE, EVERYONE! 'ERE COMES...

Narniac Attack | No. 3

[Test your knowledge on chapters 9–14]

1. Which of these creatures are not mentioned in Narnia (at least not yet)?

a) Frogs   b) Dogs   c) Armadillos

2. Which big idea was *not* part of Uncle Andrew's scheme for making money out of Narnia?

a) Building a skyscraper
b) Opening a health resort
c) Getting a gun and shooting the Lion

3. "Strike me pink!" is:

a) a rock band in Narnia.
b) a curse uttered by the Witch.
c) something a carriage driver might say if his horse started to talk.

4. Who said, "Very few of us have what could exactly be called a Nose"?

a) The Warthog
b) The Bulldog
c) The Elephant

5. Something fell out of Uncle Andrew's pockets and started to grow. What was it?

a) A bottle of brandy
b) Coins
c) A cigar

6. Where did Digory read, "Take of my fruit for others"?

a) On a cereal box
b) On the Tree of protection
c) On a garden gate

Plant Your Own
NARNIA TREE

YOU'VE just read about the Tree of protection that Digory plants from an apple. It will shield Narnia from evil for many years. Maybe you're noticing by now—trees in Narnia are much more interesting than here on earth!

For example, they:

*Grow from strange objects
(an iron crossbar, toffee)
Seem to wade through dirt like we
do through water
Talk
Bow in worship to Aslan
Fight in battles against the enemies
of Aslan*

Two
mature trees
provide enough
oxygen for a
family of four.

C. S. Lewis loved nature. But interestingly, the trees he loved first weren't even real! Here's what happened:

When he was about six, his brother Warnie made him a toy forest in a cookie tin. It was made of moss, twigs, and flowers. Lewis never forgot the happiness he felt as he looked into that miniature world of imaginary trees, grass, and flowers.

Is your family ready to celebrate the magical trees of Narnia? Here are three fun ideas:

Trees are the longest-living and largest living organisms on earth.

1. Plant a Tree of Protection

If you have a place where you can plant a tree, here's what to do:

Choose your tree. A crab apple tree just might have the magical qualities you're looking for. Crab apples are weather resistant, grow in most areas of North America, and don't get too big. Plus, they blossom beautifully in spring and have colorful leaves, and most species also bear small red or yellow fruits (tasty only to birds, though). Ask at a local plant nursery for more ideas.

Plant your tree. Your plant nursery can provide simple planting instructions. Be sure to follow expert advice on soil preparation, staking up, and watering. And *please*—out of sympathy for Uncle Andrew, be sure to plant your tree right end up!

Celebrate your tree. What makes your tree special is what it means to you. So put your imagination to work coming up with a memorable celebration. You could:

Name it. Digory's tree was the Tree of protection, and you could name yours that, too. But your family might decide to name your tree for healing, blessing, forgiveness, remembrance, or something else that's special for you.

Bury it. Collect small items—a photograph, rings, small toys, a written prayer—and seal them well inside a plastic container. Bury the time capsule near your tree.

Photograph it. Take a family photo around the tree.

Dedicate it. Read Psalm 1 together. Then hold hands around the tree and pray, asking the Lord to use the tree to remind you of its special meaning more each year as it— and your family—grows.

2. Make a Miniature Garden

Live in an apartment or just don't want to dig in the dirt? Do what Warnie did for Jack and make a miniature garden in a cookie tin or aquarium. Make your mini-Narnia with moss, stones, grass, twigs, small houseplants—you name it! Use jar lids to make small pools. You might even want to populate your world with miniature Narnian creatures and characters made out of paper or other material.

Trees help cool the earth's temperature.

3. Adopt a Tree or Forest

You don't have to plant or collect anything. You could, for example, "adopt" a Narnia tree at a local park. Or you can find your own Wood between the Worlds in a park or other forest setting where you can return often to play games and tell stories.

—*with Laurie Winslow Sargent*

Make your mini-Narnia with moss, stones, grass, twigs, small houseplants—you name it!

The smell of the Apple of Youth was as if there was a window in the room that opened on Heaven.

The END of This STORY and the BEGINNING OF ALL THE OTHERS

The Story ❧ Before sending them back to London, Aslan gives the children a warning (the race of Adam could share Charn's fate) and a command (bury the rings where no one will find them). Once home, Digory feeds his mother the magic apple, and everything starts to get better and better.

Frowsy

Having an unpleasant smell; musty

Fortnight

A period of fourteen days; two weeks

Don't forget!

Full glossary on p. 381

Grown-up Thoughts

The book closes with good news for Digory and his mother, and peaceful times for Narnia. But you can almost hear the sequel(s) in the making! That's because *The Magician's Nephew*, the sixth Chronicle published, was written to explain where Narnia came from, who created it, and what went wrong. In these ways, it reads a little like Genesis, a book of both beginnings and unfinished business. The biblical question after Genesis is, "Who will save us from the consequences of the Fall?" The Chronicle question now is similar: "Since the curse is still on Narnia, and the Witch is still out there somewhere, what will happen next—and who will save us from ourselves?"

Snoozer

Somebody slept through Aslan's last conversation with the children. Who was it?

_____

The Lion's Face

When Aslan was sending the children home, his face looked like a _____ of tossing _____ in which they were _____.

_____

Speedy

How much time had passed in London between the wreck at the lamp-post and the children's return?

_____

Healing Fruit

If you had an apple with miracle healing powers, who would you most like to give it to?

_____

"What I Learned in Narnia"

What lesson do you think these people learned from their adventures in _The Magician's Nephew_: a) Digory, b) Uncle Andrew, c) Polly, d) you?

_____

I will praise the LORD. I won't forget anything he does for me. He forgives all my sins. He heals all my sicknesses.

PSALM 103:2–3, NIRV

EAR EXAM

———

What did Professor Digory Kirke make from the apple tree after it blew down in a storm?

Answers on page 431

The Magician's Nephew: One-Sentence Edition

Pssst! Can you say it in one breath?

Soon after Digory and P_____ stumble into Uncle _____'s study, his m_____ rings take them to a Wood and then to the ruined city of _____, where Digory foolishly rings a _____ and awakens the wicked Queen J_____, who follows the kids back to England and makes trouble, but soon all of them, along with a Cabby and his h_____, end up in a place of Nothing until a _____ sings Narnia into being, and then the a_____s chase Uncle Andrew and make him their p_____, while the Lion asks Digory to fetch him an a_____ from a tree in a g_____, where the Witch t_____ts him, but she fails, and Digory returns with the _____ and Aslan says, "Well done," and he lets _____ take a healing apple back to his sick _____ in England, and then he and P_____ bury the magic r_____—and we all hope Uncle has learned his l_____!

FOUR ENGLISH schoolchildren—Lucy, Peter, Edmund, and Susan Pevensie—stumble into Narnia through the back of an ordinary wardrobe. But the Narnia they discover suffers under the wintry spell of the White Witch, who is using her powers to lead a rebellion against Aslan. Soon even Edmund has turned traitor. Then Aslan appears, and the stage is set for a most remarkable deliverance.

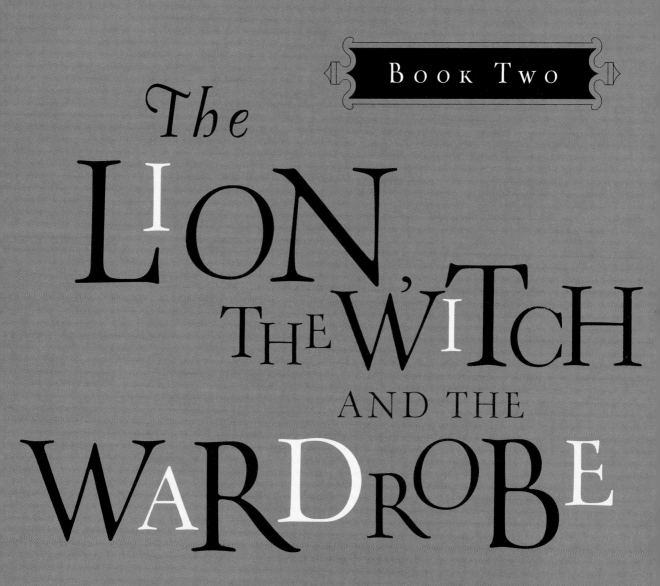

BOOK TWO

The
LION
THE WITCH
AND THE
WARDROBE

She immediately stepped into the wardrobe and got in among the coats and rubbed her face against them, leaving the door open, of course.

LUCY LOOKS INTO A WARDROBE

The Story ✸ Peter, Susan, Edmund, and Lucy have been sent to stay in a large country house with an old Professor (he's Digory, all grown up). While exploring the rooms, Lucy steps into a wardrobe full of fur coats. One step deeper and she finds herself in a snowy wood…and she's not alone!

Blue-bottle
A kind of housefly

Faun
A creature from Roman mythology with a man's body, horns, pointed ears, and a goat's tail

Wireless
A radio

Grown-up Thoughts

Lucy's entrance into Narnia through the wardrobe is one of the most magical and beloved scenes in the Chronicles. This particular wardrobe was built of wood from the apple tree that Digory planted with a seed from the Tree of protection (see last page of *Magician*). So what appears to be an ordinary closet is actually a portal to another world. The inside is bigger than the out-side—a recurring theme in the Chronicles. Lewis's wardrobe illustrates the biblical truth that the unseen spiritual world is much closer than we think.

We don't spend all our time looking at what we can see.…What can be seen lasts only a short time. But what can't be seen will last forever.

2 CORINTHIANS 4:18, NIRV

Strangers to Me

Have you ever stayed in a big, mysterious house with people you didn't know or without your parents? What did you do? Was it scary or fun?

———

Door of Wonder

Pushing past the fur coats, Lucy was afraid but also curious. Would you have kept walking into the snowy woods, or gone back first to tell someone?

———

My Personal Wardrobe

Can you think of a mysterious place you'd like to explore?

———

A Way Out

Lucy was wise to leave the wardrobe door open behind her. What other places should you never lock yourself in?

———

Brothers and Sisters

Can you already tell some things about what each of the children is like? Who is adventurous? Who is a little bossy? How would you describe your brothers and sisters, if you have any?

———

LET'S TALK ABOUT IT

WISDOM *for* NARNIACS

———

Sometimes there's just one step between the mundane and magic.

Did You Know?

The Children Who Came to Stay

During World War II, a lot of children in London were sent by their parents to stay with other families because the city was under attack by German airplanes. To escape the bombings, some schoolgirls came to stay with Lewis near Oxford. He was a middle-aged professor by then, who lived in a big, drafty house in the country.

Look It Up

Light of the World

Lucy was drawn toward the light ahead. Light makes us feel safer, doesn't it? Who does the Bible say is the light of our world? (See John 8:12.) And what is a lamp to our feet? (See Psalm 119:105.)

Uncle Jack Says

"I believe in Christianity as I believe that the sun has risen: not only because I see it, but because by it I see everything else."

But the Faun continued sobbing as if his heart would break. And even when Lucy went over and put her arms round him and lent him her handkerchief, he did not stop.

CHAPTER 2

WHAT LUCY FOUND THERE

The Story ❀ Lucy enjoys a delightful tea in the cave-home of Mr. Tumnus. He tells her about life in Narnia, then bursts into tears. All along, he confesses, he's been planning to turn her over to the White Witch. But now that he's met Lucy, he realizes he can't. Instead he leads her home.

Don't forget!

Full glossary on p. 381

Grown-up Thoughts

One of the titles on the Faun's bookshelf is, *Is Man a Myth?* Here in Narnia we encounter a world where creatures of our imagination—nymphs, naiads, dryads, and Fauns— are real, and man himself is rumored to be a myth. No wonder the Faun is startled to actually meet a "Daughter of Eve"! Before Lewis became a Christian, he described all religions as mythologies—"merely man's own invention." After his conversion, he used myths to teach eternal truth. For more on mythology in the Chronicles, see page 335.

Godly sadness causes us to turn away from our sins and be saved.

2 CORINTHIANS 7:10, NIRV

Faun-tastic!

When Lucy and the Faun meet, who seems more surprised—Lucy or the Faun? Why, do you think?

———

Snug as a Bug

Why do you think Lucy loves the Faun's cave so much? What's the nicest home you've ever visited?

———

Tears & More Tears

What made Mr. Tumnus change his mind about kidnapping Lucy? Do you think he will get in trouble with the Witch?

———

Talking Trees

"Even some of the trees are on her side," Mr. Tumnus explains. Have you ever imagined that a tree could listen or talk?

———

"Always Winter and Never Christmas"

What would *that* be like, do you think?

———

LET'S
TALK
ABOUT
IT

Her face was white—not merely pale, but white like snow or paper or icing-sugar, except for her very red mouth.

EDMUND *and the* WARDROBE

The Story ❁ Poor Lucy! No one believes her story about what happened inside the wardrobe. Edmund is the worst—he teases her unmercifully. Then one day he too finds himself in Narnia—alone, and face-to-face with a Witch.

Bathing
Swimming

Batty
Crazy or insane

Grown-up Thoughts

In some fairy tales, there are good witches as well as bad ones. But in Narnia, and in the Bible, there's no such thing as a good witch. The White Witch (like the Green Witch to come) is evil and heartless. She spreads only fear, oppression, and death. The endless winter she has draped over Narnia suggests a dead or dormant place. For your family, "always winter and never Christmas" can become a memorable picture of the spiritual deadness people experience before they find new life in Jesus.

"The thief comes only to steal and kill and destroy. I have come so they can have life…in the fullest possible way."

JESUS, IN JOHN 10:10, NIRV

Believe Me

Lucy's siblings don't believe her story. Have you ever told the truth but *not* been believed? Talk about it.

———————

Warning Signs

Edmund says and does a few things that suggest he might be headed for trouble. Things like what?

———————

"I Was Wrong"

Edmund hates admitting he's wrong. Why is it hard for most of us to do that, too?

———————

Pale Face

The woman Edmund meets says she is a queen. Any idea who she might be?

———————

Mysterious Wardrobe

Why do you suppose the wardrobe has an ordinary back sometimes, and opens into Narnia at other times?

———————

LET'S
TALK
ABOUT
IT

FAST FACT

———

In an early draft of this story, the children were named Ann, Martin, Rose, and Peter.

Answers on page 432

PLEASE, YOUR MAJESTY.
IT'S ONLY...

Narniac Attack | No. 4

[Test your knowledge on chapters 1–3]

1. Why were the children sent to the professor's house in the country?

a) *Their parents went on a trip to India.*
b) *There were air-raids in London.*
c) *Their mother was in the hospital.*

2. What was Mr. Tumnus *not* carrying when he met Lucy?

a) *The Narnia Herald newspaper*
b) *An umbrella*
c) *His tail*

3. How did Mr. Tumnus cheer himself up after talking to Lucy about winter?

a) *He sang Lucy a song.*
b) *He poured himself a cup of tea.*
c) *He played a little flute.*

4. Which one of these is *not* true about the Witch's reindeer?

a) *They wore bells on their harness.*
b) *They were whiter than snow.*
c) *Their noses were bright red.*

5. Who was driving the Witch's sled?

a) *A dwarf*
b) *The Witch*
c) *A Cabby*

CHAPTER 4

[The Queen] knew…
that this was
enchanted Turkish
Delight and that
anyone who had once
tasted it would…
if they were allowed,
go on eating it till
they killed themselves.

TURKISH
DELIGHT

The Story ◉ When the Witch discovers that Edmund is "a Son of Adam" with a brother and two sisters, she lets him eat a whole box of Turkish Delight. Of course, he wants more! He can be King of Narnia *and* have more Turkish Delight, the Witch says, but first…

Courtier
An attendant at
a royal court

Mantle
A loose, sleeveless
coat; cloak

Grown-up Thoughts

Edmund's insatiable appetite for Turkish Delight illustrates the power of lust. Lust is any sinful craving that can't be satisfied. The more we get, the more we want, even if our choices hurt ourselves and others. James described the downward cycle: "After desire has been conceived, it gives birth to sin; and sin, when it is full-grown, gives birth to death" (James 1:15). Edmund's surrender to his lust brings immediate changes in how he thinks and acts. Now he's "more than half on the side of the Witch"—and that spells trouble.

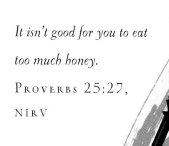

It isn't good for you to eat
too much honey.
PROVERBS 25:27,
NIRV

Royal Insults

Before the Queen decides she wants something from Edmund, she's not very nice. She asks if he's a great overgrown _____ and calls him an i_____.

_____

Secrets & Lies

The Witch wants Edmund to keep their meeting a secret. Is this a good secret or a bad one? How do you know the difference?

_____

Taking Sides

Even after hearing Lucy's frightening report, Edmund is already "more than half on the side of the Witch." How does the Witch get Edmund to side with her?

_____

Sweet Sick

By the time Edmund meets up with Lucy, he is feeling sick from too many sweets, yet he still wants more. Has that ever happened to you?

_____

LET'S
TALK
ABOUT
IT

Ear Exam

_____

What was Lucy doing with Mr. Tumnus?

Answers on page 432

Try This at Home
Make Your Own Turkish Delight
(Don't worry, it's not enchanted!)

> *2 cups granulated sugar*
> *2 tablespoons cornstarch*
> *1 cup water*
> *1/2 teaspoon cream of tartar*
> *1 tablespoon flavoring of choice:*
> *strawberry, orange, or lemon*
> *Food coloring of choice*
> *1/2 to 3/4 cup chopped walnuts*
> *or almonds*
> *Powdered sugar*

In a heavy saucepan over medium heat, combine sugar, cornstarch, and water; stir to dissolve. Whisk in cream of tartar and bring to a boil. Adjust the heat and let simmer until the mixture registers 220°F on a candy thermometer, covering it for the last 5 minutes.

Fold in your flavoring of choice, several drops of food coloring, and nuts. Pour into a greased shallow pan. Wait for the candy to cool, then cut into squares and roll in powdered sugar. Enjoy!

CHAPTER 5

> "There are only
> three possibilities.
> Either your sister
> is telling lies, or she
> is mad, or she is
> telling the truth."
> —Professor Kirke

BACK ON THIS
SIDE *of the* DOOR

The Story ❋ Back in Professor Kirke's house, Edmund denies having been to Narnia. That puts Lucy in tears, and Peter and Susan wonder if she is losing her mind. But the Professor comes to Lucy's defense. Then one day, all four children hide in the wardrobe...

Row
Quarrel

"Sharp's the word"
Quickly!

Trippers
Tourists

Grown-up Thoughts

The Professor's comments about Lucy telling lies, being "mad," or telling the truth echo Lewis's well-known conclusion about Jesus—that He was either a liar, a lunatic, or the Lord (*Mere Christianity*). The Professor also explains to the children why it's important to consider someone's *record* of truthfulness. If you're a Christian, ask yourself, "What is God's record of truthfulness in my life?" That question was the starting point for many psalms. And our answer to it can bring reassurance and gratitude during times of doubt.

Truthful words last forever. But lies last for only a moment.
PROVERBS 12:19,
NIRV

Oh, Brother!

Edmund betrayed Lucy in a very hurtful way. Why would a brother treat his own sister like this?

———

"Mind Your Own Beeswax!"

What do you think about the Professor's advice to Susan and Peter?

———

True to the End

What would you do if no one believed something you *knew* was true—and they treated you badly besides?

———

Crazy About Jesus

If you love Jesus, some people might think you are silly or crazy or even a liar. What might be the best way to talk to them about Him?

———

Who's Lying Now?

Have you ever had two people tell you different stories about an event? How did you decide who to believe?

———

LET'S
TALK
ABOUT
IT

WISDOM
for
NARNIACS

———

Telling lies is such a bother. Why, you have to *remember* them!

Did You Know?

So where is the wardrobe that inspired C. S. Lewis to create the world of Narnia? Two colleges claim to possess it, and they both might be right. The wardrobe at Westmont College (California) once stood in Warnie's bedroom. The wardrobe at Wheaton College (Illinois) was made by Lewis's grandfather. It once stood in the hall at the Kilns.

Look It Up

Someone in the Bible had brothers and sisters who thought he had gone "out of his mind." Who? (See Mark 3:21.)

Uncle Jack Says

"Christianity, if false, is of no importance, and if true, of infinite importance. The only thing it cannot be is moderately important."

EVERY DECENT house or apartment with a decent boy or girl in it has at least *one* hideaway. Come on, you know it's true! So where's yours? Under a bed, up a tree, behind a clothes hamper, in the attic, under the kitchen table?

Hideaways are important because kids have important things to do, feel, and imagine that require being in a secret place, behind a closed door, and maybe even in the dark!

A wardrobe or armoire, in case you didn't know by now, is a freestanding clothes closet. Unfortunately, most houses these days don't have wardrobes. They have closets, dressers, and built-in drawers instead.

Even if you don't have a wardrobe to play in, you can make one with just a few materials and a little imagination. Here's how:

Where's the Wardrobe in *Your* House?

HOW TO MAKE YOUR OWN MAGICAL HIDEAWAY

Closet Makeover

option 1

Get permission to turn the least-used closet in your house into a little piece of Narnia, at least for a spell. Move the contents to the garage or other safe spot. Paint large poster boards with favorite scenes from the Chronicles, and tape them inside the closet. Spread a blanket and pillows, and stock with flashlights. Take Lucy's advice and don't close the door all the way.

Wardrobe Box

option 2

At your local moving company, buy a cardboard wardrobe box (about ten dollars, less if it's used). With a box cutter or kitchen knife (*adults only, please*), cut a door about eighteen inches wide by twenty-four inches tall (or size to fit). Insert the metal hanging rod for stability, and decorate inside and out to suit your imagination.

Wardrobe Box Plus!

option 3

Buy *two* wardrobe boxes. Cut one door into the first box (the wardrobe, complete with hanging clothes), then cut another door into the second box (Narnia, complete with your decorations). Use plenty of duct tape to stick the boxes together. Now you can crawl from an ordinary wardrobe into a magical one! If you want to keep crawling—say, to Aslan's How or the Dancing Lawn—back up your single or double wardrobe boxes to a draped table or other play space.

Ten Things to Do in a Wardrobe:

Play a flute like Tumnus

Have tea and scones

Eat Turkish Delight

Discuss the book title, Is Man a Myth?

Do pantomimes of Narnian characters

Read aloud favorite parts of the Chronicles

Listen for Aslan's voice

Practice your British accent

Play Twenty Questions—"Who am I in Narnia?"

Write your own story of Narnia with you and your friends in it

In a Word

A very short history of history's most famous wardrobe

1. **Obey.** Digory brings the magical apple to Aslan.

2. **Protect.** Aslan makes the Tree of protection grow and bear fruit in Narnia.

3. **Heal.** Digory brings home a healing apple for his mother, who is ill.

4. **Plant.** Digory buries the seeds in the backyard of the Ketterley home, London.

5. **Grow.** The tree grows large and strong.

6. **Blow.** When Digory is a middle-aged professor, a storm blows the tree down.

7. **Make.** Digory uses the wood to make a wardrobe; then he puts it in his big house in the country.

8. **Visit.** One day, four children come to visit the professor.

And the rest is Narnian history!

—with Laurie Winslow Sargent

"We can't just go home, not after this. It is all on my account that the poor Faun has got into this trouble."
—Lucy

INTO *the* FOREST

The Story ❧ Now that all four children are in the snowy forest, everyone realizes the trouble they are in: Edmund is a deceiver and the Witch is very dangerous (Mr. Tumnus has been arrested and his house burned). Lucy begs the others to help her rescue the Faun, and they follow a friendly Robin.

Bagged
Stolen

Larder
A place, such as a pantry or cellar, where food is stored

Pay you all out
Get you back

Grown-up Thoughts

When Edmund's betrayal is revealed, his response is not remorse, but a further hardening of his heart against this "pack of stuck-up, self-satisfied prigs." But is his reaction that unusual? When we're caught in the wrong and embarrassed, it's tempting to label our accusers as uppity or self-righteous. This way—especially if we have no intention of repenting—we feel more justified in our wrong choices. Have you seen guilt work that way in your own life, or in your family?

In all your ways acknowledge him, and he will make your paths straight.

PROVERBS 3:6

Oops!

What slip of the tongue shows everyone else that Edmund has been lying?

———

Rescue 911

Lucy feels she owes it to Mr. Tumnus to try to save him, even though the Witch sounds dangerous and scary. Would you have done the same?

———

Verrry Suspicious

Why do you suppose that Edmund doesn't trust the Robin or the Faun and tends to think the worst of everyone else's motives?

———

The Right Side

Edmund asks Peter, "Which *is* the right side?" Based on what you've read so far, why might the Faun's side be the right one?

———

Let's Explore

If *you* had to go exploring in Narnia, which one of the four Pevensie kids would you pick to go with you? Who would you choose from your world?

LET'S
TALK
ABOUT
IT

CHAPTER 7

There's nothing to beat good freshwater fish if you eat it when it has been alive half an hour ago and has come out of the pan half a minute ago.

A DAY *with the* BEAVERS

The Story ⬩ Next thing you know, the children are following a Talking Beaver deeper into the woods. Finally they come to his home, a stick house built above a dam. A delicious meal with Mr. and Mrs. Beaver follows, but Edmund is secretly scheming for more Turkish Delight.

Gum boots
High boots made of rubber

Grown-up Thoughts

Aslan's name has great power in Narnia. But when the children hear he "is on the move," their responses vary. Edmund feels horror, Peter courage, Susan delight, and Lucy happy anticipation. Likewise, the name of Jesus is powerful, but people react to it in different ways. To nonbelievers, His name might be a joke or a swear word. But to those who believe, His is the name above every name (Philippians 2:9). Jesus is our hope, Redeemer, Savior, healer, friend, and Lord. What a privilege it is for us to honor His name and watch for Him to be on the move!

When the name of Jesus is spoken, everyone's knee will bow to worship him.

PHILIPPIANS 2:10, NIRV

Lost!

Have you ever been lost in the woods, or a mall, or...? How did you feel? What happened?

_____

What's in a Name?

When you hear the name of Jesus, what's the first thought or feeling that comes to your mind?

_____

Horrible Ideas

So, what horrible ideas do you think came into Edmund's head when he saw the valley leading to the White Witch's castle?

_____

Yum or Yuck?

Does fried trout and sticky marmalade rolls with hot tea sound good to you? What would be your favorite meal on a winter day if you were in a house on a beaver dam?

_____

Why, It's You At Last!

Do you have any ideas about why Mrs. Beaver was *so* excited to meet the four children?

_____

FAST FACT

———

A beaver's front teeth never stop growing.

LET'S
TALK
ABOUT
IT

S-s-s-sh! The trees are listening. Now take...

Narniac Attack | No. 5

[Test your knowledge on chapters 4–7]

1. Narnia seems to begin just past...

a) *London*
b) *The post office*
c) *The lamp-post*

2. What game were the children playing while Edmund and Lucy were in Narnia?

a) *Checkers*
b) *Hopscotch*
c) *Hide-and-seek*

3. Good thing Lucy left it in Narnia, wouldn't you say?

a) *Her red umbrella*
b) *Her white handkerchief*
c) *Her purple Game Boy*

4. Who said, "Merely a trifle! Merely a trifle! And it isn't really finished!"

a) *Maugrim, Captain of the Secret Police*
b) *Mrs. Beaver*
c) *Mr. Beaver*

5. Mr. Beaver went fishing...

a) *in a boat.*
b) *with a hook and worms.*
c) *with his paw.*

"Safe?" said Mr. Beaver; "don't you hear what Mrs. Beaver tells you? Who said anything about safe? 'Course he isn't safe. But he's good."

WHAT HAPPENED
AFTER DINNER

The Story ❧ After supper, Mr. Beaver tells the children some very important things about Aslan, the White Witch, and a mysterious prophecy that seems to be coming true. But during the conversation, sneaky Edmund sneaks away!

Stratagem
A clever or deceptive plan; a scheme

Jinn
A demon

Grown-up Thoughts

The children can't wait to rescue Mr. Tumnus, but Mr. Beaver tells them they need Aslan's help. The Chronicles often portray the tension between the need for personal action and the need to depend on God. The Bible tells us to choose, to stand, to take courage, to fight. It also teaches that apart from God, we can do nothing (John 15:5). Of course our children feel the tension in their own way—one minute, it's "I can do it myself," the next, it's "Help!" Use these stories to help your kids see how God is ready to help those who are ready to act.

Introducing Aslan

The Beavers are the first ones to tell the children a great deal about Aslan:

> He's not a man, he's a _____.
> He's the K_____,
> the L_____ of the
> whole wood.
> He is not safe, but
> he is _____.
> His power is much greater
> than the Witch's.
> When he _____ his mane,
> spring will return.

LET'S TALK ABOUT IT

Not Safe, but Good

What do you think that means?

_____

Treacherous

Mr. Beaver could tell that Edmund had been with the Witch and eaten her food. How?

_____

How Far Will He Go?

Do you think Edmund really will betray his sisters and brother to the Witch?

_____

EAR EXAM

Aslan wants
to meet the
children where?

The Meaning of Everything

"The Enemy of Children"

Mr. Beaver explains that the Witch is not human, but half "Jinn," half giant. She was descended from Lilith. According to Jewish legend, Lilith was Adam's first wife but refused to serve him or bear him a child. In Babylonian mythology, Lilith wandered the wilderness looking for children to hurt.

Look It Up

The White Witch wants to kill the children because of an ancient prophecy that tells of four humans who will take the throne away from her. Who wanted to find baby Jesus and kill Him because of a similar prophecy? (See Matthew 2:13–16.)

> *My help comes from the LORD,*
> *the Maker of heaven and earth.*
> PSALM 121:2

Answers on page 432

"Probably," he thought, "this is the great Lion Aslan that they were all talking about. She's caught him already and turned him into stone."
—Edmund

In the WITCH'S HOUSE

The Story ◈ Edmund stumbles through the snow toward the Witch's house, fuming about the others and making kingly plans. But at the Witch's castle, he discovers a creepy courtyard full of stone creatures guarded by a huge wolf. Then the Witch herself appears, and she is *not* pleased.

Centaur
A mythical being that is half man and half horse

Satyr
A creature from Greek mythology with a man's body, horns, pointed ears, and a goat's tail

Grown-up Thoughts

Following Edmund on his walk through the snow toward the Witch, we hear him make excuses, add up offenses (mostly imagined), decide that Aslan is "awful," and find reasons to defend the Witch. Some people would call Edmund's internal dialogue "stinking thinking." Wrong thoughts are dangerous. No wonder the Bible says we should "take captive every thought to make it obedient to Christ" (2 Corinthians 10:5).

"So I strive always to keep my conscience clear before God and man."
PAUL, IN ACTS 24:16

That Little Voice

Edmund keeps arguing against his own conscience. Have you ever had this kind of conversation with yourself? What happened?

———————

King for a Day

Edmund is looking forward to being King and already worried about "keeping Peter in his place." Have you ever wished you could be older or have more power than a brother or sister? Why is it hard to be younger?

———————

Home Improvements

What kinds of big changes does Edmund plan to make in Narnia when he is king?

———————

Lion Graffiti

Edmund drew a mustache and spectacles on the lion statue. Why do you think he did this?

———————

Who's Afraid?

Edmund said, "Pooh! Who's afraid of Aslan?" Should he be afraid?

———————

LET'S
TALK
ABOUT
IT

CHAPTER 10

*Father Christmas…
was so big, and so
glad, and so real,
that they all became
quite still. They felt
very glad, but
also solemn.*

The SPELL
BEGINS TO BREAK

The Story ◈ Everyone scrambles to get away from the Beavers' house ahead of the Witch's arrival. Then after a night in hiding, they hear the sound of bells. Is it the Witch? No, it's Father Christmas, and he's brought gifts for them all! At last, the Witch's spell seems to be weakening!

Cordial
A healing liquid

Plaguey
Bothersome

Frowsty
*Stale smelling
or slovenly in
appearance*

Grown-up Thoughts

If Aslan is a picture of God the Son, and the Emperor of the Sea is a picture of God the Father, who might Father Christmas be? Many think of him as God the Holy Spirit. Like Aslan, he already knows the children by name. And for each, he brings important gifts for them to use in Aslan's service. (For more comparisons, see John 16:13–15.) Ask your family what the three children's gifts might stand for (possible answers: Peter's armament = faith, Susan's horn = prayer, Lucy's cordial = healing).

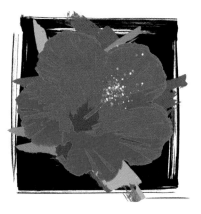

*God has poured out his love
into our hearts by the Holy Spirit,
whom he has given us.*

ROMANS 5:5

Mrs. Practical

Everyone's in a panic to leave, but Mrs. Beaver is calm and practical and thinks ahead (they'll need to eat!). Do you know anyone like that?

_____

Tools, Not Toys

None of the children got toys from Father Christmas. Why, do you suppose?

_____

Don't I Know You?

Father Christmas already knew the children by name. How would you explain that?

_____

Women & War

Father Christmas agreed that Lucy was brave enough to fight but said she shouldn't be in the battle itself. Do you think women should fight in battles?

_____

Just What I Wanted!

What is the best gift *you* have ever received?

LET'S TALK ABOUT IT

Kid Test

Beyond the Story

Lewis doesn't explain everything that happens in Narnia, or how. Some of the fun is what he leaves out! For example:

> *Where do you think Father Christmas might have been during all these years of winter? And doing what? And where did Mrs. Beaver get her sewing machine? Are there untold stories in Narnia? Make up your own story!*

Did You Know?

Roger Lancelyn Green, a close friend of C. S. Lewis, told him that Father Christmas should be dropped from the story. J. R. R. Tolkien, another friend (and author of *The Lord of the Rings*), agreed. He said Lewis was creating confusion. But the "huge man in a bright red robe" stayed in the story, and Christmas *did* finally come to Narnia!

CHAPTER 11

It didn't look now as if the Witch intended to make him a King.

ASLAN IS NEARER

The Story ❋ Edmund's hopes for Turkish Delight and a crown turn to dry bread. The Witch treats him cruelly as they race toward the Stone Table. When she hears about Father Christmas, she angrily turns some forest creatures to stone. But Narnia keeps thawing and soon…it's spring!

Dog-fox
A male fox

Laburnum
Flowering shrubs or trees having bright yellow flowers

Vermin
A person considered loathsome or highly offensive

Grown-up Thoughts

When Edmund finally sees the Witch's true colors, it's too late—the selfish schemer is now a slave. Ever been there? Most of us have. We thought we were picking Satan's pockets only to look up one day and discover we were his prisoner. But even then, when some consequences can't be undone, repentance is still possible. And so in the story: as winter in Narnia begins to melt, so does Edmund's heart. For the first time, he feels remorse and regret and "sorry for someone besides himself."

See! The winter is past; the rains
  are over and gone.
Flowers appear on the earth;
  the season of singing has come.
SONG OF SONGS 2:11–12

Captive

The Witch treats Edmund like a prisoner, giving him dry bread instead of Turkish Delight. Do you feel sorry for him?

_____

Please Don't!

The cruel Witch turned a happy party of forest creatures into statues. But what good came of that for Edmund?

_____

End in Sight

The Witch refuses to believe that the end of her reign is near, or that Aslan has returned to Narnia. Why?

_____

Signs of Spring

What happens in spring that doesn't happen in winter? How does winter remind you of the Witch and spring remind you of Aslan?

_____

WISDOM
for
NARNIACS

———

If you encounter a Witch with a wand, assume a comfortable position!

LET'S
TALK
ABOUT
IT

Answers on page 432

SPRING HAS SPRUNG, AND SO HAS THIS...

Narniac Attack | No. 6

[Test your knowledge on chapters 8–11]

1. The Witch wants to kill the children because:

a) *they are cuter than she is.*
b) *a prophecy links them with her ruin.*
c) *she is worried they will eat all her Turkish Delight.*

2. Which of these was *not* part of Edmund's plans for Narnia when he is King?

a) *A private cinema*
b) *Laws against beavers*
c) *A swimming pool*

3. What gift did Father Christmas give Susan?

a) *A bow and arrow, and a horn*
b) *A sewing machine*
c) *A dagger*

4. What was the merry party of creatures in the wood eating?

a) *Ham sandwiches*
b) *Potatoes with butter*
c) *Plum pudding*

Peter did not feel very brave; indeed, he felt he was going to be sick. But that made no difference to what he had to do.

PETER'S FIRST BATTLE

The Story ❀ Peter, Susan, Lucy, and the Beavers arrive at the Stone Table, where they encounter Aslan and a crowd of Narnians. Aslan shows Peter Cair Paravel in the distance and tells him he will be High King. Then Peter bravely rescues Susan from the Witch's wolf.

Alsatian
A German shepherd

Bane
A cause of harm, ruin, or death

Pavilion
A large and often sumptuous tent

Grown-up Thoughts

Peter's fight with the Witch's wolf is the first violence in the Chronicles that involves bloodshed and death. More battle scenes are to come, but Lewis is never gratuitously violent. Here, the attack is an act of courage and chivalry on Peter's part—he is defending Susan. The Witch, on the other hand, kills and maims out of anger, pettiness, and selfish ambition. For more on violence in the Chronicles, see page 356.

"Be strong and courageous. Do not be terrified; do not be discouraged, for the LORD *your God will be with you wherever you go."*

JOSHUA 1:9

Leadership Test

This chapter focuses on Peter becoming a leader. Do you think Peter will make a good leader and king? Why?

————————

Tools in Hand

How had Aslan already made sure that Peter would have what he needed for the fight with the wolf?

————————

More than Feelings

Peter felt more sick than brave when he attacked the wolf. Have you ever done something that required a lot of courage but you didn't *feel* brave? Talk about it.

————————

Saving Susan

Do you think that saving Susan was Aslan's way of *testing* Peter's courage? Or was it his way of showing Peter that he *already had it*?

————————

How Weird Is That?

Name three strange creatures who were crowding around Aslan at the Stone Table.

————————

LET'S TALK ABOUT IT

WISDOM
for
NARNIACS

————

Brave is what you do, not what you feel.

The Meaning of Everything

Terrible Aslan

When Lewis describes Aslan as both "good and terrible," he wasn't using the word "terrible" to mean horrible or bad. Originally, the word also meant awe-inspiring. For example, "The LORD thy God is among you, a mighty God and terrible" (Deuteronomy 7:21, KJV). Most of today's Bible translations replace the word "terrible" with "awesome."

Look It Up

A New Name

One disciple got a new name from Jesus when he answered that Jesus was the Messiah. Jesus also said that this disciple would be the leader of His new church. What was his name? (See Matthew 16:15–19.)

> *"You at least know the Magic which the Emperor put into Narnia at the very beginning. You know that every traitor belongs to me as my lawful prey and that for every treachery I have a right to a kill."*
> —the White Witch

DEEP MAGIC
from the DAWN OF TIME

The Story ◉ Poor Edmund is about to die by the Witch's knife when the rescue party sent by Aslan arrives. After a skirmish, the Witch escapes. But soon she returns to the Stone Table to claim her right to Edmund's life. Then Aslan and the Witch strike a mysterious deal.

Boggles and Cruels
Imaginary evil beings

Cheek
Sass or back talk

Minotaur
A mythical monster who was half man and half bull

Ogre
A mythical giant or monster that eats humans

Specter
Ghost

Grown-up Thoughts

In theses climactic chapters we find biblical truths about sin, sacrifice, and redemption at almost every turn. (If you're like most Narniacs, you'll return to ponder Lewis's meanings many times.) For example, notice that Edmund is rescued twice—first from the Witch's clutches, and then again from the penalty of his treachery. (How Aslan manages to both meet the requirements of the law *and* redeem Edmund's life unfolds in the next two chapters.) Probably the most moving scene is when Aslan takes Edmund for a walk and we sense that forgiveness is being granted.

Walking with the Lion

What do you think Edmund was feeling when Aslan took him for a walk? What do you think they said to each other?

———

Words in Stone

Can you remember a Bible story about laws written in stone? If so, tell it. What are some of the laws? (See Exodus 20.)

———

Traitors

Can you name three kinds of creatures that are on the Witch's side? Do you think they really like the Witch?

———

The Mysterious Trade

What do you think Aslan offered to give the Witch in exchange for Edmund's life?

———

Bad Bumps

How did the Witch and the dwarf disguise themselves?

———

LET'S
TALK
ABOUT
IT

FAST FACT

———

Lewis dedicated this book to his goddaughter, Lucy Barfield.

The Meaning of Everything

Deep Magic

The Deep Magic of Narnia refers to the law that Narnia is founded on. This law (like the Old Testament law of Moses) states that every act of treachery requires a payment of blood. "Without the shedding of blood there is no forgiveness" (Hebrews 9:22).

Kid Test

Forgiveness: Do You Get It?

Jesus promises to forgive us our sins, but He asks us to forgive one another, too. What do you think forgiveness really means? Pick one:

1. You broke my X-Box, but I'll pretend you didn't.

2. You told a mean lie about me, so I'll tell one about you.

3. You dropped my Chihuahua into a garbage can, but that's okay (because I'm a nice Christian).

4. Actually, you did all three of those things to me—and that was wrong—but I've decided not to stay mad at you, or hold those things against you. (Still, if you keep treating me this way, we probably can't be friends.)

Answer on page 432

So Bitter and Firm

See a family walking out together to name their hopes. Up ahead, a flat gray slab awaits.

When children need a destination is every time they go. So our walks—family walks—are to places with mythical names. They are ordinary, but for their names and but for the small feet that trample them excitedly once-a-walk.

The great juniper stump with five yard roots jutting the air is surrounded by a clutter of deer bones. It is Bone Stump. They come to it as archaeologists, forensic examiners, root swingers.

The pile of rusted cans in a nook of pine trees off the trail has a campfire circle by it. It is Old Miner's Camp. They come to find gold nuggets scuttled in the pine needles. To talk like leather-faced miners would, around a fire, lying to each other under stars.

There's maybe twenty others. Our walks go place-to-place for skits and for collecting.

They come to find gold nuggets scuttled in the pine needles.
To talk like leather-faced miners would, around a fire, lying to each other under stars.

And, of course, we add new places. We point and shout, "Hey guys, go look! It looks like a _____! You think it is?!" They hope all things and run ahead to make a place and name it.

But Stone Table was not at all like normal places we make. A new subdivision had gone in: Pine Meadow Ranch. The walk that night took us along a cut stone path winding beside an artificial creek, through acres of sod and newer houses. But no pines, oddly. "Did they put the rocks here? All these rocks?" asked Emmae. Elliot was throwing bank-rocks out further.

"Trucks full of rock, 'Mae," I said. I had seen the trucks.

Some wind changes and the kids decide to run ahead. Jennifer and I could talk adult again. "Look at Cam run!" she said. Cambria still keeps her arms up when she runs like when she was a toddler who expects to fall.

I take Jen's hand. We walk. Looking ahead, we watch them running together. We watch for their different styles of running. How often do we watch them together, sorting their distinctions?

I think for something Jen and I should talk about…. And then in slow frames I look again ahead at our three, just pulling themselves up on a great slab of rock. A flat gray slab moored on a peninsula of green grass.

Ho! Lord, it is Stone Table! I whisper, remembering a round of tears we'd had reading of it a few nights back.

Elliot crosses back and forth to the edges of the corners, wondering that rocks come so flat, so large. Now they are jumping together. Now Cam sits on the edge and kicks her flashing-red-lights sneakers off one side. Elliot sails off and comes running back to us. "Dad!" he cries, halfway. "It's where the mice tried to get Aslan loose!" He spits the words and sucks in air, swiping his nose with his sweatshirt sleeve. "Stone Table, Dad!"

"You found it, buddy! That rock must've been here. No way they could truck that thing in!" I vouch. Looking past Elliot, I see Emmae helping Cambria hop down and I wonder if there is anything in this world or others so safe to play on as Stone Table? So bitter once, but now so firm.

—Brian Thomasson

"Muzzle him!" said the Witch. And even now, as they worked about his face putting on the muzzle, one bite from his jaws would have cost two or three of them their hands. But he never moved.

The TRIUMPH OF THE WITCH

The Story ❧ Dinner is strangely quiet and sad. Afterwards, Lucy and Susan follow Aslan in the moonlight back to the Stone Table where the Witch's rabble tie him up, mock him, and shave off his mane. At the moment of Aslan's death, the girls look away.

Efreets

Demons or monsters of Mohammedan mythology

Incubuses

Demons

Orknies & Wooses

Only C. S. Lewis knows, but they don't sound nice

Sprites

Elves or goblins

Wraiths

Spirits that can be seen

Grown-up Thoughts

This is one of the most important scenes in all the Chronicles and one of the most clearly allegorical. Still, try to tread softly with your children, especially if they're younger. Trust that their emotional connections to the characters will sweep them up in the drama and lead them to the larger truths about the Crucifixion. "I'm aiming at a sort of pre-baptism of the child's imagination," Lewis wrote. His whole point in the Chronicles, he said, was to make it easier for children to accept Christianity when they met it. For more Bible parallels, see p. 419.

While we were still sinners, Christ died for us.

ROMANS 5:8

Commander in Chief

Aslan carefully prepared Peter for a battle with the Witch. Why, do you think?

_____

Substitute Me

Why do you think Aslan offered to die in Edmund's place? How is that like what Jesus did?

_____

Scaaary!

What did you think of all the Witch's strange workers? What are Satan's helpers called?

_____

No Resistance

How did you feel when Aslan's enemies mocked him and shaved his mane?

_____

Don't Look Now

The girls couldn't bear to look when the Witch killed Aslan. Would you feel the same way?

_____

LET'S
TALK
ABOUT
IT

EAR EXAM

_____

What did Aslan ask the girls to do to make him feel better while they walked?

Answer on page 432

The Meaning of Everything

Stone Table

Earlier in his life, Lewis visited the ruins at Stonehenge, a mysterious circle of giant prehistoric stones in southern England. Did this give him the idea for the Stone Table? One Lewis expert, Kathryn Lindskoog, notes, "The stone that is lowest at Stonehenge is called the stone of sacrifice because people suspect that humans were bound and stabbed there in evil ceremonies thousands of years ago.... It's almost certain that Stonehenge gave Lewis the idea of the Stone Table."

Look It Up

The Last Hours

Do Aslan's last hours seem familiar to you? Compare Aslan's story with the last hours of Jesus (see references):

Aslan's "last supper" (John 13)

Aslan's last night of agony (Matthew 26:36–38)

Aslan is mocked and humiliated by his enemies (Mathew 26:67–68; 27:27–31)

Aslan doesn't resist his enemies (Isaiah 53:7; John 18:7–11)

It's the girls who wait and watch (Matthew 27:55–56)

"But what does it all mean?" asked Susan.... "It means," said Aslan, "that though the Witch knew the Deep Magic, there is a magic deeper still which she did not know."

DEEPER MAGIC
from BEFORE
THE DAWN *of* TIME

The Story ❋ Susan and Lucy sob over Aslan's dead body. Meanwhile, friendly field mice chew away the ropes binding him, and at dawn, the Stone Table cracks in two. Suddenly, Aslan is alive again! After a happy romp, Aslan gives the girls a high-flying ride to the Witch's castle.

Skirl

To produce a high, shrill, wailing tone (think bagpipes)

Grown-up Thoughts

Anyone familiar with the story of Christ's death and resurrection will recognize what Lewis so lovingly accomplishes in this chapter. And with Susan and Lucy playing the part of Jesus' disciples at Calvary, your kids can experience Easter from a new perspective: children's tears at his awful death, and children's jubilation—a happy, laughing "romp"—at his glorious return to life. And they'll love knowing that the nasty Witch is really going to get it now!

For Christ died for sins once for all, the righteous for the unrighteous, to bring you to God. He was put to death in the body but made alive by the Spirit.

1 PETER 3:18

So Many Tears

Have you ever cried as hard and long as Susan and Lucy? What could make you cry that much?

_____

A Romp to Remember

Aslan played like a kitten (a *very* big one!) with the girls. How would you feel romping with a huge, friendly lion?

_____

ROAR!

Why do you think Aslan roared?

_____

Easter in Narnia

The romp in Narnia reminds Christians of the joy we feel on Easter morning. Can you think why?

_____

Deep, Deeper

Deeper Magic is a lot like what the Bible calls grace. Grace means getting a gift or favor you do *not* deserve. That's why it's called *amazing* grace! Have you received this free gift from God? If you want to know more, turn the page!

_____

LET'S
TALK
ABOUT
IT

Aslan *is* Coming Nearer & NEARER

 Ready for a riddle? *How is a boy eating a crust of bread like a winter that never ends and a squirrel family turned to stone?* Let's see. They're all crusty and cold. They sound lonely, lifeless, and somehow sad…

But what is the answer?

Here it is: *They're all pictures of a life **without** Aslan.*

Who is Aslan? Well, over the last few chapters, you've met him. He's the one who makes winter end and spring flowers pop up everywhere! He's good and kind and strong and—how to explain it!—he's willing to die for a greedy little boy named Edmund.

And there's more. Aslan can rise from the dead, defeat the Witch, and set free all the creatures locked in stone by her evil spells. Alsan can bring new life and joyful romps back to Narnia.

Now you get the picture of life *with* Aslan!

While you've been reading or listening to these stories, have you felt Aslan coming nearer and nearer to *you*? Aslan, as you also know by now, is a picture of Jesus. But unlike Aslan, Jesus is *real*. He came to earth so that you could know God and be near Him forever. He came to defeat death and bring new life to everyone who asks for it. He did all that by dying on the cross to pay the price for our sins.

You see, like Edmund, every one of us has been trapped by stupid choices and dumb lies. Everyone is stuck in an endless winter of sin, eating crusts, under the spell of death. Everyone, including you.

And even though you can't save yourself, Jesus wants to and He will. He wants to give you the free gift of endless life…right now!

> **Jesus is real. He came to earth so that you could know God and be near Him forever.**

All you have to do is say yes.

Saying yes to Jesus is something young people understand more quickly than anyone else—Jesus Himself said that. And it's so simple. Jesus explained how in a verse you might already know by heart:

For God so loved the world that he gave his one and only Son, that whoever believes in him shall not perish but have eternal life. (John 3:16)

Can you remember a time when you have said, "I believe in You" to Jesus?

If not, you can do that right now. Talk to Him in a simple prayer, like this one:

Dear Jesus,
Thank You for loving me so much. Please forgive me and save me. I believe You are God's Son. I believe You died for my sins. Come into my heart, Lord Jesus. And let me live with You forever. I belong to You now!
Amen.

If you prayed that prayer and meant it—congratulations! You have just received the free gift Jesus promised.

Now you belong to Him.

Now you are saved from the penalty of your sin.

Now you can begin to live for Jesus on earth, and look forward to enjoying Him in heaven forever.

Saying yes to Jesus is something young people understand more quickly than anyone else—Jesus Himself said that.

CHAPTER 16

*The courtyard looked
no longer like a museum;
it looked more like a zoo.
Creatures were running
after Aslan and
dancing round him
till he was almost
hidden in the crowd.*

WHAT HAPPENED ABOUT
THE STATUES

The Story ❧ Aslan breathes on the statues, and they spring to life. Then, after Giant Rumblebuffin breaks open the castle gate, Aslan leads them back to help Peter, who is fighting the Witch. Aslan leaps into battle—right on top of the Witch!—and the friends of Narnia raise a cheer.

"Blowed if I ain't"
*An expression
of amazement*

Gibbered
*Talked unintelligibly
or foolishly*

Muck sweat
*A great amount
of sweat*

**Saccharine
tablet**
*A pill the size of
an aspirin*

Grown-up Thoughts

The first thing Aslan does after defeating death is to breathe life into statues. His search through the dungeons for prisoners brings to mind Jesus' words and ministry on earth—"He has sent me to proclaim freedom for the prisoners" (Luke 4:18; also 1 Peter 3:19–20). In Narnia, the breath of Aslan changes winter to spring, stone to flesh, and despair to hope. For our families, the Holy Spirit can bring new life and set us free where we're bound. It's better than a good story—it's a truth every child deserves to hear!

Flickering Lion

Remember what it looked like as that first lion came back to life? Describe it (or go back and read it again, if you like).

————

Breath of Life

What do you think it might have felt like to come back to life after being a statue?

————

Before and After

Before Aslan's breath, the courtyard was locked in deadly _____; afterwards the whole place rang with happy _____, _____, _____, _____, _____, _____, _____, _____, _____, _____, _____, and _____.

————

Giants!

It you met a good Giant like Rumblebuffin, what would you ask him to do for you?

————

LET'S
TALK
ABOUT
IT

Ear Exam

————

What old friend did Lucy find at the castle?

The Meaning of Everything

Statues, Statues Everywhere

Lewis compared a man who has come from having only a Natural life to one who has Spiritual life as having gone through a change as great as a statue being turned into a real man. He wrote, "That is precisely what Christianity is about. This world is a great sculptor's shop. We are the statues and there is a rumor going round the shop that some of us are someday going to come to life."

Try This at Home

Frozen Stiff

See how long you and your family can hold one position like a statue without moving. Can you go ten seconds? Thirty seconds? Choose a difficult stance and see who gives up first. Then, talk about how it feels to finally be free to move.

"The Spirit of the Lord…has sent me to announce freedom for prisoners. He has sent me so that the blind will see again."

Jesus, in Luke 4:18, nirv

Answers on page 432

> "Yes, of course you'll
> get back to Narnia
> again someday....
> But don't go trying
> to use the same route
> twice. Indeed, don't try
> to get there at all. It'll
> happen when you're
> not looking for it."
> —the Professor

The HUNTING
of the WHITE STAG

The Story ❋ Lucy uses her cordial to heal the wounded, including Edmund. Then everyone journeys to Cair Paravel for a celebration. Aslan slips away, but Mr. Beaver assures them he'll be back. The children reign for years. Then, on a hunt for the White Stag, they come upon a familiar lamp-post…and decide to keep going!

Consorts
*Companions
or partners*

Foreboding
*A sense of impending
evil or misfortune*

Grown-up Thoughts

In the same way that *Magician* reads like Genesis, *The Lion, the Witch and the Wardrobe* reads like the Gospels. Here, we've seen a savior come into Narnia and pay the penalty for their disobedience. Now the followers of Aslan can go on (in the books to come) and take the adventure that shall fall to them with confidence in what the Great Lion has won for them. "Once a king or queen in Narnia, always a king or queen," says Aslan. And we, too (see verse below)—once through Christ we have become royal, no power can take it from us.

You are a chosen people, a royal priesthood, a holy nation, a people belonging to God, that you may declare the praises of him who called you out of darkness into his wonderful light. Once you were not a people, but now you are the people of God; once you had not received mercy, but now you have received mercy.
1 PETER 2:9–10

"Do You Know?"

Lucy asks Susan of Edmund, "Does he know what Aslan did for him?" Do you think they ever told him? Do you know what Jesus did for you?

___

Crabby and Cross

When an upset Lucy tells Aslan to wait while she sees if Edmund will recover, he asks her gravely, "Must *more* people die for Edmund?" Talk about this little scene. Why was Lucy crabby? What did Aslan mean by his question?

___

A Jolly Good Reign

Remember Edmund's plans for Narnia (see chapter 9)? How did things turn out differently?

___

The Bestest Parts

Think back—what parts of *The Lion, the Witch and the Wardrobe* are your favorites, and why?

___

Adventures Ahead

Susan says, "In the name of Aslan, let us go on and take the adventure that shall fall to us." What new adventures would you like to read about in Narnia?

___

FAST FACT

___

In the Middle Ages, a stag was a symbol for Christ.

Answers on page 432

YOUR WISH IS GRANTED!
FOLLOW THE WHITE STAG TO...

Narniac Attack   No. 7

[Test yourself for chapters 12–17]

1. What did Peter forget to do after killing the wolf?

a) *Make sure Susan was okay*
b) *Thank Aslan for his help*
c) *Clean his sword*

2. On what condition did Aslan agree to talk to the Witch?

a) *That she come alone*
b) *That she leave her wand behind*
c) *That she use her cell phone*

3. How did the dwarf and Witch escape during Edmund's rescue?

a) *They ran to the river.*
b) *They hid behind a large stand of trees.*
c) *They disguised themselves as a stump and a boulder.*

4. What decorated the west door of the Great Hall at Cair Paravel?

a) *Shields*
b) *Pictures of the Witch's relatives*
c) *Peacock feathers*

5. What smart battle tactic did Edmund use when he attacked the Witch?

a) *He pulled out her microchip.*
b) *He stole her broom.*
c) *He smashed her wand.*

FOLLOW THE ADVENTURES of two runaway youths, Shasta and Aravis, as they travel through the exotic but threatening land of Calormen on their way north to Narnia and freedom. Helped on their journey by the talking horses Bree and Hwin, the two also come to understand that Aslan is traveling with them toward a greater destiny than they could have ever imagined.

BOOK THREE

The HORSE AND HIS BOY

CHAPTER 1

*"Oh hurrah!"
said Shasta.
"Then we'll go
North. I've been
longing to go to the
North all my life."*

HOW SHASTA SET OUT ON HIS TRAVELS

The Story ❧ A cruel stranger on horseback visits a poor fisherman and offers to buy his son. But the boy, Shasta, decides to run away—"his life was already little better than slavery" anyway. Then Shasta discovers that the stranger's horse can talk…and he wants to run away, too!

Carbuncle
A red precious stone

Indigence
Poverty or need

Judicious
Sensible

Loquacity
Wordiness

Scimitar
A curved sword

Grown-up Thoughts

So begins one of the Chronicles' three "road trip" books (the others are *Voyage* and *Silver Chair*). A journey story is perfect for watching characters face and overcome new challenges. Along the way, they must resolve questions like, "Who am I, *really*?" "Who should I trust?" and, "Which way should I go?" In *Horse,* you'll see these as recurring themes. And as in the great journey stories of the Bible (Abraham, Jacob, Joseph, Moses, and Ruth), Shasta discovers that a Stronger Hand is weaving his experiences—both good and bad—together for a greater purpose.

Travel Itch

What do Shasta and Bree discover they have in common?

_____

Kid for Sale

Do you think the fisherman would have treated Shasta differently if he really were his father?

_____

Runaway

Can you blame Shasta for wanting to leave? Have you ever wanted to run away?

_____

Blah, Blah, Blah

What do you think about how Arsheesh and the stranger talk? Would you like to visit with them?

_____

Speak, Rover!

If you have a pet, what do you think it would say if it could talk?

_____

EAR EXAM

———

What was
Bree's
full name?

Answers on page 432

Kid Test

What Time Is It?

Shasta's adventure begins

a) While Peter is High King of Narnia

b) While Mrs. Macready is standing in the hall of the Professor's house, talking to visitors

c) While Lucy and Susan are Queens in Narnia

d) While all of the above are happening

Uncle Jack Says

"Friendship is born at that moment when one person says to another, 'What! You too? I thought I was the only one!'"

Look It Up

Baby Prince

What baby in the Bible was also found drifting on the water and was raised by adoptive parents? (See Exodus 2.)

And we know that in all things God works for the good of those who love him, who have been called according to his purpose.

ROMANS 8:28

Shasta...saw that the other rider was a very small, slender person, mail-clad...and riding magnificently.

A WAYSIDE ADVENTURE

The Story ◉ From Bree, Shasta learns the hard way how to ride a horse. One moonlit night on their way toward the great city of Tashbaan, prowling lions frighten them. Shasta and Bree get into a race across the plains with another horse and rider— a talking horse, no less, and a girl!

Canter
A horse's gait between a trot and a gallop

Cob
A short-legged, stocky horse

Copse
Woods, thicket

Grown-up Thoughts

Unseen lions roaring in the darkness push the four runaways together in fright and flight. Only after they've met do they realize that traveling together will be much safer. Have you had a "fright in the night" that later turned out to be...right? Sometimes God *causes* a troubling experience; sometimes He *allows* it. Either way, it's for our good. Joseph was sold as a slave into Egypt. Yet, looking back on his hardships, he could tell his family: "It was not you who sent me here, but God" (Genesis 45:8).

I will remember the deeds of the LORD.... Your path led through the sea, your way through the mighty waters, though your footprints were not seen.

PSALM 77:11, 19

Riding Lessons
How can you tell it took a while for Shasta to learn how to properly ride a horse?

_____

How Do I Look?
What was Bree worried about after he rolled on the grass?

_____

Boy Meets Girl
What did Shasta and Aravis think of each other? Do you think they'll become friends?

_____

Roar in the Dark
Do you think it might have been Aslan out there in the dark, helping the two children and two horses to meet each other?

_____

Scary/Not Scary
Bree is afraid of lions in the dark but not of battle. What about you? Make your own Scary/Not Scary list, then talk about it.

LET'S
TALK
ABOUT
IT

"My word!" said Bree, "if I wasn't a Talking Horse what a lovely kick in the face I could give you!"

At the GATES OF TASHBAAN

The Story ❋ Aravis is escaping an arranged marriage to an evil, much older man. Hwin, another Talking Horse of Narnia, is helping her. Then the four arrive at Tashbaan. How can they pass through unnoticed? Disguised, they finally decide, as exactly what they don't want to be—slaves and pack horses!

Dandled
Bounced (as a baby on a knee)

Inquisitive
Curious

Lineage
Ancestry

Grown-up Thoughts

Getting to know Aravis's past prepares us for how her future will unfold. For example, we see the parallels between her story and Shasta's: both were used and abused by fathers, both are longing for freedom and a better future. How will these desires be realized? Watch how Aslan deals with them individually to prepare them to receive the desires of their heart—and his.

"I do? I don't!"

Why didn't Aravis want to get married to Ahoshta Tarkaan?

_____

"Nevertheless my father..."

Is Aravis's story like Shasta's in some ways? How?

_____

LET'S
TALK
ABOUT
IT

Four Portraits

By now, we're getting to know the four main characters—Shasta, Aravis, Bree, and Hwin. Use the following words to describe each one based on what you know so far: *honest, jealous, worried, proud, boastful, brave, smart, good storyteller, humble, good listener, practical.*

_____

Meet You at the Tombs

Why is meeting at a place that's supposed to be haunted a good idea? Or do you think it's a bad idea?

_____

Thinking Ahead

Do you think the disguises will get the four safely through Tashbaan?

_____

EAR EXAM

_____

Shasta called it stealing, Bree called it _____.

Answer on page 432

The Meaning of Everything

The Grand Calormene Style

The culture, language, and dress of the Calormenes reminds many readers of long-ago Persian and Turkish empires. The city of Tashbaan that the children are about to enter is very similar to ancient Tashkent, an oasis city of central Asia that grew up along a river in the middle of a desert.

Try This at Home

Create a Disguise

Suppose you had to travel unnoticed through an enemy city—what would you dress up like? Sort through old or unusual clothes—hats, gloves, jackets, and capes—to come up with a winning disguise. Ask your mom or dad for help.

Humble yourselves before the Lord, and he will lift you up.

JAMES 4:10

You could see that they were ready to be friends with anyone who was friendly and didn't give a fig for anyone who wasn't.

SHASTA FALLS *in with* the NARNIANS

The Story ❋ The runaways push through the crowded streets of Tashbaan. Suddenly, a group of Narnians spy Shasta and decide he is a missing prince. They take him to their guesthouse and treat him royally. There, he meets King Edmund, Queen Susan, Tumnus, and other Narnians.

Avouch
To declare openly

Colonnade
A row of pillars

Minaret
A tower with a round top

Truant
Playing hooky; missing

Grown-up Thoughts

One big idea here: "You can't hide who you really are." Shasta, a poor fisherman's son who's trying to look like a slave looks exactly like…a prince! (Could this be a clue?) The early Christians were treated like criminals and enemies. But Peter told them, Remember who you *really* are—"a chosen people, a royal priesthood" (1 Peter 2:9). Of course, Shasta doesn't yet know his real identity. But already, others know it or sense it. Have you or your children ever experienced something similar—where nonbelievers know or sense that you are different?

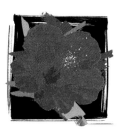

You are a chosen people, a royal priesthood, a holy nation, a people belonging to God.

1 PETER 2:9

Bright Lights

Shasta has never seen a big city before. What is his reaction when he first enters the city?

_____

Treat Me Right

Aravis is upset that she's not treated by the crowds like a rich girl. Do you think she should be treated the same as Shasta, or differently? Why?

_____

Outta My Way!

In Tashbaan, there's only one traffic regulation. What is it?

_____

The Look of Narnia

How did Narnians look and act differently from the people around them in Tashbaan? Why was Shasta attracted to them?

_____

City Folk

What's the biggest city you have ever visited? If you don't live there, would you want to?

_____

LET'S TALK ABOUT IT

FAST FACT

___

Sixty percent of the world still practices arranged marriages.

Answers on page 432

WAY! WAY! MAKE WAY FOR...

Narniac Attack | No. 8

[Test your knowledge on chapters 1–4]

1. Who do you think Shasta's real father might be?

a) A king or other royal person
b) Aravis's dad
c) The Calormene on a big horse

2. What brought Bree and Shasta together with Hwin and Aravis?

a) An accident
b) The roar of lions
c) An attack by Calormenes

3. Why was Aravis running away from home?

a) Her mother fed her mushy broccoli.
b) Her maid told her stories of life in America.
c) Her father wanted her to marry a sixty-year-old humpback with a face like an ape.

4. Why did the Narnians stop their procession through Tashbaan and pick Shasta out of the crowd?

a) He looked like a slave.
b) He looked like a pickpocket.
c) He looked like Prince Corin.

5. Where are the four friends supposed to meet?

a) At the home of Prince Rabadash
b) At the Tombs of the Ancient Kings
c) At the guesthouse of the Narnians

CHAPTER 5

"I suppose we must look like one another. Can I get out the way you've got in?"
—Shasta to Prince Corin

PRINCE CORIN

The Story ⊛ If Susan tells Prince Rabadash she won't marry him, he'll throw the Narnians in prison. Now what? Tumnus comes up with an escape plan and the Raven tells the eavesdropping Shasta how to get to Narnia by land. Then *crash!* Through the window scrambles the real Prince Corin!

Flagon
Pitcher

Fool
A cold dessert made of fruit and cream

Galleon
Sailing ship

Joust
To compete against other knights on horseback

Stoup
A beverage container; a mug

Grown-up Thoughts

Watching the Narnians' free, joyful behavior, Shasta experiences an important awakening about his identity. When the real Prince Corin crashes in, Shasta's a lost son no longer. "I'm a Narnian, I believe," Shasta tells the Prince. "Something Northern anyway." Christian families can be like the Narnians in this chapter. When we model lives of joy and purpose, unbelievers may see in us the true freedom they're seeking. Who are the watchful Shastas in your family's sphere of influence?

Through us, God spreads the knowledge of Christ everywhere like perfume.

2 CORINTHIANS 2:14, NIRV

Lobster Pots

What does the Raven's example of "easily in but not easily out" mean?

_____

Dashing Prince?

How can you tell that Prince Rabadash is probably not a person Queen Susan should marry?

_____

Strike Two

So far, we've met two men who didn't seem like promising husbands—Ahoshta (for Aravis) and Prince Rabadash (for Susan). How are the men alike?

_____

The Trust Problem

Shasta doesn't trust grown-ups because he was raised by a mean man who didn't love him. Are there grown-ups in your life that have earned your trust? How do they treat you?

_____

Good-Bye

Corin to Shasta: "I hope we meet in _____. Go to my father King _____ and tell him you're a _____ of mine." (By the way, do you think they'll meet again?)

_____

LET'S TALK ABOUT IT

WISDOM for NARNIACS

_____

"Easily in but not easily out," said the lobster in the lobster pot.

Answers on page 433

Try This at Home

_A Fine Meal After
the Calormene Fashion_

Make a Calormene-style feast, or at least one dish, at your home. Look in a cookbook for a Persian recipe or on the website for Ali Baba Restaurant: www.alibabarst.com. (Note: Calormene cuisine usually requires adults in the kitchen, or several well-trained slaves.)

While you eat, put on your turban, keep your nose in the air, and flatter everyone with fancy words. Examples:

> _"O most excellent princeling, if it please thee, pass the pepper…"_ (Answer: "To hear is to obey.")
>
> _"Treasure of my heart, more precious than carbuncles, do you like your food?"_ (Answer: "O my father, may you live forever, but this tastes _____.")

If one is nervous there's nothing like having your face toward the danger and having something warm and solid at your back.

SHASTA
AMONG *the* TOMBS

The Story ❁ Shasta hightails it to the Tombs to meet up with his friends. But no one's there. That night, a stray cat comforts the lonely boy. Later a lion roars to protect him, then turns into the cat—or is Shasta dreaming? Next day at sunset, two horses and a groom approach.

Jackal
A wild dog similar to a coyote

Jostled
Pushed or elbowed

Queue
A line of waiting people or vehicles

Skulked
Lurked, prowled

Grown-up Thoughts

Shasta's only company at the Tombs first appears as a stray cat, then as a lion roaring in the distance. Not until chapter 11 do we find out that the cat and the Lion are one. It's another example of how Aslan is both good and not safe—comforting and terrifying. Earlier, Aslan's roaring frightened the travelers for their good (it brought them together). It's fair to assume now that his roaring is frightening dangers away. See what your kids think.

LORD, even before I speak a word, you know all about it. You are all around me.... You hold me in your power.
PSALM 139:4–5, NIRV

Rush

After Shasta climbed out of the window, why was he anxious to get to the Tombs as quickly as possible?

_____

Shivers

Have you ever spent a night somewhere that made you afraid? Talk about it.

_____

LET'S TALK ABOUT IT

Cozy Cat

Shasta is comforted and kept warm at the Tombs by a cat. Have you ever felt comforted by a pet when you were scared? What happened?

_____

Roar for Real?

Do you think Shasta just dreamed about that lion roaring, or do you think it really happened?

_____

Waiting

Shasta waits for his friends all day by the Tombs, and it "seemed about a hundred hours long." Tell about a time when you were waiting and time took f-o-r-e-v-e-r to pass.

_____

Did You Know?

Lewis dedicated *The Horse and His Boy* to David and Douglas Gresham. They were the sons of Joy Davidman Gresham, a friend of Lewis's who moved from America to England to be near him. She, too, was a writer. In 1957, Jack married Joy and became stepfather to David and Douglas.

Kid Test

Your Horse I.Q.

Horses play a big part in this story. What do you know about horses? Answer true or false:

1. You should mount a horse from its right side.
2. You can tell a horse's age by its teeth.
3. A horse can't sleep standing up.
4. The world's smallest horse measures only eighteen inches at the shoulders.

FAST FACT

The roar of a male lion can be heard up to five miles away.

Answers on page 433

Want of Serious

Dad needs gravity. Kids deliver goofiness. But now the storybook opens to the desert.
The gates of Tashbaan at dusk. Tombs.

Itching for serious. I feel this way so often when I come home and hear playing. A dose of gravity for each of them. Some things gravely serious they require.

I feel like shouting...maybe "HEARKEN UNTO ME!" Or something else imperial sounding.

But the *what* foils me and little persons swarm and shriek and dart around my couch, up the stairs, under things.

I have them by bedtime, though. *The Horse and His Boy* has them and brings them to my couch every night. And when I hold it and buzz the pages a few times there is something like serious. Tonight Shasta and Aravis rendezvous at the Tombs.

Before I find my place, I think, *Why not blow it wide open? Why not just ask them and stop being bothered?* Watch as I whittle at the great partition: Parent, Child!

"What's serious to you guys? Is anything serious you think about?" *I can't believe I said it!* "Having fun is great, but what do you take serious?"

Emmae is chomping a spike of hair. She slides it out of her teeth and pours a bucket. She's our chatter-bucket.

"WellumsometimeswhenItellelliotandhe's takingthingsfrommystoreandItellhimnottoand hestilldoesandIsayelliotyoucan'teeeeevvvveeeen nnndothatorI'mtellingmommythat'sserious, yeah."

Processing. I'm processing the bucket. "I guess I want to know if…"

"Well, Daaadd?" Cam is up. I hear Jen tittering gleefully at the sink.

"Well, Caaamm?" I chide.

"You know sometimes, well, Emmae doesn't ask me for…and, umm…sometimes she doesn't even…umm…sometimes she doesn't ask, Dad." Her sea-blue marble eyes are so wide. Her phasers set to stun. It doesn't seem to matter what she means to say if those eyes are there. Her eyes *are* serious. Like the moment when we find the full moon in the viewfinder of our telescope and we switch to the eyepiece and it's…glory, a flavor of serious.

But I wasn't fishing for small crime. Really I wanted what Elliot would say to steer the talk.

He knew that. He knows how my talks work and how to kill them.

He had pulled his knees up into his pajama top. Batman's chest parachuted impossibly.

He had hooked his two front teeth over his lower lip.

He had gone bug-eyed.

He had begun to purr somewhere in his throat like a Mr. Coffee.

Could he save my thread? This rigor-mortisized little Ghandi?

Thwip. His teethed slipped back behind.

He would speak! *He will tell of a solemn, lofty, grand sort of meditation which he had when a memory verse came to mind at sunset and the clouds were just so and—*

"I tell Edwin when he can get on my bed and when he needs to get down RIGHT NOW! Usually, umm, usually it's when he'll start clawing at my raccoon hat!"

There's nothing for this, I think and find my place to read.

Where the grass ends, the desert begins. Trumpets. The gates of Tashbaan shut at dusk. The Tombs. What could be more serious? If everyone is afraid to go there, doesn't that make it a perfect place to get to?

Lord, bring them serious when they can.

—Brian Thomasson

Aravis…was so tired of Lasaraleen's silliness by now that, for the first time, she began to think that traveling with Shasta was really rather more fun than fashionable life in Tashbaan.

ARAVIS *in* TASHBAAN

The Story ❧ Now for a flashback to Aravis's story. After Shasta is taken away by the Narnians, Aravis is recognized by a childhood friend, Lasaraleen, a spoiled rich girl. But together they come up with a getaway plan for Aravis that takes them straight to the palace of the Tisroc.

Ass
Old term for donkey

Dumb
Unable to talk

Litter
A canopied couch carried by men on foot

Punt
A boat you push with a pole

Grown-up Thoughts

The parallels continue to develop in the children's stories. For example, now Aravis and Shasta are both:

* *learning how to cope in unfamiliar surroundings,*
* *getting by often by disguise and deceit,*
* *being watched over by an Unseen Hand.*

And along the way, both characters are changing. Shasta, in the "looking glass" of Corin, learns that some adults can be trusted. Aravis, in the "looking glass" of Lasaraleen, recognizes shallow, self-centered values she is coming to reject.

Glitter Girl

List what you think might be the most important things in Lasaraleen's life.

_____

Old Friends

Aravis and Lasaraleen are different, but still friends. Do you have a good friend who is very different from you? How are you different? What do you like about being together?

_____

"I'll be nobody, just like him."

Aravis still wants to go to Narnia with Shasta, even though she'll have to give up the fashionable life she used to love. What does that tell you about her?

_____

Lasaraleen's Penalty x 3

"Anyone I catch talking about this young lady will be first beaten to _____ and then _____ alive and after that be kept on bread and water for _____ _____. There."

_____

Walking Backward

Why would a king make his servants walk backward in front of him? How would you feel if you were the servant?

_____

WISDOM
for
NARNIACS

———

Your breathing isn't noisy until you try to hide.

The Meaning of Everything

Under the Spell of Arabian Nights

The Horse and His Boy shows the strong influence of the classic of Arabic literature, *The Thousand and One Nights*. That book is a collection of folk tales from ancient Arabia, Egypt, India, and Persia. The stories involve magic (like flying carpets and genies), palace intrigue, and wild adventures. The best known characters are Aladdin, Ali Baba, and Sinbad.

Look It Up

How to Get Along with Your King (or Boss)

The book of Proverbs—written by King Solomon—gives a lot of advice on how to be the favorite. They work for bosses and employees, too! What are these four rules? (See references.)

1. *A king likes servants who are _____ in their work (22:29).*
2. *A king loves a friend whose heart is _____ and whose speech is _____ (22:11).*
3. *A king values a man who speaks the _____ (16:13).*
4. *A king delights in a _____ servant (14:35).*

CHAPTER 8

"But I want her,"
cried the Prince.
"I must have her.
I shall die if I do not
get her—false,
proud, black-hearted
daughter of a dog
that she is!"

IN THE HOUSE *of the* TISROC

The Story ❀ Prince Rabadash is in a pout because the ship carrying the lovely Queen Susan has sailed away. Aravis is in a cramp because she and Lasaraleen are wedged behind a couch, listening. What they hear is the Prince making plans to attack both Archenland and Narnia.

Apophthegm
A short teaching

Inexorable
Unstoppable

Irrefutable
Beyond question

Maleficence
Harm, evil

Maxim
A wise saying

Grown-up Thoughts

In this chapter, we watch what the foolish "wisdom" of flattery gets for the groveling Ahoshta—mostly just another kick in the pants. It seems Lewis was poking fun at a culture very unlike the understated and dignified British culture he was used to. But also, he's dramatizing the fact that insincere flattery can get you into a lot of trouble.

If a man is proud, he will be made low.
But if he isn't proud, he will be honored.
PROVERBS 29:23, NIRV

Head Count

What's the problem with Aravis's hiding place?

_____

Want You, Need You

Prince Rabadash wants to marry Queen Susan so badly he can't sleep. But is that the same thing as true love?

_____

My Father

What would it feel like to be one of the Tisroc's sons? What do you think of how he treated Prince Rabadash?

_____

Grand Fool

Did you laugh at Ahoshta's terrible troubles in this chapter? What did you think was going through Aravis's mind as she watched him suffer?

_____

Battle Plans

How does Prince Rabadash plan to defeat Archenland and Narnia? What do you think will happen?

_____

LET'S
TALK
ABOUT
IT

What was your favorite trip ever? Maybe it was camping with Dad, a bus ride with Grandma, or a journey to somewhere far away like Disney World or Yellowstone or Timbuktu? In *The Horse and His Boy,* Shasta and Aravis leave the only life they've ever known behind and ride off into the unknown. Along the way, they meet new people, discover new things about themselves, and share unforgettable adventures. Road trips are like that. You never know just who you'll meet, what will happen, or where you'll end up. Maybe it's time for your family to break routine and hit the road. Experiencing the unknown invites God to surprise you with new ideas about His big, wonderful world. Fortunately, you don't have to travel far to get that getaway feeling. If you don't have a road trip already in mind, try these simple ideas:

Take a Shasta-Style Road Trip

YOU CAN BE LONG GONE SOONER THAN YOU THINK

Tomb Travelers

Travel to a pioneer graveyard or the tomb or statue of someone famous. Choose a headstone to read. Make a pencil tracing of the stone or engravings. Before you leave for home, sit with your back to the memorial and talk about what you think the person's life was like.

Thataway, Dad!

A family member shuts his or her eyes and points to a spot on the map of your state. Voilà! Your destination. Plan a one- or two-day exploration.

Blast into the Past

Take a trip to Mom or Dad's childhood town, neighborhood, or house. Or you could travel into a grandparent's past. Be sure to take pictures of then and now.

This Way to Nowhere

Pack the car and head out to nowhere. "Nowhere" might be a tiny town, an old ruin, a silly sandwich shop, an empty stretch of highway. When you get there, take family pictures, make a sign—"I've Been to Nowhere and Back!"—and head home.

End of the Line

Bus and subway lines run much further and see much more than most city kids think. Have you been to the end of the line? Take a lunch, your ticket(s), and a grown-up and start your adventure. When your time is half gone, turn around.

SIX ROAD TRIP RULES FOR TRAVELING WELL (*Even Without a Talking Horse*)

1. **Expect to wake up.** Traveling into the unknown means you have to be more alert and ask more questions. You're likely to meet strange people, see strange places, eat strange food. But all those adventures can open your eyes to yourself and the world around you. You might just wake up to the fact that you're royal born!

2. **Accept that something will go wrong.** Let's hope you don't get left at the Tombs all night by yourself, but…somewhere along the way, even the best plans fail. Things get lost. Fun fizzles. Just remember that when things go wrong, you learn more…and laugh more later.

3. **Respect safety.** Smart adventurers prepare ahead for basics like food, water, and shelter. Make sure someone knows where you're going and when you'll be back. You never know when a short walk might turn into a long trudge across the desert.

4. **Eject bad attitudes.** If you start feeling snooty like Aravis or obnoxious like Rabadash, remember that bad attitudes are like bad smells—in small spaces they stink ten times worse! So take those cranky feelings and spit 'em out the window like a wad of used-up gum. Things will get more fun right away.

5. **Collect memories.** Don't you suppose King Cor and Queen Aravis had fun in later years talking about their youthful adventures? To help you remember the good times, bring back postcards, admission tickets, maps, photos, pressed leaves or flowers. Then make a memory book of your trip.

On again, trot and walk and trot, jingle-jingle-jingle, squeak-squeak-squeak, smell of hot horse, smell of hot self, blinding glare, headache. And nothing at all different for mile after mile.

ACROSS THE DESERT

The Story Aravis escapes the city and meets Shasta and the horses at the Tombs. After sharing what they've learned, the four set off across the moonlit desert. They ride through the night, then through burning heat the next day, then to the narrow gorge that will lead them to water and Archenland.

"Faugh!"
An exclamation of disgust

Scullion
A kitchen helper

Victuals
Food

Grown-up Thoughts

The characters are in a race against time. Still, after they've made their crossing, Bree wants to eat first before continuing. Hwin reminds them that when they were not free they would have found the strength to continue from a rider's spurs. "I mean," Hwin says, "oughtn't we to be able to do more even, now that we're free. It's all for Narnia." We face the same issue every time we encounter a difficult task, and our motivation has to come from *inside*. (See Paul's advice to slaves who had become Christians, Colossians 3:22–24.)

Give thanks to the One who led his people through the desert. His faithful love continues forever.

PSALM 136:16, NIRV

Point of View

Aravis and Lasaraleen heard and saw exactly the same thing in the house of the Tisroc, but later they reacted *very* differently. How and why, do you think?

_____

Hot!

Why is Shasta unable to walk in the desert but Aravis can?

_____

Are We There Yet?

Have you ever been on a long hike or trip where you were terribly hungry or thirsty? Talk about it. How did you keep going? Was the trip worth it in the end?

_____

Horse Sense

Bree says that galloping day and night only happens in stories. His advice for a long, fast journey is brisk _____s and short _____s.

_____

EAR EXAM

———

What sang over the children during the night?

LET'S
TALK
ABOUT
IT

HEIGH-HO, BROOH-HOO! THREE CHEERS FOR GOOD OATS AND...

Narniac Attack   No. 9

[Test your knowledge on chapters 5–9]

1. Why was Prince Corin delayed in Tashbaan?

a) *He got lost in the park.*
b) *He got in several fights.*
c) *He was looking for Susan.*

2. Why did Shasta sleep with his back against the cat?

a) *He wanted to see danger coming.*
b) *He wanted to make sure ghosts wouldn't sneak up on him.*
c) *He was just doing what the cat said.*

3. To cross the desert to Archenland from Tashbaan, you have to start at the Tombs and...

a) *ride northwest straight toward Mount Pire.*
b) *ride south, keeping Mount Pire to your right.*
c) *ride east until you get to a Dairy Queen.*

4. What words best describe Lasaraleen?

a) *Dogs, horses, outdoors, leader*
b) *Reading, thoughtful, shy, quiet*
c) *Perfume, dresses, parties, gossip*

5. Calormene servants often respond by saying:

a) *"May the force be with you."*
b) *"To see is to believe."*
c) *"To hear is to obey."*

*"And now, my son,
waste no time on
questions, but obey....
If you run now, without
a moment's rest, you
will still be in time to
warn King Lune....
Run, run: always run."*
—the Hermit to Shasta

CHAPTER 10

The HERMIT
of the SOUTHERN MARCH

The Story ◉ As they're climbing hills into Archenland, Shasta and Aravis look back to see Rabadash's army advancing. The horses break into a gallop. Then a lion chases them and scratches Aravis's back. Shaken and out of breath, they find refuge with a mysterious Hermit, who sends Shasta on to warn King Lune.

Fetlock
A knob and tuft of hair on the back of a horse's leg just above the hoof

March
A border region used for defense

Rowan
An ash tree

Grown-up Thoughts

An unusual chapter packed with learning experiences:

1. Shasta learns that he really is noble—he's willing to lay down his life for his friends (John 15:13).

2. Minutes later, he finds that his new identity means that more will be required of him (Luke 12:48).

3. From the Hermit, Aravis learns how to think in a new way about "luck" and what we don't yet understand (Romans 8:28).

4. A despondent Bree grumbles his way through an important lesson in repentance (Psalm 32).

Are any of these lessons happening in your life?

The LORD is the one who keeps you safe.
So let the Most High God be like a
home to you.
PSALM 91:9, NIRV

Cat Scratch

Why do you think the lion was chasing the group? Why did it just scratch Aravis when it could have killed her?

––––––––

Hundred & What?

How old is the Hermit? Since Shasta mistook him for the King, what do you think he might have looked like?

––––––––

No Such Luck

Do you believe in luck, or do you believe that everything happens as part of God's plan?

––––––––

Run, Run, Run!

After Shasta jumps off his horse to try to save Aravis, he's given another hard task—to keep running to warn King Lune. Does that seem fair to you?

––––––––

Bree Is Blue

What did Bree learn about himself in the race from the lion? What do you think he should do to make things right?

––––––––

LET'S
TALK
ABOUT
IT

> *"I was the lion you do not remember who pushed the boat in which you lay, a child near death, so that it came to shore where a man sat, wakeful at midnight, to receive you."*
> —Aslan

The UNWELCOME FELLOW TRAVELER

The Story ❧ Shasta makes a dash for Anvard but meets King Lune and his hunting party first. The boy reports the coming attack. He is given a horse to follow the party home but soon gets lost in fog. After Rabadash's army thunders past, Aslan speaks out of the darkness.

Furlong
220 yards (201 meters)

Mettle
Courage

Grown-up Thoughts

Shasta's at the crossroads in the fog, and this is the crossroads chapter for the whole book. The prince finally meets both his earthly and spiritual Fathers (King Lune, High King Aslan). Aslan gently explains to Shasta the "why" of many confusing past events in his life, starting with his infancy, and reveals his caring role in it all. It's a moving picture of God's sovereignty.

God has said, "I will never leave you."
HEBREWS 13:5, NIRV

LET'S TALK ABOUT IT

Men in Green

What was King Lune doing when Shasta met him?

_____

Curious Expression

When King Lune first sees Shasta, he shouts, "Corin! My son!" Then he stares hard at Shasta with a curious expression. What's your explanation?

_____

Boo Hoo

Left behind in the fog, Shasta begins to feel very sorry for himself. Have you ever felt sorry for yourself after going through a tough time? Talk about it.

_____

A Crossroads in the Fog

If you can't "see a thing," how do you decide which direction to go?

_____

Only One

When Aslan told Shasta "there was only one lion," were you surprised?

_____

WISDOM
for
NARNIACS

___

When you can't see God ahead of you, look behind you for His tracks.

Try This at Home

Looking for Lion Tracks

Remember when Aslan told Shasta, "I was the lion who…"? What would happen if you looked at your life now and at what's happened to you in the past, and tried to find "Lion tracks"? Lion tracks = signs that God has been walking beside you, ahead of you, behind you to make sure that the right thing happens for you and your family.

Take a few minutes. Be quiet. Write things down. Then talk about it together. You'll be surprised at what you find! Remember, God works through happy things *and* hard things to bring you good. (Read Psalm 119:68 and Romans 8:28.)

Look It Up

Who Are You?

When Shasta asks the Voice, "Who are you?" Aslan answers, "Myself." Who else is known by a similar name? (See Exodus 3:13–14 and John 8:58.)

It took one's breath away to think of the weight that could make a footprint like that.

CHAPTER 12

SHASTA *in* NARNIA

The Story ❧ Shasta drinks water from the Lion's paw print, then walks down into Narnia where he meets friendly creatures. While a stag rushes to Cair Paravel with news about the Calormene attack, three Dwarfs treat Shasta to a huge breakfast. Two days later, Narnian reinforcements arrive, and Prince Corin is with them.

Frowsty
Stale smelling or slovenly in appearance

Haversack
Knapsack

Lintel
Crosspiece at the top of a doorway

Morsel
Bit of food

Grown-up Thoughts

After coming out of fog and darkness, Shasta finds himself in Narnia. He drinks cool water that Aslan provides (John 4:14) and walks on into a new, strange, welcoming, and wonderful world. Author Lewis makes sure the boy gets a fine "English" breakfast (courtesy of three Dwarf brothers). Then Shasta sleeps and sleeps. Something is different here. Is it the presence of the One? "Come to me, all you who are weary and burdened," Jesus said, "and I will give you rest" (Matthew 11:28).

Wheezer

Who is the first woodland creature that Shasta meets in Narnia? How does he react to Shasta's news about the attack?

_____

Yum!

The Dwarfs serve up a huge breakfast for Shasta, who has never eaten bacon, eggs, and toast. But there was one "rather troublesome" detail. What was it?

_____

Three Brothers

The Dwarf brothers' names were _____, _____, and _____.

_____

The Prince's Plan

Corin gets in another fight, then talks Shasta into sneaking into the battle with him. What do you think of Corin's plan? What do you think will happen?

_____

LET'S **TALK** ABOUT **IT**

Kid Test

Learning the Woodland Chatter of Narnia

1. "Good morning, _____."
2. "_____! Better than talking."
3. "_____ alive!"
4. Some_____ ought to tell some_____ about it with a view to doing some_____ (but only if it's remarkable news).

Uncle Jack Says

"You can't get a cup of tea big enough or a book long enough to suit me."

Share with God's people who are in need. Practice hospitality.

ROMANS 12:13

EAR EXAM

___

The great banner of Narnia shows a _____ lion on a _____ ground.

Answers on page 433

CHAPTER 13

*The ground between
the two armies grew
less every moment.
Faster, faster. All
swords out now, all
shields up to the nose,
all prayers said, all
teeth clenched.*

The FIGHT AT ANVARD

The Story ❋ The Narnians attack the Calormenes outside the castle at Anvard, while Archenlanders fight from within. Far away in the Southern March, the Hermit watches the battle in his magic pool. After Rabadash's army is defeated, King Lune brings Corin and Shasta together and asks a very surprising question.

Chide
Scold

Funk
*To shrink in fright
from doing something*

Hauberk
*Defensive armor of
woven metal*

Portcullis
Protective iron bars

Grown-up Thoughts

Having been a soldier in World War I, Lewis knew war well. And he portrays enough violence and carnage in this chapter to convince most parents (kids, too, we hope) that "war is hell." But although Lewis deplored war, he was not a pacifist. He defended the "just war"—where those who prefer peace choose to fight when attacked. At Anvard, Rabadash was the evil aggressor. "By attacking our castle... in time of peace without defiance sent," King Lune explains, the Calormenes aren't noble warriors but traitors and criminals. For more on violence in the Chronicles, see page 356.

*With your help I can
advance against a troop; with my
God I can scale a wall.*

PSALM 18:29

Just Different

Why did Queen Lucy go to battle when Queen Susan stayed back at Cair Paravel?

Young Warrior

What happens to Shasta in the battle?

Hung Up

Prince Rabadash wants to fight King Edmund, if only someone would help him get unhung from the wall! King Edmund accepts the challenge, but King Lune says Rabadash is not a worthy opponent. Why?

That's My Boy!

Why is King Lune proud of his son, Prince Corin, even though he went into the battle when he wasn't supposed to?

*"I'd sooner be eaten
by you than fed by
anyone else."
—Hwin to Aslan*

CHAPTER 14

HOW BREE BECAME A
WISER HORSE

The Story ◎ Back at the Hermit's place, the horses and Aravis are discussing their next step when Aslan jumps over the wall. Hwin greets him affectionately. The Lion explains Aravis's scratches and talks through Bree's tangled feelings. Then Shasta arrives as Prince Cor to invite Aravis to live at Anvard.

Cambric
Thin white material

Halberd
An axlike weapon

Heraldry
*Family symbol
displayed on a shield*

Grown-up Thoughts

Each of the main characters is drawn to Narnia by a deep longing, but interestingly, each one finds Aslan in his or her own way:

Shasta, through affirmation
Aravis, through discipline
Hwin, through an immediate emotional response
Bree, only after he puts aside ego and doubts

It's important as parents to remember that as we try to lead our children to God, He is also drawing them to Himself. And more than likely He will use their unique needs and interests to bring our kids to Himself.

Proud or Frightened?

Do you know people who seem stuck-up but might just be *frightened*? How could you be a friend to them?

_____

Radical Trust

When Hwin meets Aslan she says, "I'd sooner be eaten by you than fed by anyone else." What do you think she means?

_____

Story Specific

Why do you think Aslan tells people only their story, not someone else's?

_____

"You Needed to Know..."

Why did Aslan scratch Aravis?

_____

One Last Roll

Why do you think Bree was so gloomy about going to Narnia? Do you think he will be disappointed?

_____

LET'S
TALK
ABOUT
IT

FAST FACT

___

Today Bree could simply purchase a fashionable horsehair tail extension at a tail hair store as many show horse owners do.

Look It Up

Rising to the Top

Shasta, the poor fisherman's son, becomes a prince. But rising from hardship to success happens a lot in the Bible, too. Name these men:

1. He was a prisoner who became governor of Egypt. (See Genesis 41.)
2. He was a slave's baby who became prince of Egypt. (See Exodus 2.)
3. He was a shepherd boy who became king of Israel. (See 1 Samuel 16.)
4. He was a carpenter from Nazareth who became the Savior. (See Mark 6:1–6.)

Uncle Jack Says

"Every story of conversion is the story of a blessed defeat."

Our sons in their youth will be like well-nurtured plants, and our daughters will be like pillars carved to adorn a palace.

PSALM 144:12

*"Oh, not a Donkey!
Mercy! If it were
even a horse—
e'en—a—hor—
eeh—auh, eeh-auh."
And so the words
died away into a
donkey's bray.*

CHAPTER 15

RABADASH *the* RIDICULOUS

The Story ◈ Aravis is warmly welcomed by King Lune and Queen Lucy. But things do not go as well for Prince Rabadash. When he resists every kindness, Aslan turns him into a donkey. Then Cor discovers he will one day be king. The story ends smashingly for all.

Chafe
Annoy or irritate

Estre
The interior of a building

Lapsed
Onetime; returned to wild ways

Pajock
Fool

Grown-up Thoughts

A lighthearted ending brings good news for the good guys and bad news for arrogant Prince Rabadash. When the kings are wondering what to do with him, Edmund says, "Even a traitor may mend. I have known one that did." (Remember what happened in *Lion*?) But Rabadash is a slave to his own pride and returns Aslan's grace with curses. As a consequence he becomes what he is—a stubborn, foolish donkey.

Commenting on the themes of this story, Kathryn Lindskoog wrote, "Inner slavery is even worse than outward slavery; and inner freedom is even better than outward freedom."

To show mercy is better than to judge.

JAMES 2:13, NIRV

The End

Did you like how the book ended? Is there anything you would have changed?

―――――

King 1, King 2

Who do you think would have made the better king, Cor or Corin?

―――――

Mommy's Story

When Aravis became a mother, what kind of advice do you think she gave her daughters about finding the right husband?

―――――

Raba-donkey

If you'd been there, what would you have recommended as punishment for Prince Rabadash?

―――――

Free Indeed

In the end, who finds freedom in this story and who doesn't?

―――――

WISDOM *for* NARNIACS

―――

Don't act like a donkey if you don't want to turn into one.

LET'S **TALK** ABOUT **IT**

Answers on page 433

CORIN THUNDER-FIST SAYS, "PUT 'EM UP FOR…"

Narniac Attack | No. 10

[Test your knowledge on chapters 10–15]

1. On their race to the Hermit's gate,

a) Bree saves Hwin from the lion.
b) A lion saves Shasta from jackals.
c) Shasta saves Aravis from a lion.

2. When Shasta is following King Lune's hunting party, he falls to the rear. Why?

a) Shasta is barefoot.
b) Shasta is watching for the Calormenes.
c) Shasta doesn't know how to use the horse's reins, so the horse does what it wants.

3. What shows up in Aslan's paw print?

a) A toffee tree, and Shasta eats.
b) Water, and Shasta drinks.
c) A map, and Shasta uses it to find his way.

4. How does the Hermit watch the battle?

a) On the History Channel.
b) On the surface of a smooth pool.
c) From the top of Stormness Head.

5. Why is Bree *not* in a hurry to return to Narnia?

a) He's worried about getting into a battle.
b) He's worried that the Narnians won't let him in.
c) He's worried that his tail still looks funny.

A YEAR AFTER their previous adventure—but a thousand years later, Narnia time—the Pevensie kids are called back to help young Prince Caspian and his right-hand Dwarf, Trumpkin. To claim his rightful throne, Caspian must defeat his wicked Uncle Miraz. But Miraz's people, the Telmarines, have cast a pall of death and destruction over the land, and many believe Aslan no longer cares. Will he come back to save the Narnians from certain defeat?

BOOK FOUR

PRINCE CASPIAN

"This is better than being in a stuffy train on the way back to Latin and French and Algebra!" said Edmund.

The ISLAND

The Story ❖ The four gloomy Pevensie kids are on their way back to boarding school when—hurrah!—the trip is interrupted…and they're off to Narnia again. But what Narnia? They seem to be on an island of overgrown orchards and deserted courtyards.

"By Jove!"
An exclamation of surprise; Jove was a Roman god

Knight-errant
A knight in search of adventures to prove his chivalry

Playbox
A box for a child's toys and personal things (especially at a boarding school)

Grown-up Thoughts

If you've been reading the Chronicles in order, you probably recognize the author's pattern. Lewis isn't much interested in boring old England, and in most stories he can't wait to sweep his children away to enchanted Narnia. Lewis can sympathize with the Pevensies' dread of going back to school. As a boy he was sent to boarding schools where he was badly taught and miserably treated. Of course, Professor Lewis isn't against education; he's *for* kids!

"Do not worry about your life, what you will eat; or about your body, what you will wear."

JESUS, IN LUKE 12:22

School Blues

The children do *not* want to return to school after the holidays. What does that feel like?

_____

Gloom & Board

In Lewis's day, boarding schools (schools where you live all the time) were common. How would you feel about attending one?

_____

"Let's Be Practical"

Which of the children usually thinks ahead and comes up with the smart thing to do? Who is like that in your family?

_____

Quiet

Except for an occasional _____, the island was a very quiet place.

_____

Gulping Gulls?

Peter worried that soon they might be glad to eat raw gulls' eggs. Have you ever been so hungry you ate something you didn't like?

_____

LET'S TALK ABOUT IT

Ear Exam

———

The apples on the ancient tree were *what* color?

Answers on page 433

Kid Test

Travel Plans

This time the children got into Narnia by simply being pulled there by magic—*poof!* But each time the travel arrangements are different. If you haven't yet read all the books, you'll have to take a guess, but can you pick which of these is *not* a way that the children get into Narnia?

1. Through a wardrobe
2. By a magic carpet
3. Through a picture on a wall
4. By touching magic rings
5. By a train accident

The Meaning of Everything

A Roofless Church

C. S. Lewis loved to visit old ruins and castles. His description of a famous English ruin, Tintern Abbey, sounds something like the roofless Cair Paravel: "It is an abbey practically intact except that the roof is gone, and the glass out of the windows, and the floor, instead of pavement, is a trim green lawn. Anything like the sweetness and peace of the long shafts of sunlight falling through the windows on the grass cannot be imagined. All churches should be roofless. A holier place I never saw."

For long ago at a Christmas in Narnia he and Susan and Lucy had been given certain presents which they valued more than their whole kingdom.

CHAPTER 2

The ANCIENT TREASURE HOUSE

The Story ❧ Gradually, the truth dawns—the ancient castle is really Cair Paravel. The reason it's in ruins? While a year has passed in England, hundreds have passed in Narnia. In the castle's treasure chamber, the children find armor and crowns, and most important of all, gifts from a long-ago Christmas.

Dais
A raised platform

Electric torch
Flashlight

Grown-up Thoughts

Aslan's plans for the children will require them to use their gifts if they want to fulfill their destiny (remember, they're "tools, not toys"—chapter 10, *Lion*). The gifts also seem to parallel spiritual gifts mentioned in the New Testament:

> *Peter: sword and shield (leadership, faith)*
> *Lucy: healing tonic (compassion, healing)*
> *Susan: bow and arrow and horn (prayer)*

But what about Edmund, who was in the Witch's company when the gifts were first distributed? Maybe his is discernment.

For example, he uses his flashlight, a gift from home, to help the others find *their* gifts (also, see "Edmund's Torch," next page). How could you help your children discover their special gifts today?

Change

Now that they're back in Narnia, says Peter, it's no good for them to behave like *what* anymore?

_____

Edmund's Torch

At the end of *Lion*, King Edmund is described as "great in council and judgment." How do you think his flashlight might be a picture of his special gift?

_____

Pricey Gifts

How much did the children think their gifts were worth? Do you think God has given you special abilities or interests? What are they?

_____

Name Game

Peter named his sword _____, and with it he killed a _____.

_____

Your Choice

If you could have any one of the gifts the children received, which would you pick?

_____

UNCLE JACK SAYS

"Miracles are a retelling in small letters of the very same story which is written across the whole world in letters too large for some of us to see."

Answers on page 433

Try This at Home

A Treasure Chamber of My Own

Do you have a special place for treasures or souvenirs? If not, make a treasure chamber out of an old cigar box, tool chest, or lunch box. Decorate it with wallpaper, crayon, glitter, or paint. Line it with something soft and place your special things inside—a seashell, a small toy, a letter from a friend, a photograph, a ticket stub. Hide the box somewhere that only you know. Then pick a date in the future when you will "rediscover" your treasures.

Don't fail to use the gift the Holy Spirit gave you.

1 TIMOTHY 4:14, NIRV

Young in the Future Again

A name, a picture, a spark of girl-fire—suddenly, once upon a time is now.

Emmae sits alongside me on the arm of the couch as her grandfather takes us through the family tree album he's been filling. The paper whispers as his rough hands move against the pages.

He brings over a page and there is a lock of golden hair in a tiny bag; a photocopy of a marriage license with the extraordinarily dainty signature of one Lillie Belle Thomasson; and around these, yellowing pictures of a baby, a schoolgirl, a bright young woman.

"Lillie Belle. Your great-grandmother's mother, Emmae," Dad says.

"Her name was *LILLIE BELLE*?" Emmae asks sharply, girl-fire spreading across her face. (Girl-fire comes over little girls when they find in life or books another girl doing something magnanimous or being some way they'd like to be. A girl can wick up energy from once upon a

time in the instant of acquaintance and be bursting with adoration in three seconds!)

The last time I'd seen girl-fire was when we read about Susan finding the chess knight and Lucy remembering the hidden door. Emmae was rapt. "Seee, Elllllliot," she'd jeered. "Peter doesn't do *every*thing like the boss!" And later she put together the sequence and claimed with triumph: "They wouldn't have eeevvveeenn found their magic things if *Susan* didn't get that chessman in the first place!"

But now as we sit here with Grampa, staring at a single album page, you might think there wasn't much for girl-fire to go on, just that name. "It was *LILLIE…BELLE*?" she asks again.

"Indeed it was," Dad replies easily.

"She sounds like from a song, Grampa!" Her eyes are flickering with delight and her bottom lip is out and she reaches up to pop it with a finger. She's thinking, going by all her heart to find this Lillie Belle, and she can hardly bear the press of all her questions.

"Now," says her grandfather, turning the page…

"Oh! Oh! Wait, but Grampa—" Emmae says, but Grampa doesn't hear.

"Yes, and here we have your great-great-uncle. Do you know your uncle back then only signed his name with an X? Here he was, in the Union in the Civil War. That's his X, there."

"Yeah, but Lillie Belle, Grampa, but what did they call her by, you know? Just Lillie or Lillie Belle *all* the time?"

"Why, 'Lillie Belle Anne Marie, Prettiest Princess of the Land,' of course!" I tease.

Emmae grabs both feet and pulls them up to near her chin, rocking back. Dad takes his reading glasses off to wipe them and continues: "It's really quite a thing. In those days a man just made his mark…"

He glances across at Emmae and sees she's not even looking near the X. "You know, Emmae, we might have…" says Grandpa of a sudden. "Melody, do we still have that Bible, old Lillie Belle's? You can see where she's marked and written names in."

My mom goes up the hall. "It would be right in the closet if we do," she says. Emmae rocks upright and rubs her hands together.

Lillie's Bible in a ziplock bag comes out with Grandma. It looks warm yet and the Psalms look pulled on, maybe loose. The prune-colored cover is wrinkled in a thousand predictable tributaries. Her name, gilded, still tells us "Lillie Belle."

Emmae lurches for it and her grandfather winces.

"'Mae," I say, "It's sooo old, be slow with it." Slow means more than careful when there is eagerness. She smiles deeply as she brings it to her knees. *Lillie Belle was here.*

As girl-fire feasts, I decide that maybe staying young while a world ages isn't so difficult to understand as I had made it in our after-reading forum some nights ago.

Elliot and Emmae couldn't quite get how Cair Paravel had aged to crumbling while the children had only been away a year, and I told them to imagine camping in our home a thousand years from now, but tomorrow. But now I see it isn't as hard as that, and it begins when you find just one of the things from way back when.

And it can still work.

And, while it's not quite your youth formula, for these discoveries there is no charge.

And any Grampa's album is as good as any treasure chamber.

And, providing the heart is right, it's almost guaranteed to bring us further than back, to make us young in the future again.

—Brian Thomasson

"I was wondering if perhaps you were going to ask me to breakfast? You've no idea what an appetite it gives one, being executed."
—the Dwarf

The DWARF

The Story ⟐ The children rescue a Dwarf from execution. At first, the Dwarf thinks they're ghosts. But soon he's taking them fishing so they can eat. Then he lights his pipe and prepares to tell the story of Prince Caspian and Old Narnia.

Bathe
Swim

"For nuts"
Slang for "at all" or "no matter what"; similar to "worth beans"

"Garn!"
An exclamation of disgust or aggravation

The War of the Roses
A thirty-year-long civil war in England

Grown-up Thoughts

Enter Trumpkin, the Dwarf—great poet ("whistles and whirligigs!"), fearless guide, and storyteller (he narrates the next four chapters). Never mind that we don't know his name till chapter 8. Never mind that the little guy doubts Aslan's existence for most of the book. Aslan, as we'll see, believes in Trumpkin and likes him very much. Trumpkin also plays a key role in *Voyage,* shows up again in *Silver Chair,* and—your kids will be happy to know—arrives in Aslan's country at time's end.

Rescue the weak and needy;

deliver them from the hand of the wicked.

Psalm 82:4

Danger

The Dwarf says he's a
dangerous criminal. Hmmm.
What do you think?

————

Trigger Finger

Why did Susan
instinctively shoot at the
soldier, not the Dwarf?
Would you have done
the same thing?

————

Ghosts

Do you think there really
are ghosts in the forest by
the sea, or could it be a lie
intended to scare people?

————

Lion Signs

Do you see any clues yet that
Aslan has another plan for the
children in Narnia this time?

————

Haunted

The Dwarf thinks the castle
looks spooky and smells like
ghosts. What is the spookiest
place you've ever been?

————

CHAPTER 4

> *"Your Kings are in
> deadly fear of the sea
> because they can never
> quite forget that in all
> stories Aslan comes
> from over the sea."*
> —Doctor Cornelius

The DWARF TELLS OF
PRINCE CASPIAN

The Story ✦ First his Nurse and now his Tutor, Doctor Cornelius, tell Caspian stories of Old Narnia. So the fairy tales are all true! Once upon a time, animals talked and the woods were alive with fauns and dryads. Maybe, just maybe, some of them are still alive and in hiding.

Buskins
*Laced boots that come
halfway to the knee*

Dryad
*A mythical spirit of
forests and trees;
a wood nymph*

Leads
*A flat roof covered
with sheets of lead.*

Turret
*A small tower extend-
ing above a building*

Grown-up Thoughts

What if you discovered tomorrow that fairy tales were *fact* and your history books *fake*? What a shock! Such is the case for Caspian. Truths about Aslan and Old Narnia have faded into rumor, and rumor has grown into fact (ghosts in the wood, for example). This chapter is a lot about what we believe and why. Years of fearing the truth and living with a guilty conscience have left some Narnians in bondage to lies.

Can you think of parallels in your own experience?

> *Test me, O LORD, and try me,
> examine my heart and my mind;
> for your love is ever before me,
> and I walk continually
> in your truth.*
>
> PSALM 26:2–3

Story Time

Caspian loved when his Nurse told him stories. Who is your favorite storyteller?

————

Rapid Rumors

Heard any rumors lately? Rumors tend to travel faster than the truth! Why?

————

Fairy Tales

Do you know anyone who thinks the Bible is a fairy tale? What are some reasons we know that it isn't?

————

Nope, Never Happened!

Why do the Telmarines want to pretend that Old Narnia never existed?

————

Half a Man

Doctor Cornelius is part _____ and part _____.

————

LET'S
TALK
ABOUT
IT

FAST FACT

———

Of his fictional works, Lewis's favorite was his last, *Till We Have Faces.*

Answers on page 433

The Meaning of Everything

Lizzie and the Leprechauns

Jack Lewis and his brother, Warnie, grew up loving stories. Biographer Brian Sibley writes, "The family's Irish nurse Lizzie Endicott, who looked after the boys, told them wonderful stories about leprechauns and ancient gods. Listening to Lizzie's tales was for Jack the beginning of a lifelong fascination with...myth and legend. Perhaps Jack was thinking of Lizzie when...he described how Caspian's nurse told him fabulous tales of Old Narnia."

Uncle Jack Says

"Now that I am a Christian I do not have moods in which the whole thing looks very improbable: but when I was an atheist I had moods in which Christianity looked terribly probable."

> *"I believe in the High King Peter and the rest that reigned at Cair Paravel, as firmly as I believe in Aslan himself."*
> —*Trufflehunter*

CASPIAN'S ADVENTURE *in the* MOUNTAINS

The Story ❧ Caspian learns he's the rightful king of Narnia, but is in danger of assassination. His Tutor helps him escape. The next day in wild country, he gets knocked off his horse. When he comes to, he meets two Dwarfs—Nikabrik and Trumpkin (the narrator)—and a badger named Trufflehunter.

Antechamber
A smaller room serving as an entryway into a larger room

Courtier
An attendant at a royal court

Fall foul
To clash or have conflict with

Pother
A state of nervous activity; a fuss

Victuals
Food

Grown-up Thoughts

Ironically, even many of the Old Narnians themselves have stopped believing in Aslan and the old stories. "Who believes in Aslan nowadays?" says Trumpkin. But the badger Trufflehunter is a true believer and Caspian's first subject: "As long as you will be true to Old Narnia you shall be *my* King," he tells young Caspian. Have you pledged yourself to the King of kings? Then you can say with Paul, "Now to the King eternal, immortal, invisible, the only God, be honor and glory for ever and ever" (1 Timothy 1:17).

Remember Jesus Christ, raised from the dead, descended from David.

This is my gospel.

PAUL, IN 2 TIMOTHY 2:8

Run!

Without any warning, Caspian had to run away from home and everything familiar. How would that feel?

———————

Trump & Nik

Sure, they're both Dwarfs. But how are they different from each other?

———————

History 101

The Dwarfs themselves don't believe in their own history! How do you suppose that happened?

———————

The King & I

How does Trufflehunter feel about Caspian?

———————

Remember!

Who did Trufflehunter say remembers better— Dwarfs or beasts?

———————

LET'S
TALK
ABOUT
IT

Ear Exam

———

How many noble lords sailed away and never came back?

Horns and Halibuts! It time for...

Narniac Attack   No. 11

[Test Your Knowledge on chapters 1–5]

1. What did Susan find by the well in ancient Cair Paravel?

a) Peter's sword
b) A chessman
c) An apple

2. The Dwarf said being executed really helped one's *what*?

a) Sleep
b) Mood
c) Appetite

3. What is Caspian's aunt's name?

a) Prunaprismia
b) Polypropylene
c) Primadonna

4. What two stars aligned over the tower?

a) Sirius and Saturn
b) Aspirin and Benadryl
c) Tarva and Alambil

5. Why did Nikabrik at first want to kill Caspian?

a) He thought Caspian would taste good.
b) He thought Caspian would betray them.
c) He thought Caspian looked funny.

CHAPTER 6

*It gave Caspian
a shock to realize
that the horrible
creatures of the old
stories, as well as the
nice ones, had some
descendants in
Narnia still.*

The PEOPLE
THAT LIVED IN HIDING

The Story ❧ Caspian meets the Others: three silly bears, a plucky squirrel, more Dwarfs (skeptical, of course), a commanding Centaur, a big mouse, and a host of other creatures. Most of them embrace Caspian quickly. Then the magical day ends with a dance with Fauns!

Girt
Equipped with

Hag
A witch

Rook
*A bird that
resembles the North
American crow*

Smithy
*A workplace where
metal is worked by heat-
ing and hammering*

Water-butt
*A large, open-headed
container for water*

Grown-up Thoughts

Everything changes when Caspian meets Glenstorm. Before now, Caspian hadn't considered a war to rewin Narnia. But the Centaur imparts such vision and courage that "it now seemed to them quite possible that they might win a war and quite certain that they must wage one." In biblical terms, Glenstorm is a prophet—someone who discerns people and the times, hears God's voice, and then pro-claims a vital message. Is there a prophet in your life? What is he or she saying?

*In the past God spoke to
our forefathers through the
prophets...but in these
last days he has spoken
to us by his Son.*
HEBREWS 1:1–2

Profile of Pattertwig

He was far _____ than other squirrels Caspian had seen, nearly the size of a _____, and it was difficult to get him to _____ _____.

_____

Nutty No-No's

What is considered bad manners among squirrels?

_____

Glenstorm Storms In

How did Caspian's encounter with the Centaur Glenstorm change things? Have you met someone who helped you understand something important you should do? Talk about it.

_____

LET'S
TALK
ABOUT
IT

Shaky Alliances

Nikabrik is willing to side with anyone who is also the enemy of Miraz. What's the problem with this kind of thinking?

_____

In Dwarfs We Trust

Why do you think Dwarfs are so very suspicious of men?

_____

Mine & Yours

Glenstorm said it was his job to _____ the skies and the Badger's to _____.

_____

Answers on page 433

> *They were not using the Table nor sitting round it: it was too magic a thing for any common use.*

OLD NARNIA
in DANGER

The Story ❖ Doctor Cornelius brings alarming news—Miraz and his army are near. The whole party travels to Aslan's How, a better place to fight. Soon the enemy is upon them and the Narnians are being defeated. It's time to blow the ancient horn and hope that help arrives in time.

Anteroom
An outer room that opens into another room; often a waiting room

Eggs in moonshine
Foolishness

Entrenchments
Earthen trenches meant to shield warriors in battle

Sortie
An armed attack, especially one made from a place surrounded by enemy forces

Grown-up Thoughts

The group decides that Aslan or the children will most likely arrive at one of the magical places of Narnia—the How (built over the Stone Table where Aslan died), Lantern Waste (where the lamppost stood), or the castle ruins at Cair Paravel (where the High Kings and Queens once reigned). Many Holy Land sites have held sacred meaning for generations: Mount Sinai, the temple in Jerusalem, Bethlehem. Are there places that hold special spiritual significance to you and your family? Talk about it.

> *In you I trust, O my God. Do not let me be put to shame, nor let my enemies triumph over me.*
>
> PSALM 25:2

Eat or Act?

Who had the best plan for how the war council should proceed? Who interrupted it?

_____

How About the How?

Why did Caspian's party decide to travel to Aslan's How? Describe what it looks like—inside and out.

_____

Sacred

What three places do the Narnians consider the most magical? Why?

_____

Ancient Writing

What do you think the ancient writing on the Stone Table might have said?

_____

Rainy Wimbleweather

What would you say to comfort Wimbleweather? Have you ever felt like you caused your team to lose? What happened?

_____

LET'S

TALK

ABOUT

IT

WISDOM
for
NARNIACS

———

Giant Reminder:
Big doesn't always
mean smart.

The Meaning of Everything

Battle Lines

In modern warfare, armies often fight the enemy from a distance with rockets and airplanes. But in medieval times, armies fought close-up. Lines of cavalry (soldiers on horseback), archers (soldiers using bows and arrows), and foot soldiers (armed with swords or spears) faced each other and charged. The advantage of moving into battle in a line was the same as it is in football—the army could deliver a more powerful attack while getting better protection on both sides. And, as in football, the wrong move at the wrong time could lose the game for your team (ask Wimbleweather!).

Look It Up

Holy Ground

Who did God tell that he was standing "on holy ground"? What did God tell him to do? (See Exodus 3:4–6.)

"Thanks for my life, my cure, my breakfast— and my lesson."
—Trumpkin

CHAPTER 8

HOW THEY LEFT *the* ISLAND

The Story Trumpkin's story ends, and we come back to now: four schoolkids recently pulled into Narnia, and a war going badly. At first, Trumpkin is *not* impressed with what the Horn delivered. But soon the children (helped by the magical air of Narnia) prove themselves, and it's off to help Caspian.

Bows; Poop; Prow
See page 188

Hauberk
Defensive armor of woven metal

Jibe
A taunting remark

Jinn
A demon

Pelt
To move at a rapid pace

Seneschal
The chief steward or butler of a great household

Grown-up Thoughts

Susan's horn has pulled the children out of their world right into Narnia. "Golly!" said Edmund. "It's a bit uncomfortable to know that *we* can be whistled for like that." Lucy put it in a better perspective. "But we want to be here, don't we...if Aslan wants us?" Have you felt called by God to do something, said yes, then found yourself on an impossible mission? Remember *Who* called you; He doesn't speak and then not act (Numbers 23:19).

My enemies will turn back when I call out to you for help. Then I will know that God is on my side.

PSALM 56:9, NIRV

Summoned

How do the children feel about being pulled out of their world into Narnia? How would you feel?

_____

"No Offense, But..."

Why does Trumpkin think the children can't help?

_____

One, Two, Three...

Talk about the three ways Edmund, Susan, and Lucy proved themselves to Trumpkin.

_____

Four

Peter didn't do anything to prove himself...or did he?

_____

Sensitive Su

Why was Susan reluctant to beat Trumpkin? Have you ever felt that way when you were competing with a friend?

_____

D.L.F....

stands for what?

_____

LET'S **TALK** ABOUT **IT**

WISDOM
for
NARNIACS

—

Inside every child is a mighty warrior.

Try This at Home

Remember When?

Being on the sea in a rowboat prompts the children to remember the good times. Take a few minutes to recall some of your favorite memories. For example:

Someone showed up and surprised you.
You were especially happy.
It was almost time for a special holiday.
You gave or received a wonderful gift.
Things went terribly wrong, but later it seemed funny.

Share your memories. Now tell someone in your family your favorite memory that involved him or her.

Kid Test

So, Where Is Everybody?

1. Pattertwig is on the way to _____ _____.
2. Trumpkin is steering a _____.
3. Dr. Cornelius, and a lot of creatures, are inside _____ _____.

CHAPTER 9

*A great longing
for the old days
when the trees could
talk in Narnia
came over her.*

WHAT LUCY SAW

The Story The group hikes away from the water and after much trouble—a charging bear, for example—comes to a stream. Which way to go? Lucy spots Aslan on a ridge above them, and she's certain he wants them to follow him. But the others aren't, so they take a vote.

Bally
*An intensifier, slang
for* really *or* very;
similar to bloody
or blooming

Bivouac
A temporary camp

Brick
*A helpful,
reliable person*

Rush
*A rapid flow or
surge of water*

Grown-up Thoughts

The kids are having trouble navigating: Which way to go? Who to listen to? When to turn back? Against all reason, Lucy calls out to the trees and then sees Aslan. Only Edmund believes her (remembering what happened last time he doubted). Sometimes God's leading requires faith, not understanding. He told His people: "I will lead the blind by ways they have not known, along unfamiliar paths I will guide them" (Isaiah 42:16).

A Great Longing

Why do you think it was Lucy who almost woke up the trees?

_____

Wild Inside

Lucy has a horrible idea about humans in our world. What is it? Could it happen?

_____

Hesitation

Why did Susan hesitate to shoot the bear?

_____

Crazy Lucy

Do you think Lucy saw Aslan? Why don't the others believe her?

_____

Clueless

Edmund thinks girls "never carry a map in their heads." Lucy's comeback: "That's because our heads have something inside them." So…do boys have a better sense of direction than girls? Are girls smarter than boys?

_____

LET'S
TALK
ABOUT
IT

Ear Exam

———

Name at least two Narnian summer constellations.

Kid Test

Dwarf Challenge #1

Okay, *you* be Trumpkin! Finish your own Dwarfish exclamations:

"Blinkers and _____!"

"Flapjacks and _____!"

"Poodle pups and _____!"

"_____ and gooseberries!"

Kid Test

Dwarf Challenge #2

Lucy forgot that Dwarfs always snore. What else do you know about Dwarfs in Narnia by now?

1. Dwarfs come in colors _____ and _____.
2. Dwarfs are always less than _____ feet tall.
3. Dwarfs' faces are always covered with _____.
4. Dwarfs are skilled at making armor out of _____.
5. Dwarfs in battle are deadly _____.
6. Dwarfs communicate with the sound of _____.

"Now you are a lioness," said Aslan. "And now all Narnia will be renewed."

CHAPTER 10

The RETURN OF THE LION

The Story ❧ To escape whizzing arrows, the exhausted group must climb back *up* the gorge they just came *down*. Oh, bother! But that night, Aslan comes to Lucy, and it's a joyous reunion. They talk about what might have been, belief, and courage. Then it's time to wake the others.

Battledore
A flat wooden paddle used in an early form of badminton

Bracken
A widespread, often weedy fern

Slanging
To use angry and abusive language

Grown-up Thoughts

In one of Aslan's longest conversations in the Chronicles, Lucy learns surprising spiritual lessons:

She cannot know what "would have happened," but anyone can find out "what will happen" if they obey.
The older Lucy gets, the larger Aslan will appear.
She must follow Aslan, even if it means doing so alone.
Nothing happens the same way twice.

What a gift it would be to have just such an intimate conversation with our Lord! One day we will—in person! (See John 10:27–28; 14:1–3.)

"My sheep listen to my voice; I know them, and they follow me."
JESUS, IN JOHN 10:27

Back up the Gorge

Retracing their steps was hard going, but still, "everyone felt more cheerful." Why, do you think?

———

Follow Me

Aslan wanted Lucy to follow him even if the others wouldn't. What do you think might have happened if she had?

———

"I Had Hoped..."

Lucy hoped Aslan would magically make everything perfect again. Have you ever asked God to do that?

———

Magic Mane

When Lucy buries her face in Aslan's mane, she feels "lion-strength" going into her. What do you think that might feel like?

———

Always Bigger

What do you think Aslan meant when he told Lucy that the older she grows, the bigger he will be?

———

LET'S TALK ABOUT IT

WISDOM
for
NARNIACS

———

The more we grow, the bigger God gets.

Answers on page 434

Narniac Attack   No. 12

[Test Your Knowledge on chapters 6–10]

1. Who were the first creatures Trumpkin introduced Caspian to?

a) *Bulgy bears*
b) *Five black Dwarfs*
c) *Glenstorm the Centaur*

2. Who cried because of a mistake in battle?

a) *Reepicheep*
b) *Wimbleweather*
c) *Trufflehunter*

3. What is the *Splendor Hyaline*?

a) *A nymph*
b) *A ship*
c) *A hotel*

4. Who said that girls never carry a map in their heads?

a) *Caspian*
b) *Columbus*
c) *Edmund*

5. Why did Aslan faintly growl at Lucy during their talk in the woods?

a) *She stepped on his toe.*
b) *She asked why he took so long.*
c) *She wanted to blame her brothers and sister.*

CHAPTER 11

*They felt as glad as
anyone can who feels
afraid, and as afraid
as anyone can
who feels glad.*

The LION ROARS

The Story ⚜ The little group follows Lucy, who follows Aslan, and one by one they finally see the Lion. When they near Alsan's How, he roars. All of Narnia is shaken. Trees bow in worship, and a wild band of ancient people arrive to throw a grape party.

Bilge
Stupid talk or nonsense

Blown
Out of breath

Grousing
*Grumbling or
complaining*

Rum
Strange or unusual

Tig
A game among children

Tinker
*A traveling mender of
metal household utensils*

Grown-up Thoughts

This is a chapter of forgiving and forgetting. Susan and Peter reconciled with both Lucy and Aslan. And Lucy was right: Susan didn't have to say much to Aslan; he knew her tears were real. He called her by name and told her, "You have listened to fears." Then he breathed courage into her. It's a beautiful end to a wrongheaded, wrong-spirited detour—and an encouraging picture of mercy at work.

*Be kind and compassionate to one
another, forgiving each other,
just as in Christ God forgave you.*

EPHESIANS 4:32

Forgiven

If you were Lucy, would you have been able to forgive Susan as easily?

_____

Glad and Afraid

Have you ever felt glad and afraid at the same time? If you have, talk about it.

_____

Dwarf Toss

Why do you think Aslan liked Trumpkin even though Trumpkin hadn't believed in him until now? Would you like to be tossed that way by Aslan?

_____

Fears in the Ears

What fears had Susan been listening to? How can fears lead a person away from what God wants?

_____

Time to Romp!

Why do you think Aslan roared? What did you think about the strange, wild romp?

_____

LET'S
TALK
ABOUT
IT

> *"Either Aslan is dead, or he is not on our side. Or else something stronger than himself keeps him back."*
> *—Nikabrik*

SORCERY *and* SUDDEN VENGEANCE

The Story ❧ Inside Aslan's How, Trumpkin, Peter, and Edmund overhear Nikabrik proposing an evil plan to Caspian. It involves a Hag, a Wer-Wolf, and conjuring up the White Witch. Yikes! When Caspian thunders his opposition, a fight breaks out. Time for Trumpkin and the boys to join in!

Addled
Rotten

Cantrip
A magic spell; a witch's trick

Pasty
A meat-filled pastry

Sentinel
Guard

Venison
Deer meat

Grown-up Thoughts

You can't miss the clear contrast between Nikabrik's "logical" unbelief, and the against-all-odds faith of Caspian and Trufflehunter. Nikabrik is quick to turn to evil power when good power doesn't seem to be coming through. But the badger knows better. He prophetically declares, "Help will come. It may be even now at the door." David often faced enemies with no help in sight. His advice? "Be strong and take heart and wait for the LORD" (Psalm 27:14).

Let no one be found among you... who practices divination or sorcery, interprets omens, engages in witchcraft, or casts spells, or who is a medium or spiritist or who consults the dead.
DEUTERONOMY
18:10–11

Power Play

Nikabrik's theory is that any power that will work is as good as another. What would you say to him?

———

Tired of Waiting

Have you ever prayed for something and it seemed like God took too long to answer? What happened?

———

It's at the Door

What did Trufflehunter say might even now be at the door? And was it?

———

Gone Sour

Caspian is sad about Nikabrik's death and wonders if he would have become a good Dwarf eventually. What do you think?

———

Resurrection Speculation

Did Nikabrik's comments about Aslan's resurrection remind you of anything from the Bible?

———

LET'S TALK ABOUT IT

Kid Test

Witch Is True…and Witch Is False?

T or F: A Witch in Narnia can be either good or bad.

T or F: Witches are never mentioned in the Bible.

T or F: Witches in Narnia are always part human.

T or F: Witches in Narnia wear black pointy hats.

Look It Up

"What's *Taking* So Long?"
Read 1 Samuel 13:6–14. Like Prince Caspian, King Saul was anxiously waiting for help. When the prophet Samuel didn't show up at the set time, Saul took matters into his own hands. What was the tragic consequence?

EAR EXAM

———

Who said, "No one hates better than me"?

*"We don't know
when he will act.
In his time, no
doubt, not ours.
In the meantime
he would like us
to do what we can
on our own."*
—Peter

The HIGH KING
IN COMMAND

The Story ❧ Peter comes up with a plan—he'll challenge Miraz to one-on-one combat. Fortunately, Miraz's men play on his pride to get him to accept the challenge. Meanwhile, the animals vie for the highest ranking position, "marshal of the lists."

Chafe
Annoy or irritate

Dastard
A sneaking, malicious coward

Dotard
Someone whose age has impaired his intellect

Fell
Capable of destroying; lethal

Jackanape
A mischievous child

Lily-livered
Cowardly; timid

Grown-up Thoughts

The Narnian army benefits from the fact that Miraz's own men are not loyal to him. Why should they be? They've watched the impostor scheme and murder his way to power. As far as Sopespian and Glozelle are concerned, if Miraz wins, nothing will change for them; if he dies—oh well, things might improve! In this chapter we suddenly see the chinks in the enemy armor—selfishness, disloyalty, and pride. "Do not those who plot evil go astray?" (Proverbs 14:22).

For the LORD your God is the one who goes with you to fight for you against your enemies to give you victory.

DEUTERONOMY 20:4

Peter the Great

How does Peter show himself to be a wise and brave king?

————

Miraz the Not-So-Great

Miraz's men are willing to see him die. What does that tell you about him as a leader?

————

Mouse Denied

Who thought having Reepicheep as marshal was a bad idea? Do you agree?

————

Bear Pause

Why doesn't Trumpkin want the Bulgy Bear to be marshal?

————

Double Dare!

Has anyone ever challenged you to a dare or a fight? What happened?

————

LET'S
TALK
ABOUT
IT

FAST FACT

———

Lewis wrote all
the Chronicles
with a dip pen
and a bottle of ink.

The Meaning of Everything

*A Knight's Rules of Combat
(A Joust Is Not a Jest)*

In the Middle Ages (A.D. 500 to 1500), disagreements were sometimes settled by a *joust*, or one-on-one combat, between two knights. One knight challenged another (often in writing, as in this chapter), stating what the grievance was, what could be won or lost, and how and where the fight would take place. *The lists* were the narrow lanes, divided by rails, down which the opposing knights charged on horseback. A *marshal of the lists* was a referee who kept things organized and enforced the rules.

Kid Test

Meet You at the Joust

King Peter has decided: The three marshals will be Giant _____, the Centaur _____, and a B_____ _____. (Sorry, R_____! Humans are _____ of mice.) Dinner at _____. Combat at _____ _____ _____ _____.

Answers on page 434

Everyone was awake, everyone was laughing, flutes were playing, cymbals clashing.

HOW ALL WERE VERY BUSY

The Story ❧ Peter is winning his fight when Miraz's own men finish him off, and a battle ensues. Giants, mice, Bears, Telmarines all go at it—whew!—but it's the Awakened Trees who send the Telmarines running. Meanwhile, Aslan is romping through Beruna freeing schoolchildren and healing the sick.

Attend
Pay attention

Inspector
A school official

Order-mark
A demerit or penalty

Rushes
Stiff marsh plants

Silvan
One that lives in or frequents the woods

Tussock
A clump of growing grass

Grown-up Thoughts

A scene of blood and battle suddenly gives way to a joy-filled romp with Aslan at work and at play—a picture of Jesus and His disciples traveling the back roads of Judea and Galilee, spreading joy, loving children, setting ordinary people free. Lewis is playing, too. The deliverance of Gwendolen, for example, is a jab at the kind of education he detested (and had suffered through). He knew children would love this part! Wouldn't your children love to have Aslan interrupt a boring class day with a joyful romp?

Battle Nerves

Edmund was so worried watching Peter fight that he bit his lip until it bled! What were you feeling while Peter was fighting Miraz?

_____

The Trees Are Coming!

What would you do if you saw walking, talking trees? Would that seem scary or fun?

_____

School's Out!

What kind of school do you think Gwendolen attended? Would you like Aslan to interrupt your school sometime?

_____

Glad Tidings

How did Aslan bring justice and joy to Beruna?

_____

"I've Been Waiting..."

Why do you think the sick woman knew it was Aslan and not just a big lion?

_____

LET'S TALK ABOUT IT

Ear Exam

___

What was the name of Gwendolen's teacher?

The Meaning of Everything

Boring, boring, boring as...tapioca!

Lewis didn't think parents or schools should squash children's imaginations or try to explain away God as an impersonal force. He once wrote: "A girl I knew was brought up by 'higher thinking' parents to regard God as perfect 'substance.' In later life she realized that this had actually led her to think of Him as something like a vast tapioca pudding. (To make matters worse, she disliked tapioca.)"

Look It Up

Who else turned water into wine? (See John 2.)

Let them praise his name with dancing and make music to him with tambourine and harp.

PSALM 149:3

Answers on page 434

It's time for you to write and illustrate your own Chronicle of Narnia. Truth is, C. S. Lewis would be very happy if you did. "Write stories to fill up the gaps in Narnian history," he told readers. "I've left you plenty of hints." ❋ Hint, Hint. ❋ Need a place to start? Write what would happen if... ❋ Aslan came on a romp to your school. ❋ You went to the grocery store on the back of a Centaur. ❋ You were in charge of a party at the Dancing Lawn.

MAKE YOUR OWN BOOK

"Once Upon a Time According to Me"

Or, pretend you're somebody you've met in the Chronicles and write one of these titles:

The End of History: What Actually Happened When That Horrid Lion Ruined My Class, by Miss Prizzle, Beruna School

Why I Suck My Paws… by Bulgy Bear

Or put yourself in the story. In Narnia, almost anything is possible:

Prince Bob, by Bob Trumble, Nacogdoches, Texas

My Secret Adventure on Board the Dawn Treader, by Meredith Mosby, Bristol, England

What Happened When Eddie from Chicago Jumped into a Pool in the Wood Between the Worlds in Search of the Perfect Pizza, by Eddie Berretta, Chicago, Illinois

How to Make Your Book

Once you have a story in mind, you need a book to put it in. Here's how to make one in less than half an hour (grown-up help recommended).

What you need:

❊ One 8-1/2" x 11" piece of card stock or heavy scrapbooking paper, in color of your choice. Texture or fiber flecks make it look more like a real book cover.

❊ One strip, about 10" long, of colored masking tape. Wider tape is better. Pick a color that looks good with your cover color.

❊ Needle and thread.

❊ Four to seven pieces of good quality paper—25% cotton bond works best. Four sheets make 12 book pages; seven make 28.

❊ Glue stick.

Make the book cover:

1. Cut card stock in half horizontally to get two 5-1/2" x 8-1/2" pieces.

2. Lay your strip of colored masking tape on a table in front of you vertically, sticky side up. Roll the top and bottom tips of the strip under, sticking them to the table temporarily.

3. Hold your card stock pieces vertically. Now lay them down along the right and left edges of the tape strip, leaving a sticky gap between them. Gap should be just wide enough for your pages.

4. Carefully pull tape ends off table, then fold in and stick down.

Make the inside pages:

1. Neatly stack your pieces of paper together, then fold in half.

2. Unfold. Along the inside crease, sew two stitches, each about as wide as a staple, to hold the pages together. Knot in back.

3. Refold pages. Insert sewn binding into the sticky middle of your book cover.

4. Glue the first page to the inside front cover, and the last page to the inside back cover.

5. Make the first loose page your title page, and the back of it your dedication and copyright page. Now you're ready to write your own Chronicle of Narnia!

—with Laurie Winslow Sargent

But all night Aslan and the Moon gazed upon each other with joyful and unblinking eyes.

CHAPTER 15

ASLAN MAKES A DOOR *in the* AIR

The Story ❀ Aslan heals Reepicheep's tail, then all dance and feast. Five days later, it's time for good-byes. Aslan tells Caspian he is human—a "son of Adam." The Telmarines, humans too, can either stay in Narnia or return to our world. Then Aslan erects a door in the air for the children's passage back to England.

Canny
Careful and shrewd

Fray
A scuffle; a brawl

Litter
A canopied couch carried by men on foot

Mazer
A large drinking bowl or goblet made of metal or hardwood

Pleasantry
A humorous remark or act

Grown-up Thoughts

In this final chapter, Lewis provides us with the history of the Telmarines. They're humans after all. Aslan tells Caspian that being a son of Adam is, "both honor enough to erect the head of the poorest beggar, and shame enough to bow the shoulders of the greatest emperor on earth." Lewis is stating the human condition—shamefully fallen, yet gloriously made in the image of God, and loved by Him.

"Praise and glory and wisdom and thanks and honor and power and strength be to our God for ever and ever. Amen!"

REVELATION 7:12

Ready or Not

Aslan told Caspian about being the new king, "If you had felt yourself sufficient, it would have been a proof that you were not." What do you think he meant by that?

Stay or Go

If you were a Telmarine, would you have stayed in Narnia or gone home to our world?

Private Talks

What do you think Aslan might have said to Susan and Peter when they were alone?

Eat Dirt!

The trees are quite happy to do just that. What's the worst thing you ever had to eat?

The Whole Book

What was your favorite part of *Prince Caspian*? Which characters would you like to read more about in future books?

WISDOM
for
NARNIACS

If you think you don't need help for a big task, that's probably proof that you do.

LET'S
TALK
ABOUT
IT

Answers on page 434

BEFORE YOU STEP THROUGH THE DOOR IN THE AIR, TAKE...

Narniac Attack   No. 13

[Test your knowledge on chapters 11–15]

1. Why did Aslan toss Trumpkin in the air?

a) *To put a good scare into him*

b) *To get him to shut up*

c) *Because he liked him*

2. Why weren't the Dwarfs afraid to summon the White Witch?

a) *Everyone knows a Witch can't harm a Dwarf.*

b) *Dwarfs had gotten along with her all right.*

c) *They thought the Witch was part Dwarf.*

3. In Peter's letter to Miraz he lists which title for his brother Edmund?

a) *Duke of Lantern Waste*

b) *Count of Dracula*

c) *Duke of Hazzard*

4. What kind of lesson was Gwendolen in the middle of when Aslan came by?

a) *History*

b) *Math*

c) *Literature*

5. What kind of dance did Bacchus and Silenus begin?

a) *A harvest dance*

b) *A dance of plenty*

c) *A square dance*

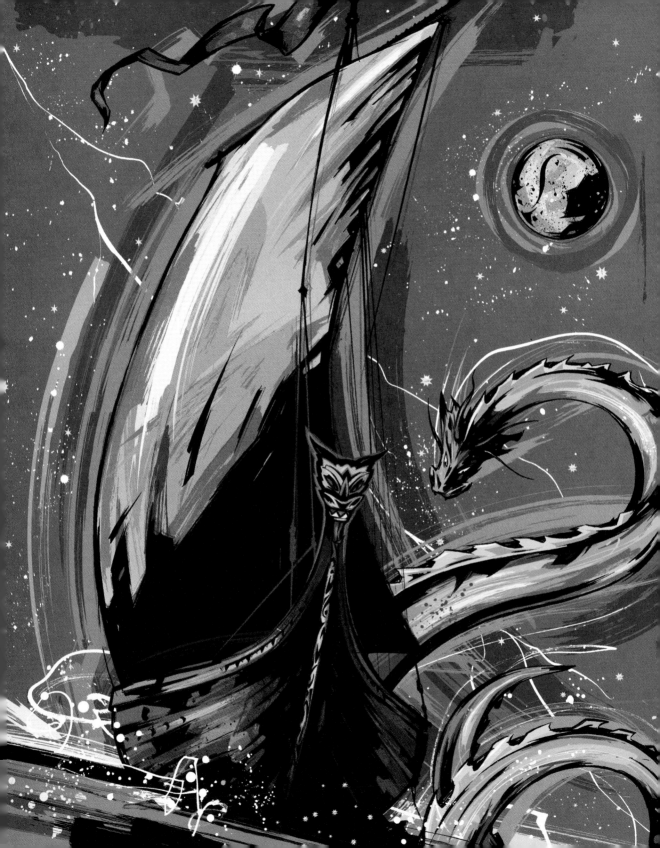

SET SAIL WITH CASPIAN, now King of Narnia, as he searches for seven nobles gone missing during Miraz's evil reign. On board are Edmund, Lucy, their disagreeable cousin Eustace, and a chivalrous mouse named Reepicheep. The voyagers island-hop eastward toward Aslan's country. Along the way they meet dragons, battle a Sea Serpent, and liberate a tribe of Monopods while learning to face the fear and darkness in their own hearts.

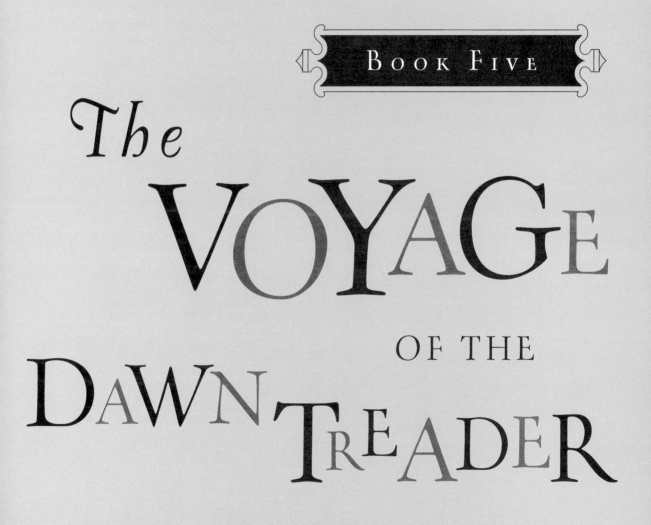

BOOK FIVE

The
VOYAGE
OF THE
DAWN TREADER

Eustace was crying much harder than any boy of his age has a right to cry when nothing worse than a wetting has happened to him.

The PICTURE
IN THE BEDROOM

The Story ❦ Once again, Edmund and Lucy are magically transported to Narnia. Only this time, it's through a picture of a boat—and they're with their obnoxious cousin, Eustace. On board, the Pevensie kids are thrilled to see long-lost friends, while Eustace cries and begs to go home.

Balmier
Crazier

Flagon
Pitcher

Masters
Teachers

Grown-up Thoughts

In this, book 5 of the Chronicles, Lewis unfolds another enchanting answer to the question: "How do you get to Narnia?" The official answer, of course, is, "Well, by magic, silly." In *The Voyage of the Dawn Treader*, it's a magic of imagination. The scene where the picture comes to life is a common fantasy for kids, and yet another way that the author teaches the biblical truth that there is more to life than meets the eye. Like Edmund in *Lion*,

Eustace mocks the idea of a "secret country"—only to soon find himself in it.

If I rise on the wings of the dawn,
if I settle on the far side of the sea,
even there your hand will guide me,
your right hand will hold me fast.
PSALM 139:9–10

"Scrubb's the Name"

What do you think Lewis meant when he said Eustace Clarence Scrubb almost deserved his name?

_____

Harold & Alberta

Would you like to call your Mom or Dad by their first name? Would they let you?

_____

Cool Mouse

How did Reepicheep respond to Eustace's insults? What does that say about him?

_____

Crybaby

Eustace cries and wants to go home, while Lucy is excited to have an adventure. Do you think Eustace will change his mind soon?

_____

Picture This

Have you ever looked at a picture of a place and wished you could *go* there? If you could, what picture would you choose?

_____

LET'S
TALK
ABOUT
IT

FAST FACT

____

When Clive Staples (Lewis) was five, he decided to change his unfortunate name to "Jack."

The Meaning of Everything

"Modern Folk"

Lewis describes Eustace's parents as people whose lifestyle reflects the "latest new thinking." Harold and Alberta are against meat, tobacco, and alcohol, for example, things that Lewis enjoyed. Later, we learn that Eustace attends a school that's soft on punishment, and he's read "all the wrong books." Lewis was happily old-fashioned, and he worried that fads and silly ideas were replacing traditional values. Here, he's not so much attacking these lifestyle choices (lots of smart people are vegetarians, or don't smoke or drink) as he is poking fun at how some people seem to be slaves to whatever thinking is "new."

Did You Know?

Lewis had a special love for ships, as did his brother, Warren. As a boy, Lewis traveled by ship between his home in Ireland and school in England.

Say It Again, Sailor!

If you want to sail with Caspian and his crew of adventurers, you have to know what's what on board ship! The *Dawn Treader* was a dromond, a small medieval ship powered by one sail and (if necessary) oars. To make sure you're ready for sea, match the number on the part of *Dawn Treader* with the description below.

1. Aft—toward the rear (stern)
2. Aloft—up in the sails or rigging
3. Bow—front end; AKA the prow
4. Deck—the platform that runs from one side of the ship to the other
5. Forecastle or fo'csle—the raised decking at the bow, often with cabins below for the crew
6. Fore—toward the front (bow)
7. Hull—the outer body of a ship; the part that floats in the water
8. Keel—the backbone of the ship running from bow to stern along the bottom of the hull
9. Mast—the vertical pole that supports sails and rigging
10. Poop deck—the raised decking at the stern, often with cabins below for the captain
11. Rigging—ropes (lines) that secure spars and sails
12. Sail—a large piece of fabric that catches the wind and moves the ship forward
13. Spar—a strong pole that supports sails or rigging
14. Stern—rear end; astern is toward the stern
15. Yard—the spar that hangs from the mast and supports the top of a sail

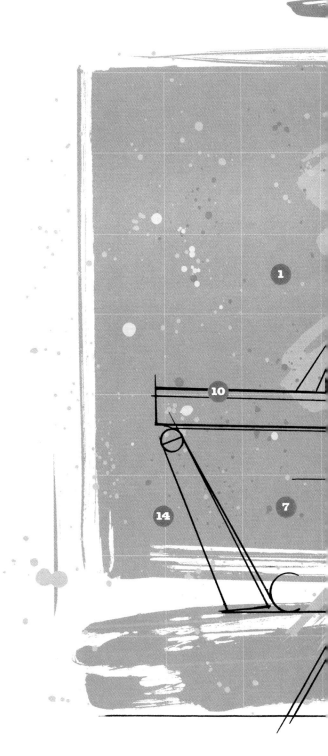

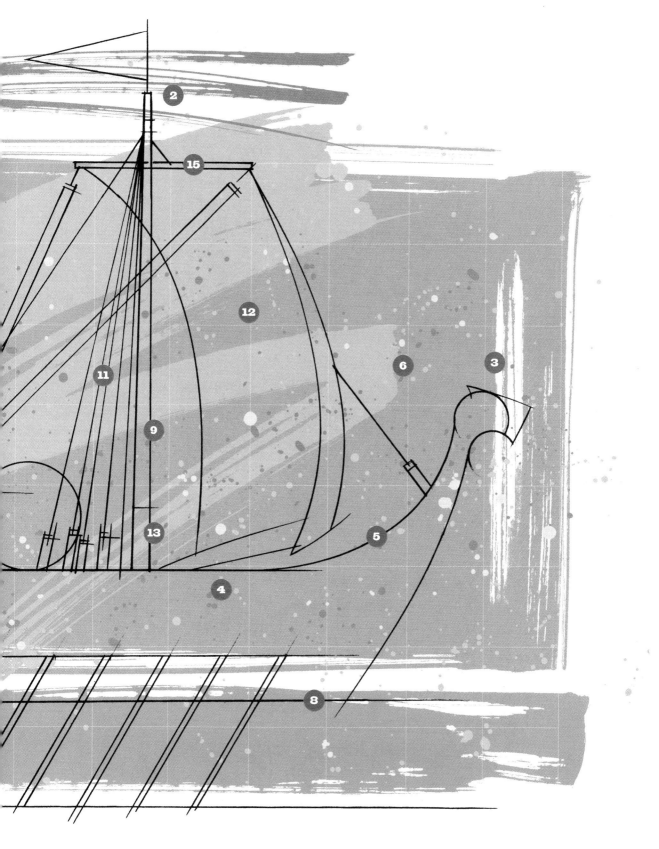

> *"But do you think...Aslan's country would be that sort of country—I mean, the sort you could ever sail to?"*
> *—Lucy*

ON BOARD
The DAWN TREADER

The Story ● The children learn that Caspian is on a voyage to find the missing seven lords, while Chief Mouse Reepicheep is intent on reaching Aslan's country. Poor Eustace, though, is intent on spreading misery. Even after Lucy heals his seasickness with her enchanted cordial, he's as obnoxious as ever.

Cheek
Rudeness or back talk

Corporal punishment
Spanking

Kinsman
A male relative

Poltroon
A coward

Rapier
A long, slender, two-edged sword

Smote
Rebuked or chastened

Trice
An instant

Grown-up Thoughts

Reepicheep's verse tells him that he will finally find all he seeks in Aslan's country. Does this sound a lot like your own desire for heaven? In *Mere Christianity* Lewis wrote, "I must make it the main object of life to press on to that other country and to help others do the same." His words echo the heroes of faith: "They were longing for a better country—a heavenly one. Therefore God is not ashamed to be called their God, for he has prepared a city for them" (Hebrews 11:16).

A man who is wise says gracious things. But a foolish person is destroyed by what his own lips speak.
ECCLESIASTES 10:12, NIRV

Destination Forever

Reepicheep wants to find Aslan's country. What is the name of the place where God lives?

_____

Noble Quest

Caspian wants to find some good men who disappeared a long time ago. What does this tell you about Caspian's character?

_____

Troublemakers

Do you know any people like Eustace? For example, they say mean things to other people, and only get nastier when you're nice to them? What's the best way to get along with them?

_____

Dear Diary

When Eustace writes in his journal, how does he describe events?

_____

Spanked by a Mouse

How did you feel when Reepicheep swatted Eustace?

_____

Ear Exam

___

How much time has passed in Narnia since the children were last here?

LET'S

TALK

ABOUT

IT

Answers on page 434

Kid Test

Ships Ahoy!

How do you feel about being on a ship?

"I feel sick and turn green just thinking about it."

"Fine—as long as we don't leave port!"

"I'd love to ride on a ship someday."

"I'm already a seasoned sailor."

Look It Up

What happened to the prophet Jonah when he ran away to sea? (See Jonah 1–2.)

The Meaning of Everything

Brave Mouse on Board

Lewis loved mice, which might explain why Reepicheep is featured so often in the Chronicles. As a boy, Lewis had a pet mouse and wrote stories about a heroic mouse who conquered Cat-Land. Many years later he wrote to an American girl: "I love real mice. There are lots in my rooms at college but I have never set a trap. When I sit up late working, they poke their heads out from behind the curtains just as if they were saying, 'Hi! Time for *you* to go to bed. We want to come out and play!'"

"In a civilized country like where I come from," said Eustace, "the ships are so big that when you're inside you wouldn't know you were at sea at all."

The LONE ISLANDS

The Story ❖ On the Island of Felimath, Caspian and the others are taken captive by slave traders. Caspian is quickly sold to—surprise!—the missing Lord Bern. Bern cautions Caspian against trusting Governor Gumpas. He suggests a plan that will keep everyone safe.

"Blimey"
Exclamation of surprise

Carrion
Dead or decaying flesh

Fief
Piece of land

Jabber
Endless talking

Moved
Requested

Over-awed
Intimidated

Taking on
Showing emotion

Grown-up Thoughts

Here's an opportunity to talk with your kids about the evils of slavery: Why is it wrong to treat people like property that you can own, buy, or sell? How has the United States sinned in the past on this issue? You could also look together at how God responded to the captivity of the Israelites when they were in Egypt. (See Exodus 3:7–8.)

We are no longer slaves of sin.

ROMANS 6:6, NIRV

Slaves of Sin

The Bible tells us that after we receive Jesus, we're no longer "slaves of sin." What do you think that means?

_____

Yakety Yak

Why do the slave traders think Reepicheep is more valuable than Eustace?

_____

Secret Identity

Why did Caspian want to hide his true identity?

_____

Knees First

As soon as Lord Bern learned that Caspian was King, he fell on his knees. What does kneeling in front of someone mean? Have you ever gotten on your knees to pray?

_____

Meanwhile, Back in Narnia...

Who did the King leave in charge in Narnia?

LET'S
TALK
ABOUT
IT

"No interviews without appointments except between nine and ten p.m. on second Saturdays."
—*Gumpas*

WHAT CASPIAN DID THERE

The Story ❧ When Caspian confronts Gumpas about the slave trade, the governor spouts a lot of flimsy excuses and bureaucratic nonsense. Caspian replaces him with Bern as the Duke, saying, "Enough governors!" Then he breaks up the slave trade and rescues his friends, even "Sulky" (guess who that is).

Bilious
Sickly, greenish

Languid
Lacking energy or vitality; weak

Liege
Lord

Pike
A long spear

Pincers
A tool with jaws for grasping

Postern
A small rear gate

Tribute
Taxes

Grown-up Thoughts

King Caspian arrives unexpectedly at Narrowhaven to find that Gumpas is not truly serving him. Gumpas had been able to set the standards of what "serving" his people meant—until the real King showed up! This echoes Jesus' warning about the servant who is not prepared for his master's coming. Jesus said that those who are not faithful when the master arrives will lose what they have to those who are (Matthew 25:28-29). Which is what happened when Lord Bern replaced Gumpas.

Imagine That!

Caspian wisely used Gumpas's own imagination to gain the upper hand. How is this smarter than having an actual battle?

_____

Sulky

Eustace was so ungrateful to be rescued, do you think Caspian should have left him behind?

_____

Gumpas Bumpus

Why did Caspian fire Governor Gumpas and give his job to Lord Bern?

_____

Impromptu Parade

How did the parade happen? Have you ever been part of a parade?

_____

Bad Eggs

What do you think Caspian meant when he compared progress to an egg going bad?

_____

LET'S TALK ABOUT IT

WISDOM
for
NARNIACS

———

Your strongest weapon may be your opponent's imagination.

The Meaning of Everything

Backwards Progress

Lewis enjoys poking fun at bad government and fake progress in this chapter. For example, Governor Gumpas is called "his Sufficiency"— not much of an honor, when you think about it. Gumpas accused Caspian of turning back the clock, but of course, the clock in the Lone Isles definitely needed to be reset! Lewis wrote in _Mere Christianity_ that if a clock is wrong, setting it back might be the most sensible thing to do.

Uncle Jack Says

"We all want progress, but if you're on the wrong road, progress means doing an about-turn and walking back to the right road; in that case, the man who turns back soonest is the most progressive."

"Therefore keep watch, because you do not know on what day your Lord will come."

JESUS, IN MATTHEW 24:42

> *"Lucy gives me a little of her water ration. She says girls don't get as thirsty as boys. I had often thought this but it ought to be more generally known at sea."*
> —*Eustace's diary*

The STORM
AND WHAT CAME OF IT

The Story   Leaving Narrowhaven, the *Dawn Treader* sails into a terrible storm, then into dead calm. Water must be rationed and everyone is suffering. Eustace's diary is crammed with ugly opinions about everything and everybody. When they drop anchor at another island, he slips away to escape work. Then the fog closes in.

Becalmed
Made calm; still

Buskins
Laced boots that come halfway to the knee

Cataract
A great downpour or waterfall

Listing
Leaning over or to one side

Odious
Hateful

Prig
A conceited, annoying person

Grown-up Thoughts

Through Eustace's diary, Lewis gives us a front-row seat to Eustace's amazing talent to convince himself of his own innocence and of others' wrongdoing. He seems to be getting worse, if that's possible—"He had persuaded himself that they [the others] were all fiends in human form." What he fails to see, though the reader doesn't, is that the real monster is in the mirror.

People who refuse to work want things and get nothing. But the longings of people who work hard are completely satisfied.
PROVERBS 13:4, NIRV

Stormy Weather

Stormy weather can change your mood or force you to change plans. Has that ever happened to you?

_____

Lazy & Lonely

Eustace didn't want to work hard. But he also got lonely. What advice would you have given Eustace on how to feel happier? Do you think he would have taken it?

_____

Thirsty Thief

Could you tell that Eustace was planning to steal some water? How did he try to make it sound in his diary?

_____

Water for a Whiner

Lucy made up a reason to share some of her water with Eustace. How did he respond? Who does the Bible say you should give water to? (See Proverbs 25:21.)

_____

Ear Exam

———

What important part of the ship was lost except for a stump?

LET'S
TALK
ABOUT
IT

Storms past. Seas calm. Time for…

Narniac Attack | No. 14

[Test your knowledge on chapters 1–5]

1. What does Eustace call his mother?

a) *Rosemary*
b) *Alice*
c) *Alberta*

2. How did Eustace react when he first got out of the water and on board the *Dawn Treader*?

a) *He blubbed like a baby.*
b) *He pulled Reepicheep's tail.*
c) *He laughed at Lucy's wet hair.*

3. Why is Caspian sailing east?

a) *To look for delinquent governors*
b) *To locate seven lost lords*
c) *To torture Eustace*

4. What was the name of the slave merchant who captured the group?

a) *Tuck*
b) *Pug*
c) *Slick*

5. During the storm, which of these did *not* go overboard?

a) *The poultry*
b) *The chess set*
c) *A man*

Sleeping on a dragon's hoard with greedy, dragonish thoughts in his heart, he had become a dragon himself.

The ADVENTURES OF EUSTACE

The Story ❧ Dragonish thoughts in his heart, Eustace falls asleep on a dragon's treasure hoard and wakes up to find—oh, horror!—he's turned into a dragon. When the others spot a dragon on the beach, they're frightened. But wait until they discover the truth.

Blighter
A persistently annoying person

Constancy
Holding firm without wavering or changing one's mind

Shamming
Pretending

Grown-up Thoughts

You could title this chapter, "Eustace Meets Himself." Monsters in training, beware: Try hard enough, long enough, and you'll succeed. But there's an even more sobering lesson: each of us is *born* Eustace—dragonish and hateful. The Bible calls it a sin nature. Lewis simply took the truth of Romans 3:23—"all have sinned and fall short of the glory of God"—and made it look like dragon scales on an obnoxious little boy.

So how can we be saved?

All of us have become like someone who is "unclean." All of the good things we do are like polluted rags to you.

ISAIAH 64:5-6

Boring Bookworms

Eustace had read none of the "right books." What kind of books do you think a boy should read?

_____

Treasure Pleasure

How was Eustace planning to spend his treasure?

_____

Boy Poison

Rhince suggested that maybe the dead dragon had "ate the little brat and died of him." Was Eustace _that_ bad?

_____

Dragon Dreams

Did the story make you want to be a dragon? Or did you begin to feel sorry for Eustace?

_____

Tongue-Tied

What do you think will be the hardest part of being a dragon for Eustace—and the greatest relief to everyone else?

_____

LET'S TALK ABOUT IT

> "The very first tear he made was so deep that I thought it had gone right into my heart. And when he began pulling the skin off, it hurt worse than anything I've ever felt."
> —Eustace

HOW THE ADVENTURE ENDED

The Story ◦ Eustace makes himself useful as a Dragon, but he's miserable. Then one morning, he meets Aslan. The Lion helps Eustace to shed his dragon skin and become a boy again. He has not changed completely, but the "cure" has begun.

Billy-oh
A great amount

Ejaculation
A sudden, short exclamation

Mouldy
Moldy

Quoit
A flat metal ring used in a throwing game like horseshoes

Grown-up Thoughts

Don't miss the chance to talk with your children about the salvation message here, even if it's later. Eustace's story is an unforgettable picture of passing from spiritual death to new life in Christ. The boy can't strip away his own scales; he needs Aslan to do it for him. We can't save ourselves, either; only God in His mercy can do that. Jesus said: "No one can enter the kingdom of God unless he is born of water and the Spirit. Flesh gives birth to flesh, but the Spirit gives birth to spirit" (John 3:5–6).

Therefore, if anyone is in Christ, he is a new creation; the old has gone, the new has come!

2 CORINTHIANS 5:17

Eustace Fire-Breath

How did the group treat Eustace when they discovered he was the dragon? Would you have done the same?

———————

My Life as a Dragon

Was it a good idea for Eustace to be a dragon for a while before he met Aslan? Why?

———————

"I Can't Do It Myself"

On his own, Eustace couldn't stop being a dragon. Who is the only One who can change you deep in your heart and make you a new person?

———————

Dunked

Does Eustace's dip in the pool remind you of anything?

———————

That Hurts!

Eustace said it *hurt* but *felt good* when Aslan pulled off his dragon skin. What could that mean?

———————

LET'S TALK ABOUT IT

Ear Exam

———

Who was Eustace the dragon's "most constant comforter"?

Kid Test

Do You Know Your Dragons?

1. Most dragons are:

a) green.   b) purple.   c) red.

2. Dragons usually breathe:

a) bubbles.   b) smoke.   c) fire.

3. Another famous dragon is named:

a) Doug.   b) Puff.   c) Barney.

4. Dragons like to eat:

a) people.   b) other dragons.   c) large fish.

Look It Up

Falling Scales

What unlikable man became a Christian, and later, "something like scales" fell from his eyes? (See Acts 9:17–18.)

Try This at Home

Dragon Night

Since dragons can't talk, everyone agrees that they will not speak for an entire evening, including at dinner. (It's harder than you think!) Meanwhile, what can you do to be as helpful as Eustace was?

Answers on page 434

Going Dragon

Why would Eustace lie down for those claws to undragon him forever…
especially if it was going to hurt?

Eustace going dragon was sort of a surprise to us. It made us uncomfortable, even in pajamas. I couldn't get ready to talk about it so I kept reading and feeling the question-eyes on me night after night.

The last thing we stopped to talk about was how Eustace walked a knife ridge with sheer cliffs on either side in the rain and fog without falling. Didn't Shasta take a walk like that? Walking north and north forever through the fog?

But Eustace was a fusspot. A real snotty-pants. We felt bad when the only dragon that could eat him up and died. And worse when he saw the gleamings in the lair. His thoughts of being rich in Calormen made us twist.

We ended there and all to bed.

When we came to read next, we met the

Eustace was a fusspot. A real snotty-pants. We felt bad when the only dragon that could eat him up and died.

dragon, Eustace. We watched him fall immediately on a carcass and scarf it greedily to the bones.

I wanted to talk about going to bed with dragonish thoughts and getting what's due. It didn't take, though. I could tell they were transfixed. Eustace was not so terrible to them. He was power. He was fire in his breath. He was vaulting over mountains with his great bat wings.

Useless Eustace was better art now! He tore pines out by the roots and roasted boars in a breath. He gave rides and I gave up fishing for the moral. Elliot's eyes gleamed when I read the dragon parts. He got me gleaming too and relishing the power. Power always seems best to Elliot and me. Power makes us gleam at each other when we see something powerful on TV or hear thunder outside. Anything like that.

And later, when it started to seem like Eustace would be just another Clifford, but mopey all the time, Elliot asked me, "What about all that treasure, Dad?"

"I…I guess he doesn't want it, El. He wants to be a kid again…" But even as I spoke, I brooded in my own heart-lair:

What a waste! He made such a perfect dragon! And with both might and wealth he could own the whole island and take on anything that opposed his illimitable reign! He could give himself to what he was all along! No arrow could pierce his armor and no foe could stand before him!

I knew then that we had all caught it, so the misery of Eustace was hard for us to understand. And it got harder when we read how he went to Aslan for a cure. Why would Eustace lie down for those claws to undragon him forever…especially if it was going to hurt?

As the lion worked to bring our Eustace out, I grasped for something to help us each accept the story: "Maybe Eustace didn't want to die like he saw the other dragon die…'member that? How he was right there when the other dragon died?" I finally said, so unsatisfied myself. But even as I spoke, bared now as I was, I prayed,

Lord, we are a dragon family!

—Brian Thomasson

"The King who owned this island," said Caspian slowly, and his face flushed as he spoke, "would soon be the richest of the Kings of the world."

TWO NARROW ESCAPES

The Story ◈ Two very close calls: First, a huge Sea Serpent tries to smash the *Dawn Treader* into matchsticks. Then a mysterious lake of gold tempts Caspian to be the richest king in the world. But when Aslan walks by, the spell of greed is broken.

Baccy
Tobacco

Coracle
A small, rounded boat

Cricket
An outdoor game played by two teams of eleven players each using bats, a ball, and two goals called wickets

Cricket pitch
The field where you play cricket

Vermilions
Vivid red colors

Grown-up Thoughts

When the normally noble Caspian contemplates the potential riches of the golden pool, he gets that "flushed" look and begins scheming to protect his discovery. Yet it's not the pool itself but the greed it arouses in Caspian that's threatening. Having money isn't wrong, but the Bible says that "the love of money is a root of all kinds of evil" (I Timothy 6:10). Do you believe Christ can rescue us from the lust for wealth just like Aslan did for the explorers?

People who want to get rich fall into temptation and a trap and into many foolish and harmful desires that plunge men into ruin and destruction.

1 TIMOTHY 6:9

Brain vs. Brawn

When the Sea Serpent attacked, swords were useless. Who saved the day with a bright idea?

_____

Golden Dreams

Have you ever dreamed of finding buried treasure or suddenly becoming very rich? Would having a lot of money change how you behave or treat other people? (Be honest!)

_____

Pull Together, Push Apart

The Sea Serpent inspired the crew to fight as a team; the gold water made them start squabbling. Why the difference?

_____

Who's the Boss?

At the pool, Caspian and Edmund argued about who was really in charge. Who do you think was right?

_____

Gold? What Gold?

How did Aslan protect the rest of the crew from the temptation of the gold? Can Jesus protect us from temptation in the same way?

LET'S
TALK
ABOUT
IT

CHAPTER 9

> *"So there we all
> were so ugly we
> couldn't bear to look
> at one another."*
> —the Chief Voice

The ISLAND OF THE VOICES

The Story ❧ Things keep getting stranger. On an island of invisible beings who make thumping noises, it's up to Lucy to discover the spell that will make them visible again. But will she also encounter the evil Magician who made them disappear?

Come up to scratch
Measure up

Enmity
Hatred; ill will

Muck sweat
A great amount of sweat

Parley
To have a discussion, especially with an enemy

An ugly furrow to plow
An unpleasant job

Grown-up Thoughts

The invisible but very silly beings display exuberant and unwavering allegiance to their Chief. Maybe Professor Lewis was poking fun at the mindless yes-ism that passes for loyalty (in classrooms? in faculty committees?). Maybe he's having fun with an ancient report of one-legged beings from the Greek writer Pliny. Maybe he's saying, "Friends, there are worse fates than being ugly!" Or maybe, after all his fun with Eustace, he's asking, "Just being agreeable isn't enough now, is it? A bloke must still do some thinking!" See what your family thinks…and read on!

Now faith is being sure of what we hope for and certain of what we do not see.

HEBREWS 11:1

"Yes, Boss!"

Why do you think the beings agree with everything their leader says? Is this a good thing to do?

———————

Ugly or Unseen?

How would it feel to be uglified? How about invisible? Which would you rather be?

———————

No C Me

If you could be invisible for one day, what would you do?

———————

A Scary Task

The invisible beings asked Lucy to do what they were afraid to do themselves. Would you say yes like Lucy does?

———————

Do You Hear Voices?

When Lucy heard the strange thumping and then voices, what did you think was happening?

———————

Mysterious Enemies

How do you fight an enemy you can't see? What kinds of invisible enemies do Christians fight? (See Ephesians 6:12.)

———————

W I S D O M
f o r
N A R N I A C S

———

It's better to be seen and not pretty than not seen at all.

LET'S TALK ABOUT IT

"RIGHT YOU ARE! RIGHT YOU ARE!" IT'S...

Narniac Attack   No. 15

[Test your knowledge on chapters 5–9]

1. Who tried to steal water after the big storm?

a) *Drinian*
b) *Reepicheep*
c) *Eustace*

2. Why didn't Eustace know what a dragon was?

a) *He was already becoming a dragon himself.*
b) *He thought the dragon looked like a teacher he once had.*
c) *He had read the wrong books.*

3. How did Aslan turn dragon Eustace back into a boy?

a) *He threw him into a pool of water.*
b) *He breathed on him.*
c) *He read him the right books.*

4. What did Caspian use to test Goldwater Lake?

a) *His sword*
b) *A bunch of heather*
c) *His nose*

5. What was the name of the invisible Chief's daughter?

a) *Gypsy*
b) *Cindy*
c) *Clipsie*

CHAPTER 10

*"I will say the spell,"
said Lucy. "I don't
care. I will." She
said I don't care
because she had a
strong feeling that
she mustn't.*

The MAGICAN'S BOOK

The Story   Oh, to be "beautiful beyond the lot of mortals"! Lucy is terribly tempted by the spells in the magician's book—even blurts one out. Then she reads the most lovely story she's ever read but…immediately forgets it! When finally she speaks the spell for the Duffers, Aslan appears, and Lucy must give an account.

Mead
*An alcoholic drink
made from honey*

Don't forget!
*Full glossary
on page 381.*

Grown-up Thoughts

Lucy utters a spell to know what people think of her. What a strong human urge that is! Of course, the consequences of that kind of eavesdropping are nearly always painful (unless you're dead and listening to eulogies at your own funeral). Ecclesiastes 7:21-22 comes to mind: "Do not pay attention to every word people say, or you may hear your servant cursing you—for you know in your heart that many times you yourself have cursed others."

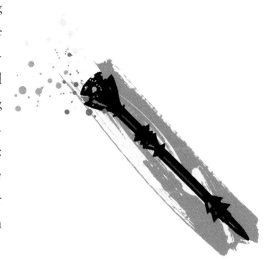

Mirror, Mirror

Why was Lucy tempted to be more beautiful than any woman? Do you see any similarities with Caspian's temptation to be the richest king?

———

Growl

What stopped Lucy from saying the spell to be beautiful?

———

Don't Look Back

Aslan reminded Lucy that "no one is ever told what would have happened." Why is this probably a good thing?

———

"The Loveliest Story I've Ever Read"

What do you think the story was?

———

Oops!

Have you ever said things about a friend that you didn't really mean? What happened?

———

Danger

Lucy was afraid of the magician. But what was the real danger?

———

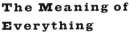

Ear Exam

———

What two girls did Lucy eavesdrop on?

Answers on page 434

The Meaning of Everything

Weaving Spells, Breaking Enchantments
Both spells that tempted Lucy in the magician's house could have hurt her and others. But in Narnia (unlike in our world), not all spells are bad. C. S. Lewis once wrote, "Do you think I am trying to weave a spell? Perhaps I am. But remember your fairy tales. Spells are used for breaking enchantments as well as for inducing them." In Narnia, magic and spells are available to both sides—good and evil. For more on magic in the Chronicles, see page 337.

Look It Up

Beautified
What woman in the Bible let God use her good looks to help rescue a nation from death? (Hint—she won a nationwide beauty contest.)

Charm is deceptive, and beauty is fleeting; but a woman who fears the LORD is to be praised.
PROVERBS 31:30

The Monopods went with them...agreeing with one another in loud voices till Eustace said, "I wish the Magician had made them inaudible instead of invisible."

The DUFFLEPUDS
MADE HAPPY

The Story ❧ Coriakin the Magician serves Aslan and has only good intentions. What a relief! Lucy is charmed by the Monopods, but she's unsuccessful in trying to convince them they aren't ugly. Then Reepicheep shows them how to use their feet for boats, and the fun begins.

Astrolabes (and other big words)
Ancient instruments of navigation

Brick
A helpful, reliable person

Chaplet
A wreath or garland for the head

Girdle
A belt or sash worn around the waist

Grown-up Thoughts

Could *anyone* be as silly as a Dufflepud? Let's see: Sometimes in our relationship with God we…

❧ *vacillate between thinking God is ready to pounce and pretending He's not there.*
❧ *listen to the loudest voice.*
❧ *talk and live as though two contradictory truths are both true.*
❧ *work against the good God is trying to work for us.*
❧ *insist on doing things the hard way.*
❧ *resent how we're made instead of celebrating it.*

But, like Coriakin and his Dufflepuds, God cares for us, and "remembers that we are dust" (Psalm 103:14).

The LORD protects the simplehearted.
PSALM 116:6

A Lot Like Us

How do people sometimes act like silly Dufflepuds?

———

Eye of the Beholder

The Magician made the Dufflepuds look better. Why did *they* think they were uglified?

———

Good Magician

How surprised were you that the Magician was actually Aslan's servant? (Remember Uncle Andrew from *Magician*?)

———

"Bless Them!"

The Magician cares for the Dufflepuds in spite of their silly ways. How is that like God and us?

———

State of Fear

What had seemed scary to Lucy when she first climbed the stairs now seems amusing. What changed?

———

Smarter Duffer?

Do you think the Dufflepuds will ever get smarter?

———

LET'S
TALK
ABOUT
IT

Oh, I Wish I Were a Dufflepud!

The Dufflepuds aren't too bright, and they make life harder than it has to be. But they sure are easy to get along with! Ever wonder what it might be like to be a Dufflepud?

How to Act Like a Dufflepud:
Take Silly Shortcuts

Dufflepuds (trying so hard to be smart) come up with, well, *interesting* ways to save time and work. Like:

Washing the plates and knives before dinner to save time afterward

Planting boiled potatoes so when they dig the potatoes up, they won't have to cook

Um, what is wrong with these ideas? And, by the way, can you invent some silly shortcuts of your own? For example, something having to do with...

making your bed

doing homework

brushing your teeth

saying good-bye to a friend

How to Talk Like a Dufflepud:

Step 1: Always be oh-so-agreeable. The Dufflepuds agree with everything their Chief says and everything each other says. In fact, they agree with everything *even if it is the exact opposite of something they already agreed with!* Handy Dufflepud-isms:

"Right you are!"

"Couldn't have said it better!"

"Keep it up!"

"That's the truth!"

"Well said! Well said!"

How would your family react if you talked this way all through dinner?

Step 2. Only say what's oh-so-obvious. Not only do the Dufflepuds agree with what others say, they make sure everything *they* say can't be disagreed with. Remember these Dufflepud-isms?

"When a chap's hungry, he likes some victuals [food]."

"It's getting dark now; always does at night."

"Ah, you've come over the water. Powerful wet stuff, ain't it?"

Try making up your own Dufflepud-isms. Start by coming up with two phrases that state the obvious or mean the same thing. For example:

"Megan's asleep, so she's certainly not awake."

"Look! Now that the sun is shining, it's sunny!"

Then ask your fellow Dufflepuds to agree with you:

You: "Megan's asleep, so she's certainly not awake."

Chorus of Dufflepuds: "Ohhh! Asleep, yes! Well said! Well said! Asleep, not awake! You're s-o-o-o right!"

How to Look Like a Dufflepud:
Stop Being a Biped.

That means it's only one "leg" for you. And it's easier than you think. All you have to do is:

Skateboard

Snowboard

Surf

Pogo

Hop around in one of Dad's big work boots

"Wait. Hop around you say?"

"Oh, right you are! Right you are! Keep it up!"

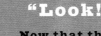

"Look! Now that the sun is shining, it's sunny!"

Lucy...whispered, "Aslan, Aslan, if ever you loved us at all, send us help now." The darkness did not grow any less, but she began to feel a little—a very, very little—better.

The DARK ISLAND

The Story ❧ When the *Dawn Treader* sails into total blackness, things get creepy. Then, when they rescue Rhoop (missing lord #4), they learn that this is a place where nightmares come true. Yikes! Lucy calls on Aslan for help, and soon an albatross leads the ship back into the light.

Boatswain
A crew member, especially one in charge of the smaller boat(s) on deck

Boon
A timely blessing or benefit

Grog
Alcoholic liquor, especially rum diluted with water

Impeachment
Accusation against

Poltroonery
Great cowardice

Grown-up Thoughts

A scary chapter where...nothing dangerous actually happens! But aren't nightmares and darkness like that? Of course, the fears they evoke are real enough. Thankfully, whenever we're afraid, we can call on God. "They cried to the LORD in their trouble, and he saved them.... He brought them out of darkness and the deepest gloom.... Let them give thanks to the LORD for his unfailing love" (Psalm 107:13–15).

In the Dark

Most of us are at least a little afraid of the dark. Why do you think that is?

_____

Bad Dreams

Can you think of anything more scary than having a bad dream come true? Does one come to mind?

_____

Nothing to Fear

Lucy realized that there really never had been anything to fear. Was this true?

_____

"Help!"

Soon after Lucy called out to Aslan to save them, he led them into the light. What does God promise He will do when we cry out to Him?

_____

Big White Bird

Who do you think the albatross was, or was sent by?

_____

Rhoop's Ordeal

How would being in the dark for years on end make _anyone_ act or feel? Do you think Rhoop called on Aslan?

_____

LET'S **TALK** ABOUT **IT**

Ear Exam

——

What three words did Aslan say only to Lucy?

Answer on page 435

The Meaning of Everything

That Was Scary!

Lewis took children's fears seriously. Paul Ford, a Lewis scholar, writes: "So important did Lewis consider night-fears that he extensively revised the ending of this twelfth chapter for the pre-1994 American editions of VDT. His aim was to correct any impression...that night fears are unreal and ultimately laughable and that they can be obliterated altogether." For more on fear in the Chronicles, see page 356.

So we say with confidence, "The Lord is my helper; I will not be afraid."

Hebrews 13:6

> *"I've seen something like it before. It was a knife like it that the White Witch used when she killed Aslan at the Stone Table."*
> —Lucy

The THREE SLEEPERS

The Story ● The ship arrives at an island where three old men sleep at a banquet table. Odd, but—oh well—at least Caspian has found the last missing lords. But odder still, they won't wake up! Is it the food? A spell? A trick? Then a beautiful girl glides up to explain.

A bowshot
The distance that an arrow can be shot

Fall to
Begin an activity energetically

"I pledge you"
"I toast you"

Grown-up Thoughts

This chapter makes you want to pinch yourself. Everything seems gauzy, improbable, unreal—like sleepwalking. Or is it? Edmund wonders if the beautiful girl can be trusted (he's had bad experiences with beautiful women—remember the White Witch?). But when he asks, "How are we to know you're a friend?" she answers, "You can't know. You can only believe—or not." The adventurers must proceed with all the wisdom they can muster. Some things are known, some aren't. But Aslan's presence is everywhere apparent, so they press on. Less like sleepwalking, then, and more like "faith walking," wouldn't you say?

He has taken me to the banquet hall, and his banner over me is love.
SONG OF SOLOMON 2:4

Afraid to Feast

This island seems full of magic. Would you have been afraid to eat here? What do you think will happen?

———————

Purple Smell

Do smells remind you of colors, like they did Lucy? Name a color for each of these smells: pizza, sawdust, crayon, rain on your face, rain on a hot sidewalk, Dad.

———————

Old Rugged Knife

The knife that killed Aslan has special meaning. What was used to kill Jesus and has special meaning for Christians?

———————

Kiss the Princess

Did you recognize the famous fairy tale Caspian referred to? Any idea why he's so anxious to end the enchantment?

———————

Believe—or Not

The girl told Edmund that he can't know anything for sure, he can "only believe—or not." Is that true for Christians, too?

———————

LET'S TALK ABOUT IT

FAST FACT

———

Kids can find recipes for food from the Chronicles in *The Narnia Cookbook* by Douglas Gresham.

Answers on page 435

Look It Up

The food at Aslan's table is eaten and renewed each day. What food in the Bible worked the same way? (See Exodus 16:4.)

Try This at Home

A Feast Fit for Lords and Ladies

If you had to eat the same feast every day for the rest of your life, what would your banquet menu look like? Say or write down your order (ask mom or dad for help):

Appetizer #1_____

Side dish #1_____

Side dish #2_____

Main course

#1_____

Main course

#2_____

Dessert #1_____

Dessert #2_____

Beverages_____

Oh, and this too:

_____

Now ask someone else to rate your banquet:

a) Awesome!

b) Pretty good.

c) Weird.

d) Disgusting.

> *"Even in your world, my son, that is not what a star is but only what it is made of."*
> —Ramandu

The BEGINNING
of the END OF THE WORLD

The Story ❧ The pretty girl's father is Ramandu, a magician and "retired" star. He explains that to break the sleepers' enchantment, the *Dawn Treader* must sail to the World's End and leave someone behind. Guess which valiant Mouse claims that honor?

Bequeath
To pass something on to another; hand down

Quay
A wharf or reinforced bank where ships are loaded or unloaded

---

Don't forget!
Full glossary on page 381

Grown-up Thoughts

This chapter is full of dreamy sequences and heavenly allusions. Ramandu's Island seems haunted by eternity. The bird bringing the fire-berry to Ramandu's lips is reminiscent of the seraph bringing a live coal to Isaiah's lips (Isaiah 6:6–7). When Ramandu and his daughter raise their arms and sing while the sun rises, Edmund describes it as the most exciting moment of the trip. Is it a preview of a morning in heaven? Psalm 108:1–2:

My heart is steadfast, O God;
I will sing and make music with
all my soul.
Awake, harp and lyre!
I will awaken
the dawn.

Then the righteous will shine like the sun in the kingdom of their Father. He who has ears, let him hear.

MATTHEW 13:43

Only the Chosen

Caspian doesn't want just any crew member to continue the voyage with him. What is he looking for?

_____

All the Way to the End

At first, some of the crew don't want to go further. But what changes their minds?

_____

Left Behind

Why is Reepicheep willing to be left behind at the End of the World? Would you be?

_____

Pittencream's Folly

Do you feel sorry for Pittencream? Have you ever missed out on something because you were afraid or not sure what kind of time you'd have?

_____

Old Star

Ramandu is an old star that is getting younger every day when he eats the fire-berry. How would you like to be a star in the sky?

_____

WISDOM
for
NARNIACS

———

Great unenchantments are never achieved by men deceived.

ENOUGH WITH THE LION KISSES! IT'S TIME FOR…

Narniac Attack | No. 16

[Test your knowledge on chapters 10–14]

1. What spell in the Magician's book did Lucy *almost* utter?

a) *A spell to be smarter than Susan*

b) *A spell to know what her friends think of her*

c) *A spell to be the most lovely woman ever*

2. Which of these is *not* true about the Dufflepuds?

a) *They were beautiful before they were "uglified."*

b) *They are not good at taking shortcuts to chores.*

c) *They always agreed with their Chief.*

3. After Lucy calls for Aslan, what leads them into the light?

a) *A large white dove*

b) *An albatross*

c) *The sound of singing*

4. Why did the three lords fall asleep at Aslan's table?

a) *Because they wouldn't clean their plates*

b) *Because one of them touched a special knife*

c) *Because they were arguing*

5. What is special about the sleep on this island?

a) *It only comes once you've eaten too much.*

b) *You only snore a little bit.*

c) *You don't have any dreams.*

Answers on page 435

"It must be exciting to live on a thing like a ball. Have you ever been to the parts where people walk about upside-down?"
—Caspian

THE WONDERS OF THE LAST SEA

The Story ❂ The Last Sea is filled with wonders. Looking over the ship's rail, Lucy sees magnificent Sea People living in an underwater city. Then Reepicheep discovers that the water is no longer salty, but sweet. "Drinkable light," he calls it. The End of the World must be very near!

Coronet
A small crown worn by princes and princesses

Cutting
A place where train tracks cut into a hillside

"Drat!"
An exclamation of annoyance

Kraken
A sea monster in Norwegian legend

Grown-up Thoughts

Now that the explorers are near the End of the World, the water is clear as light—and tastes like it, too. How different from the Dark Island! There, Lewis explored the terror of complete darkness; now he ponders the joy of pure light. In 1 John 1:5 we read, "God is light; in him there is no darkness at all." So it makes sense that the nearer the voyagers come to Aslan's country, the more they are transformed by his light.

At one time you were in the dark. But now you are in the light because of what the Lord has done. Live like children of the light. The light produces what is completely good, right and true.

EPHESIANS 5:8–9, NIRV

Out of Darkness

Why do you think it gets lighter and lighter the closer the ship comes to Aslan's country? Who is "the Light of the World"?

————

Drinkable Light

What do you think light would taste like? What would dark taste like?

————

Dangerous Beauty

Why did Drinian want to keep his crew from seeing the beautiful Sea People? Would you want to visit a world under water?

————

A Horse, of Course

Have you ever seen a sea horse? How would it feel to ride on a huge one?

————

Falling Off

Why don't people fall off the "underneath" part of Planet Earth?

————

LET'S
TALK
ABOUT
IT

> *"This was the very reason why you were brought to Narnia, that by knowing me here for a little, you may know me better there."*
> —*Aslan*

The VERY END
OF THE WORLD

The Story ◈ Oh, the wonders at the World's End! A sea of flowers, a wall like a glass wave, a world behind the sun! The *Dawn Treader* turns back for Narnia, Reepicheep paddles on for glory, and after a last meal with Aslan, it's back to Aunt Alberta's bedroom for the children!

Baited
Tormented with insults

Lessoned
Instructed or taught

Grown-up Thoughts

This chapter is filled with biblical parallels (see page 425). But the most profound passage is where Lewis states his reasons for bringing Lucy (and his readers) to Narnia from Earth: "That by knowing me here for a little, you may know me better there." Lucy finally says it best for everyone: "It isn't Narnia, you know," she sobs to Aslan. "It's *you*." For us, the wonders and everlasting delights of heaven will surely be indescribable. But nothing will surpass the joy of being at home forever with Him—Jesus, our Savior, Lord, and King.

The city does not need the sun or the moon to shine on it, for the glory of God gives it light, and the Lamb is its lamp.

REVELATION 21:23

Heaven Can Wait

Caspian longed to go on to Aslan's country, but it wasn't his time yet. Do you know anyone who can't wait to get to heaven?

_____

Bridge Builder

What do you think Aslan meant when he called himself a Bridge Builder over a river? What river must we cross to reach eternity?

_____

All About Aslan

What are Lucy and Edmund sure they'll miss most back in England? What would you tell them if they were your friends?

_____

Lion & Lamb

Do you know why we call Jesus both a Lion and a Lamb in the Bible? Why do these two animals tell us so much about Jesus?

_____

LET'S
TALK
ABOUT
IT

WISDOM
for
NARNIACS

——

By knowing Aslan a little in Narnia, we can know him better here.

Kid Test

Finding Him Here

Aslan told Lucy he brought them to Narnia so they would know him better back in England. Has your voyage on the *Dawn Treader* helped you know God better here? Talk about it. For example, what have you learned about:

> What God wants for all His children?
> What Jesus might say to you if you met Him?
> How Jesus' disciples must have felt when they were around Jesus?
> What you should be afraid of?
> What you don't ever need to be afraid of?

Look It Up

Breakfast on the Beach

Who ate a breakfast of fish on the beach with Jesus? (See John 21.)

Uncle Jack Says

"God cannot give us a happiness and peace apart from Himself, because it is not there. There is no such thing."

ON THE RUN from bullies at school, Eustace and Jill open a door in a wall…and step into Narnia. What they don't know is they've been summoned by Aslan to help find the missing Prince Rilian, son of Caspian. Fortunately, the children find an unforgettable Marsh-wiggle named Puddleglum to guide them. The three set off for the dangerous North, there to face child-eating giants and the deep darkness of Underland, where their mission will face its ultimate test.

BOOK SIX

The SILVER CHAIR

"What's the matter?" [Jill] said. And to show that she was not afraid, she stood very near the edge indeed; in fact, a good deal nearer than even she liked.

BEHIND *the* GYM

The Story ❧ On the run together from bullies at Experiment House, Eustace and Jill Pole find a door into Narnia. They travel through a forest to a high cliff, where Jill loses her balance. But it's Eustace who falls trying to save her. Suddenly a huge lion is lying next to Jill, blowing.

Blithering
Senseless or foolish

Head
Headmaster, principal

Hols
Holidays, school vacation

"Oh, Lor!"
Short for "Oh, Lord!"

Tick
An annoying bug that sucks blood

Grown-up Thoughts

Jill is a proud little girl whose pride leads to a big fall. (Scriptures come to mind: "So, if you think you are standing firm, be careful that you don't fall!" and, "Pride goes before destruction, a haughty spirit before a fall.") Safe to guess Jill has lessons to learn in Narnia, wouldn't you think? But consider the "new" Eustace! Okay, he's still a little pompous, but now at least he's patient, caring, and a good listener. The unhappy citizens at Experiment House can't help noticing. But readers notice even more—the boy has walked with Aslan, learned from him, and wants what he wants.

Bully Behavior

Why do you think some kids enjoy being mean to other kids? Have you ever teased someone or been teased yourself?

Silly Magic

Eustace knows that you can't *make* Aslan act with magic or anything else. All you can do is ask. Is God that way, too?

Strange Schools

No one seems to be in charge at this school. Do you think there's such a thing as too much freedom at school?

Don't Look Down

Why did Jill go so close to the edge of the cliff to begin with?

Blub Blub

What other Chronicle begins with someone "blubbing"?

LET'S
TALK
ABOUT
IT

WISDOM
for
NARNIACS

If you've no fear of heights, get ready to take a fall.

The Meaning of Everything

Experiments in Education

Lewis argued against "value-free" education in his book *The Abolition of Man.* Many experimental schools sprang up in England and America during the 1950s and '60s. But Lewis favored classical learning that championed positive moral values in a caring environment. At Experiment House, kids have freedom but hardly any direction or discipline. The result? Children who become either bullies or victims, and teachers who look like fools.

If you are proud, you will fall.

PROVERBS 16:18, NIRV

CHAPTER 2

*"I have swallowed
up girls and boys,
women and men,
kings and emperors,
cities and realms,"
said the Lion.*

JILL IS GIVEN A TASK

The Story ❧ A thirsty Jill meets Aslan again by a stream where she—very nervously—takes a drink. Then Aslan explains her mission: to find a lost prince. He gives her four signs to help her succeed and tells her to memorize them. Then, he blows and she too is off to Narnia!

"By Jove!"
*An exclamation
of surprise; Jove was
a Roman god*

Cheek
Rude, impolite

Grown-up Thoughts

Jill's famous encounter with Aslan at the stream echoes the story of the Samaritan woman at the well with Jesus (John 4). As with Jesus and the woman, Aslan knows all about Jill and her pride, and he invites her to drink. Their conversation reveals that while Aslan isn't safe, Jill really is "dying" of thirst and has no choice—"there is no other stream." Think of Jesus' words: "Whoever drinks the water I give…will never thirst," (John 4:14), and "I am the way and the truth and the life. No one comes to the Father except through me" (John 14:6).

Who's to Blame?

How did Jill react after Eustace fell? Why wasn't she more worried about him?

Good Answer

When Aslan asked about the boy, what did Jill admit she did wrong? Have you ever acted like this?

No Other Stream

Aslan invited Jill to drink, but she was afraid. What would you have done?

Gulp

What do you think Aslan *really* meant by saying he'd swallowed people whole?

Memorize This

Jill needs to memorize the signs if she's to succeed. Why does the Bible teach Christians to memorize God's Word?

No Guarantee

Why do you think Aslan didn't promise Jill that she would succeed?

LET'S
TALK
ABOUT
IT

Kid Test

Flying Lessons

Lots of stories tell about children who get to ride on the air somehow. What are your favorites? Which ride would you choose if you had the chance to fly:

> On a magic carpet
> On a flying horse
> By Aslan's breath
> In a hot air balloon
> In a jet
> By sprouting my own wings

Look It Up

Jesus met a woman at a well. What was special about the water He offered to her? (See John 4:10-13.)

FAST FACT

Lewis's mother took him to Trafalgar Square, London, when he was a boy. It features statues of four lions.

"Anyone who drinks the water I give him will never be thirsty."

JESUS, IN JOHN 4:14, NIRV

Everyone Can Come

She sleeps outside the circle now, but Aslan can still gather her home right on time.

These days Cambria is getting sleepy early. Or she is not making the connections at only five.

While we read Narnia, she'll lie on her side near the bottom of the stairs with her cheek propped on her blankie, curled around one of her kind of books.

I feel bad because I made the don't-bring-other-books-and-toys-to-story-time rule. So Cam has imagined that outside some perimeter my rule can't reach. "Yeah, but, Dad, it's just…tonight I don't…Daaaad…" she'll begin to say when tsked a little. But she will not be definitive because she knows what's holy to us. She leaves me where I can take it that she's especially tired, especially wanting left alone, or especially afraid about what's happening in Narnia that night.

But she still comes running over to us for the pictures and to ask her questions about them. When she finishes, she scrambles back to nest.

If I really want to keep her these days, I've learned to ask her on my lap. But then I must settle the inevitable who's-on-Daddy's-lap wars.

You see, three books ago I ended these by saying: "You guys are getting too heavy now. And Daddy just ate. Everyone just sit and I will show around the pictures." And for three books since: *pax coucho.*

Now I have to end these wars by fiat just to get Cam: "Cam sits here tonight," I icily decree. Up she crawls, quickly and with delight. (Yes, I seem ridiculous, self-controverting, defunct really. But for all of us together, that's the price.)

And only minutes later—maybe seconds—I feel Cam's small body inanimate.

Only minutes later—maybe seconds—I feel Cam's small body inanimate.
She's out. "Seeeeee, Dad! Every time Cammie goes to sleep."

She's out. "Seeeeee, Dad! Every time Cammie goes to sleep. She just doesn't want to listen to what's going on. So you might as well let one of *us* sit on your lap. Wouldn't that be graaaand?" says Emmae, ending with her head cocked to one side, her eyes wide and fluttering. Cambria starts a little at the voice, opens her eyes heavily, contracts herself more into her sleeping shape, and slips off again. With us, but away.

And we read on.

And I am anxious as to every line she misses.

We read of Aslan blowing Scrubb off the terrible edge, then Jill. (First Jill needed talking to about the signs, the rule for her, the reasons.)

"Guys, it's just this golden breath!" I interrupt myself and say, excited.

"Yeah, Dad, but I don't get how you can fall but then like Aslan could blow you then?" says Elliot looking up at the ceiling.

"Wait, what!?" asks Emmae. "I thought she just pushed Eustace 'cause she slipped."

"There's no difference between slipping off, getting pushed, and being blown off when it's Aslan there!" I exclaim, setting down the book to free my arms. I make a cliff with a fist and sweep the top with my other hand. Then I put that hand below and make as if to catch who I swept off.

Emmae bites her pinkie tip and scrunches up her eyes and the top of her nose. I go back to reading.

Later, when I tuck them in bed, I'm pulling Cam's covers up to her chin and up to the chins of her batch of dollies when she jolts awake again. She looks straight at me and says, "Dad…Dad I was just dreaming of a store where everyone—where a sign's up that says 'Zero ages to old guys can come in' so the store is full of everyone. Isn't that funny, Dad?"

"It can be, Cam…" is all that comes to me to tell her. I look over at Emmae and see her roll her eyes. We all know Cambria, and that she loves including. "Everyone can come" could be her main theme easily. Perhaps that's all that keeps her somewhat close, waiting for me to think better.

Despite my rules and all our joking, we'd love Cam with us at the couch again. And I think there's hope she'll come, for Aslan has that knack for holding over and regathering: Remember Pole? And how he blew Scrubb more slowly to be there for her when she came?

—Brian Thomasson

"Then the King was an old friend of yours!" said Jill. A horrid thought had struck her.

The SAILING
of the KING

The Story ❋ The children get to Cair Paravel in time to witness the King's speech before he sets sail. But they botch Aslan's first sign when Eustace doesn't recognize Caspian. Things look up, though, when Trumpkin shows them to a hot bath, a huge meal, and a warm bed in the castle.

Doddering
Wobbly

Kettledrums
Large, barrel-shaped drums

Muffed
Botched; bungled

"Oh, dry up!"
"Stop talking!"

"So keep your hair on"
"Stay calm"

Grown-up Thoughts

When Trumpkin hears that Jill and Eustace have been sent by Aslan, he welcomes the grubby "man-cubs" and treats them to the best Cair Paravel has to offer. How easily we miss those people God sends our way. They might be strangers, failures, or the little ones at our feet. But the Bible reminds us, "Do not forget to entertain strangers, for by so doing some people have entertained angels without knowing it" (Hebrews 13:2).

Starting a quarrel is like breaching a dam; so drop the matter before a dispute breaks out.
PROVERBS 17:14

Time Travel

About how many Narnian years have passed since Eustace's last visit?

———

Old Ain't Over

Why do you think Eustace got so upset to discover that Caspian was now old? What do you think about getting old?

———

Bicker Fest

Why aren't Jill and Eustace getting along? Do you think they'll find a way to make peace?

———

Hearing Aid

It's frustrating when you can't hear well. How should you treat someone like Trumpkin?

———

Welcome Strangers

Why did Trumpkin change his tune about the "grubby man-cubs"? Have you ever welcomed strangers at your house?
Why is it often a hard thing to do?

LET'S
TALK
ABOUT
IT

"You see," explained Glimfeather, "most of the creatures in Narnia have such unnatural habits. They do things by day, in broad blazing sunlight (ugh!) when everyone ought to be asleep."

A PARLIAMENT
OF OWLS

The Story ● After dark, Glimfeather flies the children to a ruined tower for a secret meeting of owls. They learn the sad story of Prince Rilian's disappearance and that Trumpkin, on the King's orders, would prevent them from seeking the Prince. Maybe the Marsh-wiggles can help.

A blab
A person who reveals secrets

Crew
Kind or type

Fusty
Smelling of mildew or decay; musty

Give over
Give up, abandon

Maying
Going on a spring outing

Physic
Medicine

Grown-up Thoughts

Trumpkin, Caspian's friend and overzealous servant, means well—to follow his King's orders wholeheartedly. But the King would never want his order to supersede one from Aslan. It's not the law that matters so much as the spirit of the law. When the Pharisees questioned Jesus about His Sabbath miracles, He said, "If any of you has a sheep and it falls into a pit on the Sabbath, will you not take hold of it and lift it out? How much more valuable is a man than a sheep!" (Matthew 12:11–12).

Direct me in the path of your commands, for there I find delight.

PSALM 119:35

The King's Man

Eustace was worried about being disloyal to the King. Why did he doubt the owls at first?

___

Green Beauty

The Narnians are pretty sure the serpent and the beautiful woman are the same. Why?

___

LET'S
TALK
ABOUT
IT

That's an Order

Trumpkin means well by following the King's orders. But whose orders are even *more* important?

___

Caspian's Bride

Men said "the blood of the stars flowed in her veins." What did they mean? (Hint: Read the last page of *The Voyage of the* Dawn Treader.)

___

Lost Cause?

Already thirty brave men have disappeared while seeking the lost Prince. Why should Eustace and Jill have any hope of success?

___

Fast Fact

___

With this chapter title Lewis is giving a wink to Chaucer's poem, "Parliament of Fowls."

Kid Test #1

Secret Dilemmas

Drinian kept the Prince's secret, but it was the wrong thing to do. Glimfeather held a secret meeting—but it was the right thing to do. When should you *not* keep a secret? Choose the right two:

1. When the secret could put someone in danger
2. When the secret is just too juicy to keep to yourself
3. When to keep the secret would mean betraying someone
4. When you don't like the person who told you the secret

Kid Test #2

What Will Happen Next?

Now that the owls have a plan:

1. Jill will fall off the owl she's riding—but Eustace will catch her.
2. The kids will wake up in a mysterious wigwam and eat eel soup.
3. The Marsh-wiggles will refuse to help the humans.
4. Eustace will discover that Glimfeather is not really on their side.

Answers on page 435

"Got to start by finding it, have we?" answered Puddleglum. "Not allowed to start by looking for it, I suppose?"

PUDDLEGLUM

The Story ◎ Eustace and Jill meet a Marsh-wiggle named Puddleglum. He is friendly enough, but overly glum and pessimistic—and yet his friends call him "flighty." After spending the night in his wigwam, the three spend the day preparing to journey together to the ruined city of Giants.

Bittern
A marsh bird

Bobance
Flashiness, boasting

Snipe
A marsh bird

Tinder-box
A box of flammable contents used to kindle a fire

Victuals
Food

Grown-up Thoughts

Meet Puddleglum, one of Narnia's funniest creatures (not that he knows it). Okay, the Marsh-wiggle doesn't come off as too promising a companion at first! He's long, thin, froglike, and muddy in both complexion and outlook. But this Eeyore of the Chronicles turns out to be an Aslan-sent guide for the long journey ahead. Oddly, his dire outlook will often prompt the kids to find sound reasons for hope. For example, responding to Puddleglum's pessimism in this chapter, Eustace wisely insists that the quest cannot be so hopeless as he makes it sound, or Aslan wouldn't have sent them.

May the God of hope fill you with all joy and peace as you trust in him, so that you may overflow with hope by the power of the Holy Spirit.

ROMANS 15:13

Meet a Marsh-Wiggle

His face was long and _____ with rather _____ cheeks, a _____ nose, and no _____. The hair which hung over his large _____ was greeny-_____. His expression was _____, his _____ muddy, and you could see he took a _____ view of life.

———————

Eeyore in Narnia

Puddleglum is pretty gloomy (funny, too). Remember Eeyore in *Winnie-the-Pooh*? Do you know anyone like that?

———————

Cheer Me Up!

How about you? Are you usually more cheerful or worried?

———————

A Boy's Hope

Why does Eustuce believe that the quest can't be as hopeless as Puddleglum makes it sound?

———————

Giants?

Jill doesn't like the idea of meeting giants. Just how big do you think they'll be?

———————

WISDOM
for
NARNIACS

———

Puddleglum's Rule of Thumb: The good thing about bad things is there's always a worse thing that didn't happen (yet).

LET'S **TALK** ABOUT **IT**

GOT TO START BY *TAKING* IT, DO WE? NOT ALLOWED TO BE *GIVING* IT OUR BEST SHOT? OH, I SHOULD'VE KNOWN…

Narniac Attack | No. 17

[Test your knowledge on chapters 1–5]

1. When Jill was crying behind the gym, how did Eustace help her calm down?

a) He gave her a lecture.

b) He told her to stop blubbing.

c) He gave her a peppermint.

2. The third sign that Aslan gave Jill was:

a) Watch for a beautiful lady wearing green.

b) Do what the writing on a stone tells you.

c) Follow the first person who uses Aslan's name.

3. What did the nearly deaf Trumpkin think the children's names were?

a) Killed and Useless

b) Trill and Hopeless

c) Chilled and Undressed

4. Rillian's mother was killed by:

a) A slug bite

b) A spider bite

c) A giant worm bite

5. Why were the Marsh-wiggles' wigwams so spread out?

a) The land was swampy except for a few spots.

b) They liked their privacy.

c) They didn't like the looks of each other.

They could think about nothing but beds and baths and hot meals and how lovely it would be to get indoors. They never talked about Aslan.

The WILD WASTE
LANDS OF THE NORTH

The Story ⊚ Traveling north, Puddleglum and the children walk past giants who are too busy quarreling to notice them. Later, they meet a Knight and a beautiful lady on horseback. She encourages them to visit the friendly giants of Harfang. Puddleglum is suspicious, but the kids are already thinking about dinner!

Balustrade
A railing to prevent people from falling

Bivouacked
Set up a temporary camp

Brain-wave
Smart thinking

Cairn
A mound of stones erected as a memorial or marker

Cock-shies
A throwing contest

Shoals
Areas of shallow water

Grown-up Thoughts

Puddleglum's gloomy predictions so far haven't come to pass. But in this chapter we sense that hiding in Puddleglum's negative nature is a lot of life wisdom—about giants and mysterious strangers, for example. The children, however, just want to get comfortable. In fact, they become so intent on getting to Harfang that they stop thinking about Aslan and Jill stops repeating the signs. Don't we often operate the same way? We set out to do God's will but get distracted by what *we* want. Pretty soon, we're off track and heading for giant problems.

Big Blubberers

Did the quarreling, crying giants remind you of anything you've read in this book so far?

_____

Worrywart Wiggles

Eustace said Puddleglum is always wrong. Do you agree?

_____

Strange Beauty

By now, are you suspicious of beautiful women in these stories? Why do you suppose evil beings often look so attractive?

_____

Warm Bed on the Brain

What happened when the children started thinking only of the comforts they expect to find at Harfang?

_____

Giants!

How did the Israelites respond to rumors of "giants" in the Promised Land? See Numbers 13:26–28.

_____

LET'S
TALK
ABOUT
IT

Ear Exam

_____

If we break our _____ getting down the cliff, at least we're safe from being _____ in the river.

Answers on page 435

Kid Test

What's Your Giant I.Q.?

1. The _Guinness Book of World Records_ lists Robert Pershing Wadlow as the tallest man in history. How tall was he?

(a.) 7 ft. 11 in.   (b.) 8 ft. 11 in.   (c.) 11 ft. 1 in.

2. What is the name of the most famous giant in the Bible?

3. What is the name of the most famous giant ape in the movies?

4. What is the name of the giant who sells vegetables?

5. Who found a giant at the top of a beanstalk?

Uncle Jack Says

"If you look for truth, you may find comfort in the end; if you look for comfort you will not get either comfort or truth."

I have hidden your word in my heart so that I won't sin against you.

Psalm 119:11, NIRV

> *However tired you are, it takes some nerve to walk up to a giant's front door.*

THE HILL OF THE STRANGE TRENCHES

The Story ❧ It's snowing as they trudge toward Harfang through a maze of trenches. At the giants' door, a towering porter welcomes them. Once inside, he offers Puddleglum some liquor. Oops—the wiggle overdoes it! Next thing you know, two tired kids and one drunk wiggle are summoned to meet the giants!

Funk
To shrink in fright from doing something

Guffaw
A hearty, boisterous burst of laughter

Jerkin
A short, often sleeveless coat, usually of leather

Pat
Completely or perfectly

Pluck
Courage and determination

Portcullis
Protective iron bars

Grown-up Thoughts

When Puddleglum drinks too much, his rationalizing is humorous—"better make sure," "but is it the same all the way down?" "This'll be a test." But it's sad, too, and a recognizable pattern for most of us. We each face different giants, but we all tend to sip our way, one excuse at a time, from little test into big trouble.

> *Wise people see danger and go to a safe place. But childish people keep on going and suffer for it.*
>
> PROVERBS 27:12, NIRV

No Sign of Signs

Why did Jill become angry when Puddleglum asked about the signs?

Blue Face

Have you ever been as cold as Jill and Eustace were? So cold your face turned blue? What happened?

LET'S TALK ABOUT IT

What, Me Scared?

Once again, Puddleglum told the children not to *look* scared. Why is this good advice?

Knock, Knock

How would you feel if you had to knock on a giant's door?

Plan B

Would you have advised the three to do something else? Like what?

Respectabiggle

Puddleglum gets drunk and can't talk or think straight. Why is that a really bad idea in the giants' castle?

> *"You two youngsters haven't always got very high spirits, I've noticed. You must watch me, and do as I do."*
> —Puddleglum

The HOUSE *of* HARFANG

The Story ◈ On the Queen's orders, the three guests are bathed, fed, and cared for. That night Aslan comes to Jill in a dream. The next day, when she sees the words "Under Me" carved into the flat hill, she realizes they have missed the third sign. The threesome hatch a plan to escape Harfang.

Caraways
Confections made from the fruit of the caraway plant

Cock-a-leekie
A soup made with chicken broth and leeks

Comfit
A piece of fruit, a seed, or a nut coated with sugar

Gasometer
A large drum-shaped tank used as a storage container for fuel gas

Grown-up Thoughts

When the travelers realize they've missed the third sign, Puddleglum makes an important statement: "Aslan's instructions always work: there are no exceptions." That's true with God as well. His way, His plan, His commands are always *perfect* (Psalm 19:7–11). Yet, because we're not, we need God Himself to bridge the gap. Without His mercies and help, God's good plan in our lives would be unreachable. Watch with your children as Aslan brings his good plan to completion with patience, power…and second chances.

Let the morning bring me word of your unfailing love, for I have put my trust in you.

Psalm 143:8

Giant Instincts

What is your impression of the giants so far? Can they be trusted?

––––––––

Babied

The Nurse babies Jill and brings her toys too young for her age. What does it feel like to be treated younger than you are by a grown-up?

––––––––

Just a Dream?

Who do you think was behind Jill's dream? Do you think God can work through dreams?

––––––––

Sneaky

Do you think the children's plans to sneak out during daylight will work? Have you ever tried to be sneaky? What happened?

––––––––

Giant for a Day

If you could be a giant for one day, what would you want to do?

––––––––

LET'S
TALK
ABOUT
IT

EAR EXAM

–––––

What giant toy did Jill dream about?

Answers on page 435

The Meaning of Everything

Physics and Possets

Jill's crying prompted the Queen to prescribe "physics" and "possets." What are they? Lewis was referring to two medicines that were given to ill children a hundred years ago. Physics would purge the digestive system. *Ewww!* A posset was sweet spiced hot milk curdled with ale or beer. *Yuckk!* Did the treatments work? Not usually, but at least the grown-ups felt like they were doing *something!*

Look It Up

Can you think of three Bible characters God spoke to through a dream? Let these hints help you guess, and then look up the passages:

1. A father is warned to flee with his baby and wife. (See Matthew 2:14.)
2. His brothers became very jealous. (See Genesis 37:5.)
3. He saw a ladder to heaven. (See Genesis 28:12.)

CHAPTER 9

*MAN. This elegant
little biped has long
been valued as a
delicacy. It forms
a traditional part of
the Autumn feast.
—the Giants'
Cookbook*

HOW THEY DISCOVERED SOMETHING WORTH KNOWING

The Story ❧ When the three friends discover they've been eating a Talking stag, they're heartsick. Then they discover something worse—humans and a Marsh-wiggle are featured items on the giants' dinner menu! Time to walk, then dash for safety. They find it far underground.

Biped
*An animal with
two feet*

Scullery
*A small room
adjoining a kitchen,
in which
dishwashing
and other kitchen
chores are done*

Grown-up Thoughts

Puddleglum is horrified to discover that he's been eating a Talking stag. He says, "We've brought the anger of Aslan on us," and imagines they are under a curse because they didn't follow the signs. Wouldn't you think, though, that not following the signs is the more grievous error because at points it was intentional? Eating the stag was at least an error of understanding, not of will. Maybe that's why Aslan never raises the issue with Puddleglum or the children in the pages to come.

*Even the darkness
will not be
dark to you; the
night will shine
like the day,
for darkness
is as light to you.*
PSALM 139:12

Silly Jill

How did she fool the giants? When she grows up, will she make a good undercover agent or actress?

———

But My Pig Likes Me!

Have you ever raised birds or animals on a farm, come to love them, *then* had to butcher them or sell them for food? If so, talk about it.

———

Man-Pies on the Menu

Do you think the Lady of the Green Kirtle was familiar with giant appetites—and sent the children on purpose?

———

Worse or Worser?

Puddleglum can't decide which would be worse—being eaten or meeting a dragon in this dark place. What do you think would be worse?

———

How to Sneak Away from a Giant

"Steady, _____," said Puddlglum. "Don't look _____. Don't walk too _____. Whatever you do, don't _____."

———

LET'S
TALK
ABOUT
IT

WISDOM
for
NARNIACS

———

Never dine
with Giants when
you are on
the menu.

Answers on page 435

Look It Up

Boy Versus Big Guy

Read the exciting story of David and Goliath (1 Samuel 17). Then take this quiz:

1. Goliath was _____ feet tall. (v. 4)
2. King Saul told David, You can't fight Goliath! You're only a _____! (v. 33)
3. David killed Goliath with one _____ from his sling. (v. 49)
4. Afterward, David did *what* to the giant's head? (v. 51)

Kid Test

What Will Happen Next?

Now that they're really in the dark:

1. The group will battle giant bats.
2. Puddleglum will suddenly get more optimistic.
3. They will meet coal miners from West Virginia.
4. They'll find that Aslan is in the dark with them, too.

Earthmen, no two alike, rubbed shoulders with them in the crowded streets, and the sad light fell on many sad and grotesque faces.

TRAVELS WITHOUT *the* SUN

The Story ❧ Now captives of the Warden and his armed Earthmen, Puddleglum and the children are taken through dark caverns, then by boat to a castle in an underground city. There they meet the mysterious Black Knight again…and something's wrong with his face!

Coil
A disturbance; a fuss

Jest
An object of ridicule; a laughingstock

Sepulcher
A burial vault

Strait
Affording little space or room; confined

Grown-up Thoughts

You could title this chapter, "Puddleglum Turns Positive." Twice he is the one who speaks truth and encouragements. "There *are* no accidents. Our guide is Aslan," he declares. But oh, how dark and depressing Underland feels: "You began to feel as if you had always lived on that ship, in that darkness, and to wonder whether sun and blue skies…had not been only a dream." If anyone in your family has struggled with depression (as Lewis did), you'll find opportunities here for helping your children understand it better.

You, O LORD, keep my lamp burning; my God turns my darkness into light.

PSALM 18:28

Puddleglad?

Does Puddleglum seem different now?

_____

Gloomy Gnomes

What would it be like to never see the sun?

_____

Accident Free

Puddleglum says that there are no accidents. What do you think he means? (Read Romans 8:28.)

_____

Old as the Son

Puddleglum says Aslan was alive before the words "Under Me" were ever cut in stone. How long has Jesus been alive? (See Colossians 1:17.)

_____

Knight in the Dark

Do you trust that the Black Knight knows and is telling the truth? Why?

_____

Father Time

What would happen if there were a Father Time and he fell asleep?

_____

FAST FACT

——

Lewis based the character of Puddleglum on his pessimistic gardener, Fred Paxton.

LET'S **TALK** ABOUT **IT**

Answers on page 435

Somebody turn the light on! It's time for...

Narniac Attack | No. 18

[Test your knowledge on chapters 6–10]

1. What do the children call Puddleglum sometimes?

a) A glum bum
b) A wet blanket
c) A sad sack

2. How tall was the Giant Porter who answered the door?

a) Taller than a telegraph pole
b) Taller than an apple tree
c) A little shorter than the castle door

3. Which of these was _not_ a toy offered to Jill by Nurse?

a) A woolly lamb
b) A drum
c) An X Box

4. What talking animal did Puddleglum and the children eat by accident?

a) A bear
b) A rabbit
c) A stag

5. What literary figure did the Black Knight look like?

a) Romeo
b) Odysseus
c) Hamlet

"I adjure you to set me free. By all fears and all loves, by the bright skies of Overland, by the great Lion, by Aslan himself, I charge you."
—Prince Rilian

In the
DARK CASTLE

The Story ❖ The three listen to the knight's story without believing him much. They come back after he's been tied to the silver chair to watch his daily "fit." Suddenly, he cries out in Alsan's name. Quick! It's the fourth sign! After he's cut loose they discover his real name—Prince Rilian.

Chamberlain
The head steward who manages a noble or royal household

"Faugh!"
An exclamation of disgust

"Fie"
Used to express distaste or disapproval

Grown-up Thoughts

Plenty of big ideas to think about together:

❖ The difference between enlightened belief and spiritual deception. For example, why does the Knight's worship of the Queen sound like a cult, not true devotion?

❖ The symbol of the silver chair. What might it stand for in your life?

❖ How disciples grow through failures.

❖ Look at how Jill's independent streak is being shaped into fiery but wise courage. She confronts the Knight as he's laughing over the plan for invading Overworld. "I don't think it's funny at all," she announces. "I think you'll be a wicked tyrant."

Spellbound

The Knight couldn't tell right from wrong, or choose his own future. Who was he allowing to decide for him?

_____

"You're No Good, But..."

Which of the three was the first to decide they should cut the Knight loose? (Hint: It was the same person who told him, "You'll be a wicked tyrant.")

_____

All Tied Up

What do you think would have happened if the children hadn't cut the Knight loose?

_____

Ten Years Later

How would you feel if you woke up one day and discovered you had missed ten years of your life? What would you do first?

_____

LET'S
TALK
ABOUT
IT

Ear Exam

———

What was the Witch doing while the children were talking with the Prince?

Answers on page 435

The Meaning of Everything

The Spell of Addiction

You might know someone whose life is being ruined by an addiction to alcohol, drugs, or other controlling sin. In a very real way, addicts are "spellbound"—they lose track of who they really are, and become slaves to a substance or behavior. The "spell" hurts them and others around them. Later Prince Rilian could say, "Now that I am myself I can remember that enchanted life, though while I was enchanted I could not remember my true self." Thankfully, with God's help, addicts can break the ropes that bind them to their "silver chair."

Trust in the LORD with all your heart.
Do not depend on your
own understanding.
Proverbs 3:5, NIRV

Eustace, Jill, and Puddleglum spent so much time in the Underworld in the dark that they "began...to wonder whether sun and blue skies and wind and birds had not been only a dream." ❋ Have you ever been stuck in the dark for too long, maybe when the electricity went out in a storm? No hot water. No stove or microwave. No TV.

Turn Out the Lights & Go

GNOME

HOW TO SPEND ONE NIGHT IN THE UNDERWORLD

What a bother!

Still, it can be exciting, too. You make do with candles and flashlights. You eat funny food. And you tell stories in the dark. So…for one whole evening, decide as a family to go gnomish. It's time to make yourself at home in the dark.

Here's a family plan (parents required):

Turn off the light.
Turn off lights, tape over the light switches, put blankets over the windows, unplug the night-lights.

Flicker while you work.
Do your homework by candlelight, flashlight, a camping lantern, or a warm, crackling fire.

Spread a bedspread for dinner.
On the floor, eat a cold dinner together. No cooking allowed.

Play "Puddleglum in the Gloom."
Think of something bad about living in the dark, and then something worse that won't happen.

It's so dark I can't see your face, but…at least I can't see you sticking out your tongue at me!

These crackers taste crummy, but…at least we aren't eating liver and onions!

Now that I can't see to brush my teeth… I think my hair looks terrific!

Now that I can't see to brush my teeth…I think my hair looks terrific!

Get the picture? Now make up your own.

Flip out.
All evening, anyone who accidentally flips a light switch or turns on an appliance is sent to the silver chair (pick one in your house) and must play zombie for ninety seconds (no smiling or talking) while everyone else tries to make him or her laugh.

Pop up.
Cook some Jiffy Pop in your fireplace. (Remember the old foil pan with popcorn for camping, that you shook to cook?) Or roast some good old-fashioned marshmallows and make s'mores.

Talk in the dark.
Make beds or roll out sleeping bags in the living room. Talk in the dark about a time you got scared. Or read your favorite scary chapter from the Chronicles by flashlight with a blanket over your heads.

—with Laurie Winslow Sargent

CHAPTER 12

> "I'm on Aslan's side
> even if there isn't
> any Aslan to lead it.
> I'm going to live as
> like a Narnian as I
> can even if there
> isn't any Narnia."
> —Puddleglum

The QUEEN OF UNDERLAND

The Story ❧ When the Queen sees that Rilian is free, she tries to enchant the group and convince them that Narnia isn't real. But Puddleglum resists her lies and bravely snuffs out her magic fire. Finally, she turns into a serpent and attacks Rilian, but Rilian and Puddleglum save the day.

Ark
A chest

Queue
A line of waiting people or vehicles

'Ware
Short for beware

Grown-up Thoughts

Lots to consider here about doubt, deception, and defense of the faith. The Witch's tactics and arguments echo those who tell Christians: "You only imagine a God because you want there to be one. It is only a fairy tale." Lewis struggled with doubts about the claims of Christ, and was for a time an atheist. But after his conversion, he wrote, "Now that I am a Christian I do not have moods in which the whole thing looks very improbable: but when I was an atheist I had moods in which Christianity looked terribly probable."

"I have come into the world as a light, so that no one who believes in me should stay in darkness."

JESUS, IN JOHN 12:46

Fairy Tales

How did the Queen try to convince the group that they were just making things up?

————

I Remember Now!

Who did the best job of fighting for the truth? Who remembered Aslan?

————

You're Making Him Up

Have you ever had someone try to talk you out of believing in God? What happened?

————

Hard to Think

Why does a powerful temptation make it hard to think straight?

————

Me? Enchanted?

Lewis says, "The more enchanted you get, the more you feel that you are not enchanted." Have you ever talked to someone who seemed hopelessly "enchanted" about something or someone? Describe what happened.

————

LET'S
TALK
ABOUT
IT

"Doubtless," said the Prince, "this signifies that Aslan will be our good lord, whether he means us to live or die."

UNDERLAND
WITHOUT THE QUEEN

The Story ◉ The Underworld is awash in strange activity. The city is falling apart and flooding, and the Earthmen look like they're preparing to attack. The four rescue the horses and set off. Only when Puddleglum catches a gnome do they learn the truth: The Earthmen are on their side!

Device
A graphic symbol or motto, especially in heraldry

Whipcord
A strong twisted or braided cord sometimes used in making whiplashes

---

Don't forget!
Full glossary on page 381

Grown-up Thoughts

By this time, most readers can't *wait* to get back up to the light! But will the four get out alive? When Rilian discovers the lion on his shield, he says, "Aslan will be our *good* lord, whether he means us to live or die." It's easy for families to assume that God's best always means our comfort or safety. Yet even when bad things happen, God can only be *good*. Paul wrote: "If we live, we live to the Lord; and if we die, we die to the Lord. So, whether we live or die, we belong to the Lord" (Romans 14:8).

For to me, to live is Christ and to die is gain.

Paul, in Philippians 1:21

Lion Sign

How did the Prince respond to the appearance of the Lion on his shield?

_____

Apologies

Why did Eustace and Jill apologize to one another before they left the room?

_____

Whistling in the Dark

Why was the Prince feeling so much less alarmed by the dangers than the others?

_____

Teething Ring

A wiggle's hands aren't "silly soft hands" like ours, but "even a Marsh-wiggle gets tired of being _____."

_____

I'm on Your Side

Have you ever thought someone was against you (like the Earthmen) when really they were on your side? What happened?

_____

LET'S
TALK
ABOUT
IT

Ear Exam

———

What was the name of Prince Rilian's horse?

Answers on page 435

Kid Test

Before and After

1. Before, the Knight called him Frog-foot. After, "friend _____?" Who was he?
2. Before, it was the Knight's armor. After, the Prince called it "a movable _____, and it stinks of magic and _____."
3. Before, he called the Witch "my _____." After, he called Aslan "our good _____."

Look It Up

Hardship 101

The Prince knows he might die while serving Aslan. Just because we love God doesn't mean bad things won't happen. The apostle Paul served God faithfully, yet he faced many hardships. Do you know which of these he suffered?

1. Beaten with 39 lashes five different times
2. Stoning
3. Three times beaten with rods
4. Shipwrecked
5. Went without food or water for days

CHAPTER 14

> "I know you
> Overlanders live
> there," said Golg.
> "But I thought it was
> because you couldn't
> find your way down
> inside. You can't really
> like it—crawling
> about like flies on top
> of the world!"

THE BOTTOM
of the WORLD

The Story ▪ Golg explains how the gnomes have been enchanted all these years by the Queen. When the other gnomes learn she's dead, it's party time! Then they head toward their even-further-below home, Bism. The Prince is tempted to go along, then Puddleglum reminds him of his father.

Pillar box
A letter box

Squib
A small firecracker

Grown-up Thoughts

We're just "flies on top of the world"? Now that's a perspective shift! Great stories do that—they draw us into other lives, then give us a fresh viewpoint on our life now. In this chapter, Golg assumes it would be awful to live with nothing but blue sky overhead. Jill sees things *very* differently. Jesus told unforgettable stories (parables) to surprise people with a new view of the truth. Are any of your family members stuck in one point of view? Try a perspective shift: *What would it feel like to be the youngest kid around here? Mom juggling household duties? The family pet?*

Further Down

The Prince wanted to go on an adventure down into Bism. Jill didn't. Who would you have sided with?

_____

'Nome Noggins

The Queen put only glum, dark thoughts in the gnomes' heads. How does what you think change what you do?

_____

Safe at Last

Killing the Witch saved not just the Prince but the gnomes as well. How is that similar to when we put a really bad person in prison?

_____

Up, Up, Ouch!

How did you feel when the Narnians were traveling up toward the surface, but the tunnel was getting smaller and smaller…and then the light went out?

_____

Cheap Caskets

Puddleglum said, "You must always remember there's one _____ thing about being trapped down here: it'll save _____ expenses."

_____

LET'S
TALK
ABOUT
IT

Answers on page 436

WISDOM
for
NARNIACS

———

In every age evil may look different, but it means the same thing.

Try This at Home

My Very Own Strange World

Golg described rubies you can eat and diamond juice you can drink! What? An after-school _jewelry snack_? Imagine you are creating another world for a story. How would you change the ordinary "rules" for living on earth? For example:

> We walk upright on our feet.
> We laugh out of our mouth.
> Our sky is blue.
> Oranges are for eating.
> Stealing is against the law.
> We keep dogs as pets.

Turn everything upside down…then write or tell a short story about your very own strange world!

Even though I walk through the valley of the shadow of death, I will fear no evil, for you are with me.

PSALM 23:4

CHAPTER 15

> *"Those Northern
> Witches always
> mean the same
> thing, but in every
> age they have a
> different plan for
> getting it."*
> —the oldest Dwarf

THE DISAPPEARANCE
OF JILL

The Story ◦ When Jill disappears above them, the three below in the dark fear the worst. But Jill has been pulled out by Narnians into a moonlit Narnian night. Soon enough, Dwarfs and Moles free the others. Everyone rejoices, then Rilian tells his story and all finally see the Witch's scheme.

Dryad

A mythical spirit of forests and trees; a wood nymph

Faun

A creature from Roman mythology with a man's body, horns, pointed ears, and a goat's tail

Pert

Sassy or bold; overly self-confident

Grown-up Thoughts

Consider that last line again: "Those Northern Witches always mean the same thing, but in every age they have a different plan for getting it." We know that Satan's schemes for every age have the same purpose—"the thief comes only to steal and kill and destroy," Jesus said (John 10:10). But their appearance changes. For each generation, Satan's lies look "new and improved." One of our most important jobs as parents is to expose the old lies underneath the new deceptions, and point our kids toward the unchanging Truth.

> *The night is nearly over; the day is almost here. So let us put aside the deeds of darkness and put on the armor of light.*
>
> ROMANS 13:12

Big Lie

The Witch tried to make the Prince steal something that was already rightfully his. What was it?

_____

Blue Light Special

While the children were underground, they saw a pale, bluish light. What was it?

_____

Snow Steps

Do you think you would like to learn the Snow Dance? Or just watch?

_____

Worth It All

Jill decided that the quest had been worth all the pains it cost. Would you feel the same way?

_____

Is Puddle Still Glum?

Puddleglum has been a great encourager when everything seems darkest. Then once back in Narnia, he expects only the worst again. Why do you think that is?

_____

WISDOM
for
NARNIACS

———

Evil changes its appearance, but its plans never change.

LET'S
TALK
ABOUT
IT

Narniac Attack | No. 19

[Test your knowledge on chapters 11–15]

1. What did the Prince say would happen if he was unbound from the chair?

a) He would eat Puddleglum in a frog pie.
b) He would turn into a serpent and attack them.
c) He would tie them up and torture them.

2. Why did Puddleglum step on the Witch's fire?

a) His feet were itching.
b) He wanted to dance to her music.
c) He was trying to stomp out the enchantment.

3. What did the Witch do when her enchantments failed?

a) She waved her wand.
b) She turned into a serpent.
c) She disappeared into a puddle on the floor.

4. What was the name of the Queen's horse?

a) Snowflake   b) Snowshoes   c) Snowball

5. Who said, "I have left half of my heart in the land of Bism"?

a) Prince Harry
b) Prince William
c) Prince Rilian

6. Who were the dancers in the Snow Dance?

a) Fauns and dryads
b) Deer and dwarfs
c) Centaurs and centipedes

CHAPTER 16

*"Think of that no
more. I will not
always be scolding.
You have done the
work for which I sent
you into Narnia."
—Aslan*

THE HEALING
of HARMS

The Story ◈ The children ride Centaurs to Cair Paravel, arriving in time to see King Caspian die. Then Aslan whisks them to his Mountain, where they watch him bring Caspian back to life, ready for heaven. Only one thing left to do—give those bullies at Experiment House a nasty fright!

The Head
*Headmaster,
principal*

Rapier
*A long, slender,
two-edged sword*

Grown-up Thoughts

After all the cold, dark threats of the previous chapters, this one reads like a homecoming. Which it is: Rilian to his kingdom, Caspian to Aslan's country, and the kids back to England. You'll see Bible parallels all over the place: in Aslan's graciousness about the children's failures, his tears over the dead King, the life-giving blood from his paw, his farewell breath on Eustace and Jill. For your kids, the best part might be how Aslan enters the grubby, oppressive world of Experiment House and "fights" for Eustace and Jill. Which God will do for us, too (Joshua 23:10).

*The LORD is good, a refuge
in times of trouble. He cares for
those who trust in him.*

NAHUM 1:7

LET'S
TALK
ABOUT
IT

Hungry?

Why do Centaurs eat so much for breakfast?

_____

Special Kids

How many children in Narnia have ever ridden on Centaurs, and what were their names?

_____

Nine Names

The Centaurs told the children the nine names of Aslan and their meanings. What do you think they were? What nine names would you give Aslan?

_____

"Well Done!"

The children must have felt really good when Aslan told them, "You have done the work I sent you to do." What person would you most like to hear say, "Well done!" to you?

_____

Most x 4

What was your most favorite part of _Silver Chair_? Your most favorite character? The most scary moment? The most surprising thing that happened?

_____

Fast Fact

———

Lewis also considered titling this book _The Wild Wastelands, Night Under Narnia, Gnomes Under Narnia,_ or _News Under Narnia._

The Silver Chair: One-Sentence Edition

Pssst! Can you say it in one _breath?_

Jill and Eustace came through a w_____ into N_____ only to find themselves sent on a q_____ for Aslan that involved four s_____ and a gloomy guide named P_____, who knew they shouldn't visit the g_____s, but they did anyway, and almost got e_____, but escaped into an underground world of g_____ who worked for a wicked Q_____ and brought them all to her c_____ where they discovered the Black K_____ tied to a s_____ chair, but when cut loose, he turned out to be Prince R_____, and that made the Queen try to e_____ them all, but she failed and turned into a s_____ and lost her h_____, which was good news to the gnomes, who helped the heroes escape from the crumbing U_____ , and J_____ climbed up a hole into N_____ again and Rilian became K_____, and A_____ helped Jill and Eustace scare the b_____ at Experiment H_____— hurrah!

In Narnia's final days, an evil Ape tricks Narnians into thinking Aslan wants them to work for the cruel Calormenes. King Tirian and the few remaining loyalists seem helpless to stop the lies. The real Alsan answers Tirian's prayer by sending Eustace and Jill to help, but still a terrible fate approaches. Just when all that's good and beautiful in Narnia is about to be destroyed, a Door opens into Aslan's presence, and to a new Narnia where the Great Story is just beginning.

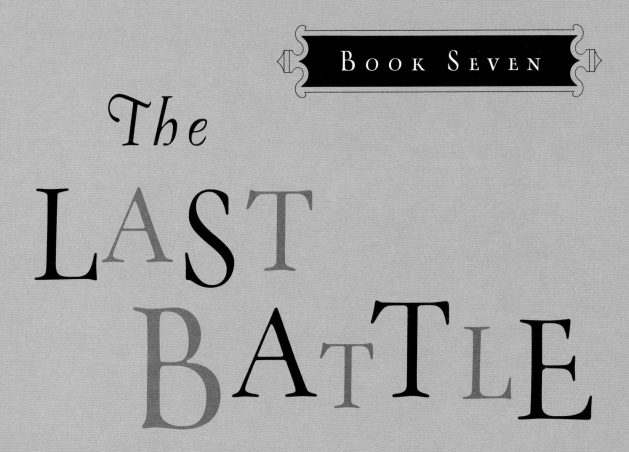

BOOK SEVEN

The
LAST
BATTLE

CHAPTER 1

*"You know you're
no good at thinking,
Puzzle, so why
don't you let me
do your thinking
for you?"*
—*Shift*

BY CALDRON POOL

The Story ❧ It's the last days of Narnia. An ugly but clever old Ape named Shift completely dominates a donkey named Puzzle. When they discover a lion-skin floating in Caldron Pool, Shift gets an idea—a donkey dressed up in a lion suit could pass for Aslan himself!

Pannier
*A basket with
carrying straps*

**"Turn and
turn about"**
*"Let's take
equal turns"*

Grown-up Thoughts

Lewis sets up the drama to come in this heartbreaking but inspiring last Chronicle by introducing us to Shift. What a perfect name for this evil Ape! He ruthlessly manipulates his "friend," twists truths, and shifts blame. He convinces Puzzle that not only is Aslan pleased that he's wearing the skin, he is commanding it. Shift tells Puzzle that if he wears the skin, he'll be just like Aslan, and "Everyone would do whatever you told them." Do you recognize one of the oldest lies in the Book?

*"Keep watch! Be careful that
no one fools you. Many will come
in my name. They will claim,
'I am the Christ!' They will fool many."*
Jesus, in Matthew 24:4–5

Shifty Shift

How can you tell that Shift is up to no good?

———

Puzzled

Why do you think Puzzle lets Shift treat him the way he does? Have you ever had a friend who tried to control you by putting you down?

———

Boom!

What do you think that thunderclap *really* meant?

———

Power Play

Shift points out that everyone will do what Puzzle says if they think he's Aslan. How could this work to Shift's advantage?

———

End Times

This story takes place in the last days of Narnia. Do you think our world is coming to an end soon?

———

WISDOM
for
NARNIACS

———

If you don't think for yourself, someone else will do it for you!

Kid Test

What Friends Are For

Shift tells Puzzle over and over that he can't think and he's not clever. He makes him do all the work, and he doesn't care about his feelings. But that's not what friends are for! Which two of these four statements do you think Puzzle should say back to Shift?

1. "I'm smarter than you, Shift! You're just a stinky old Ape."
2. "Okay! But once people think I'm Aslan, I'll make sure you never see another banana!"
3. "I know wrong from right, and what you're saying is wrong, and I won't do it."
4. "A true friend wouldn't try to take advantage of me like this."

Look It Up

The only talking animal in the Bible was a donkey like Puzzle. She, too, was mistreated. What was her owner's name? (See Numbers 22:21–35.)

"I wonder," said Jewel, "whether Aslan might not come though all the stars foretold otherwise. He is not the slave of the stars but their Maker."

The RASHNESS
OF THE KING

The Story ◈ Has Aslan returned to Narnia? King Tirian wants to believe the rumors. But then he learns that Dryads are being murdered in Aslan's name. Tirian and Jewel, a Unicorn, set off for Lantern Waste. When they find two Calormenes brutalizing a Talking Horse, they attack.

Dryad
A mythical spirit of forests and trees; a wood nymph

Fell
Capable of destroying; lethal

Felled
Cut down

Nymph
A mythical maiden who lives in nature

Sloth
Laziness

Grown-up Thoughts

Is King Tirian fearless or reckless, or both? The King didn't listen to Roonwit's caution about going to Lantern Waste alone. And, he was "too angry to think clearly." Before long he and Jewel have attacked and killed two unarmed men. What is the difference between righteous anger and rash anger? See what your family thinks. Here might be a rule of thumb: Righteous anger focuses on setting wrong things right…and doesn't result in more sin. (See Exodus 2:11–12; Proverbs 14:16.)

The end of all things is near. Therefore be clear minded and self-controlled so that you can pray.

1 PETER 4:7

Wow!

Jewel said that the news of Aslan's arrival was "too beautiful to believe." How would you feel if you knew that Jesus was coming to your house tomorrow?

———

First to Last

Tirian said reports of Aslan's return spread through Narnia in this order: first, by birds, then from _____, then came the _____, then a dark Man from _____, then, last night, a _____.

———

Sky Signs

Roonwit said the stars don't lie, but men do. How are stars in Narnia different from our stars?

———

Not Safe, But...

The Narnians all seem to remember that Aslan is *not* tame. But what are they forgetting that he *is*?

———

Hot Heads

Do you think that killing the Calormenes was the right thing for Tirian and Jewel to do?

———

LET'S
TALK
ABOUT
IT

EAR EXAM

———

The Dryad who died was the nymph of what kind of tree?

The Meaning of Everything

Written in the Stars

Astrologers try to predict the future by studying the stars—a practice the Bible condemns. In Narnia, though, stars are not just lifeless burning objects, but intelligent beings (remember Coriakin, the retired star in *Voyage*?). Roonwit is certain the stars can be trusted and that they would have foretold Aslan's coming. For us, the Bible is God-breathed truth (2 Timothy 3:16), and we can trust what it says about the future (Matthew 24:42).

Look It Up

Brotherly Love

Jewel and the King love each other like brothers and have saved each other's lives in war. What two men in the Bible "became one in spirit," and one saved the other's life? (See 1 Samuel 18:1-4.)

"Would it not be better to be dead than to have this horrible fear that Aslan has come and is not like the Aslan we have believed in and longed for?"
—King Tirian

The APE IN ITS GLORY

The Story Tirian and Jewel realize they've committed murder, and so decide to give themselves up to Aslan. But that proves difficult. The Ape, who says he now speaks for Aslan, announces cruel plans for Narnia. What's worse, he declares that Tash of the Calormenes and Aslan are the same god!

Sapient
Having great wisdom and discernment

'Ware
Short for beware

Grown-up Thoughts

This chapter, like many to come, mirrors biblical descriptions of the end times. "Do not believe every spirit," John wrote, "but test the spirits to see whether they are from God, because many false prophets have gone out into the world" (1 John 4:1). The Narnians are confused because the new Aslan speaks, acts, and responds *differently* than the Aslan they've always known. Is he true or false? The Narnians need to practice "spiritual discernment" before it's too late.

Be on your guard. Your enemy the devil is like a roaring lion. He prowls around looking for someone to chew up and swallow.

1 PETER 5:8, NIRV

Conspiracy

What do the Calormenes want out of their alliance with the Ape? Do you think they'll get it?

———————

Very Strange

How does the Ape's Aslan sound different from the Aslan the Narnians know?

———————

Not So Close!

Do you think Aslan wouldn't want the people "crowding round him," as the Ape claims?

———————

Dress Up

Why do you think the Ape put on fancy clothes and claimed to be a Man?

———————

Nuts!

How did you feel watching the squirrels hand over all their precious nuts to the Ape?

———————

LET'S
TALK
ABOUT
IT

Oh Where, Oh Where Has That Little Lamb Gone?

It's villainy. It's chaos. It's war. But as Narnia draws to a close, the huddled fretful children are having only lamby thoughts.

You might expect *Last Battle* to be about some epic combat—a frightening stand-off where everything hinges on an outcome and there are high hopes for the mettle of certain among the heroes, that they will prevail.

I certainly did, and as I read to Elliot, Emmae, and Cam this last book, I delighted to watch the makings of the clear outlines of bold villainy and most noble good forming against our favorite backdrop: Narnia!

Seeing the conflict broaden with every chapter was my satisfaction, perhaps because I've learned how war stories go. But taking my sampling glances every paragraph or so, I began to see the kids were clearly not so assured. They were afraid now, now outraged, now pitifully afraid again. Elliot kept hauling on his ears and locking his forehead between his knees. Cam had dug her toes deep between the cushions. Emmae was pinching down feathers, one by one from pillow seams.

By the time Tirian and Jewel handed themselves in for the killing of the Calormenes, my three were low, low, and sickened with Ape-contempt. "The monkey gets the king's sword now? *He* gets to wear it?" Elliot said, writhing with the shame of it.

With no relief for them in sight, I wondered if I should let them in on my certainty. (Some parents do at scary parts in stories.)

But just then a plucky lamb shuffled forward to call the Ape out. I thought, *Perfect! A little standing up for right from a little lamb is just what my little worriers need tonight.*

"Mmmm… Can you go back and read that what he said 'gain, Dad?" asked Emmae.

"Err…sure, 'Mae, let's see…" I said and read the lamb part again. His thesis was…*clear*—clear like the waters of that easternmost sea—and perhaps that was what the kids liked about him from the start. This book had been trick upon trick, and now there was a clear voice speaking clearly.

The little lamb was brave to speak, and his message was the goodness of the lion. So we read his part twice, which seemed enough to me, and then marched on TO WAR!

…But when the kids freed Tirian, Emmae asked if they would also untie the lamb.

"The lamb? I think the lamb's okay," I said.

"No, Dad, that monkey prolly chained him up too. Remember he spitted at him?"

…And later when Eustace and Jill were trying on mail shirts and helmets in the armory, our lamb came up again: "You think the lamb is coming to help too, Dad?" they asked me.

"Lambs aren't… I don't think he's coming, kids."

…And just as Tirian and the others were regrouping after rescuing Jewel and smuggling out the donkey, Elliot asked, "What about…

Did they also get the lamb out of there?"

Maybe it had turned into a game by that point. They knew they could miff me by insisting on lamb-status updates. The little lamb, the little lamb, the little lamb had become their theme, drowning out my drums of war. "Oh where, oh where has that little lamb gone? Oh where, oh where can he be?" I teased them, but they kept on asking after the lamb; sometimes to rib Dad, sometimes in earnest.

Even amidst the fury of the last battle itself, with spears flying and innocents being herded into the stable, would you believe our lamb stepped forward again? "I hope they don't ass-idenally get the lamby. How would they not ass-idenally hit some good guys, Dad?" Cam interjected.

"It's war, Cam. It's a war," I said numbly.

And at last toward the end where there was an illustration of the creatures streaming into New Narnia, passing before Aslan as they did, the kids leaned in to see if they could pick out their beloved lamb amongst the entrants and Elliot said with joyful certainty and poise, "He was there, Dad, even in, you know, the other book? Where they sailed so far and finally they met the lamb. Remember, Dad? Over where Reepicheep stayed behind? That was him!"

At that time too, you may recall, his message was the goodness of the lion.

—Brian Thomasson

CHAPTER 4

"Oh Aslan, Aslan,"
he whispered. "If you
will not come
yourself, at least
send me the helpers
from beyond
the world."
—King Tirian

WHAT HAPPENED
THAT NIGHT

The Story During the night, the little creatures of Narnia bring food and drink to the captive King. Then, as Tirian watches, a stiff-looking lion appears to a crowd in the firelight. *That's no Aslan!* Tirian decides. Desperate, he prays for help, and soon he's staring at seven people in another world!

Don't forget!
Full glossary
on page 381

Grown-up Thoughts

Tirian draws encouragement from remembering the history of Narnia and Aslan's goodness. Isaiah 46:9 says, "Remember the former things, those of long ago; I am God, and there is no other." When you consider that Tirian has never seen Aslan (or any lion), his prayer is an inspiring act of faith. Jesus told his disciples, "Blessed are those who have not seen me but still have believed" (John 20:29, NIRV).

Indeed, in our hearts we felt
the sentence of death. But this
happened that we might not rely
on ourselves but on God.

2 CORINTHIANS 1:9

Loyal Critters

The small animals who fed Tirian wanted to be loyal to the King *and* to Aslan. Why was this so hard?

_____

"Don't Be Mad!"

The beasts didn't understand why Aslan was angry with them. Have you ever felt that way with a friend or parent? What happened?

_____

Remember When?

What did Tirian remember about Narnian history that helped him?

_____

Help!

Even though Tirian had never seen Aslan, he prayed to him for help. What does this tell you about the King?

_____

Strange Travels

Who do you think those seven people in Tirian's vision might be?

_____

WISDOM *for* NARNIACS

___

If it looks like a lion, walks like a donkey, and behaves like an Ape—oh, it's probably not Aslan!

LET'S TALK ABOUT IT

Answers on page 436

Narniac Attack | No. 20

[Test your knowledge on chapters 1–4]

1. Who taught Shift how to sew?

a) *His brother, Shuffle*
b) *The Dwarfs*
c) *A Marsh-wiggle*

2. What was the name of the Cat who coolly questioned the Ape?

a) *Felix*
b) *Garfield*
c) *Ginger*

3. What did the Calormenes smell like?

a) *Sugar and spice*
b) *Pepperoni and cheese*
c) *Garlic and onions*

4. Which of these was fed to the King by the small beasts?

a) *Cheesecake*
b) *Birthday cake*
c) *Oat-cakes*

5. Who was King Tirian's great-grandfather's great-grandfather?

a) *Caspian the Tenth*
b) *King Rilian*
c) *King Arthur*

Chapter 5

*Then she added...
to Tirian,
"I'm sorry we've
been so long.
We came the
moment we could."
—Jill*

HOW HELP CAME TO
THE KING

The Story   Not long after the King's vision, Eustace and Jill arrive. They set him free, and he leads them to an old tower stocked with wonderful armor but wretched food. Tirian outfits everyone in Calormene suits of mail and they hatch a plan to attack in disguise.

Battlement
A low, notched wall running along the edge of a roof, used for defense

Firkin
About nine gallons

Garrison
A military post

Mail shirt
Flexible armor made of metal rings, chain, or scales

Smithied
Made from metal

Grown-up Thoughts

If we don't feel God's presence and don't see Him at work, does that mean He's absent? If you've ever endured fiery trials, you understand the question well. "Faith is being... certain of what we do not see," the Bible says. Certain? Truth is, most of us don't feel anything close to certainty until later. Only in looking back can we see how God was at work. Speaking of which, what do you make of Tirian's well-stocked tower and the key to it in his pocket? Coincidence or providence?

*The name of the LORD is a strong tower;
the righteous run to it and are safe.*

Proverbs 18:10

Here We Come!

After all the dangers and hardships from their last visit to Narnia (in *Silver Chair*), why do you think the children are eager to come back?

———————

Disguised

Jill loves a disguise. Do you feel the same way? Of course, others in this story are already pretending to be someone else. Who?

———————

Aliens

How did walking next to people from another world make King Tirian feel? How would you feel?

———————

Cool King

What evidence is there that the King is thinking clearly now, not impulsively?

———————

Yechh!

What do you think the mysterious "paste" was on the King's sandwich?

———————

Try This at Home

Undercover in Narnia

Wearing a costume is only part of pulling off a good disguise. Can you *act* the part? Choose a night to have everyone in the family assume the identity of a Narnian—no dress-up help allowed. Then, during dinner, make sure you talk and act like your character would. To figure out who from Narnia is at the table, ask questions like, "Are you an animal?" "Are you on Aslan's side?" "Did you go underground with Jill and Eustace?"

Look It Up

What person in the New Testament had a vision of people asking for help? (See Acts 16:9–10.)

Fast Fact

———

The story of a donkey in a lion-skin first appears in an ancient Roman fable by Avianus.

CHAPTER 6

*"If she was a boy,"
said Tirian, "she'd be
whipped for
disobeying orders."
And in the dark no
one could see whether
he said this with a
frown or a smile.*

A GOOD NIGHT'S WORK

The Story ◈ Jill proves she's the best and bravest pathfinder, so she leads the way as the children and Tirian return to Stable Hill. Then, while the King rescues Jewel, Jill slips away. But she's back shortly with Puzzle in tow, a lion-skin still tied to his back!

Jiggered
Surprised

Malapert
Disrespectful

Mattock
A hoe

Rive
To split

Smite
*To attack or
damage by hitting*

Grown-up Thoughts

This chapter could be titled, "You Go, Girl!" Jill isn't afraid of the dark, the enemy, or the unknown. If you remember her courage in the Underworld of *Silver Chair*, her daring leadership here won't surprise you. Lewis has been accused by some of being a sexist for how he portrays gender roles. See what your family thinks. And, what do you imagine Jill might say?

*Be on your guard;
stand firm
in the faith;
be men of courage.*

1 CORINTHIANS 16:13

Girl Power

Can you list three ways Jill showed skill and courage in this chapter?

_____

Face in the Dark

When Tirian said Jill would be whipped for disobeying orders, do you think he was smiling or frowning?

_____

Rough Stuff

Eustace and Jill have to skin rabbits and wake up in the middle of the night to attack the enemy. Would that be an awesome adventure to you, or just awful?

_____

Gift-Wrapped Guard

This time, Rilian ties up the Calormene soldier, then apologizes. Before, he killed a guard. Why the difference?

_____

Missing Puzzle

How do you think the Ape might explain his disappearing "god"?

_____

LET'S
TALK
ABOUT
IT

EAR EXAM

___

The Narnia North-Star is called the _____-Head.

Answer on page 436

The Meaning of Everything

Sirs and Dames—A Guide to Knighthood

Eustace says if Jill were a man, she should be knighted. What is knighthood, anyway? In medieval times (A.D. 500–1000), a knight was any male warrior of nobility. Later, knighthood had to be earned through a military exploit. In modern Britain, knighthood is bestowed on outstanding citizens—male or female—by the Queen. A male knight is addressed as "Sir," a female as "Dame."

Kid Test

Equipped for Narnia

The Narnian air makes you stronger and more "grown-up," but Jill and Eustace have also practiced their skills. If you went to Narnia, what would you be good at?

Hunting with a bow and arrow
Leading quietly in the dark
Making a meal out of unusual items
Finding your way by the stars
Going about in disguise

Get your cheers or jeers ready! It's time to praise or plaster the creatures in the Chronicles who deserve fame or shame. No witches, sea serpents, or humans need apply. Only humanlike creatures qualify. Did they choose to be brave or cowardly, wicked or good? That's how they make it to the top (or bottom) of our list.

CREATURE
Hall *of* Fame & Shame

Creature Hall of Fame
CHEERS!

Mr. Tumnus, *kind Faun and friend of Lucy*

Honored for: Refused to turn Lucy over to the White Witch in *Lion*. In *Horse*, he hatched a brilliant plan for the Narnians to escape Tashbaan.

Quotable: "Of course I can't give you up to the Witch; not now that I know you."

Weak Moment: At first he agreed to work for the Witch.

Greatest Moment: When he led Lucy back to the lamp-post.

Prize Awarded: A new tea set made of fine porcelain.

Reepicheep, *valiant Chief Mouse, warrior, explorer*

Honored for: Always ready to fight for an honorable cause. Never wavered in loyalty or courage.

Quotable: "I thought I heard someone laughing just now. If anyone present wishes to make me the subject of his wit, I am very much at his service—with my sword—whenever he has leisure."

Weak Moment: When his honor was motivated by vanity. Aslan said, "I have sometimes wondered, friend, whether you do not think too much about your honor."

Greatest Moment: Only character to not face death. Taken up into Aslan's Country in his little boat.

Prize Awarded: A gold-plated rapier and five pounds of cheese.

Puddleglum, *brave Marsh-wiggle*

Honored for: Wisdom, common sense, and courage. He saved Eustace and Jill from many dangers.

Quotable: "The bright side of it is that if we break our necks getting down the cliff, then we're safe from being drowned in the river."

Weak Moment: Puddleglum got drunk at the giant's house.

Greatest Moment: When he stamped out the Witch's fire with his bare feet.

Prize Awarded: His wigwam back, only better than ever and newly renovated.

Trumpkin, *loyal but skeptical Red Dwarf, AKA D.L.F. (Dear Little Friend)*

Honored for: Stood up to Nikabrik to save Caspian's life. Fought Nikabrik, the Wer-Wolf, and the Hag.

Quotable: "Lobsters and lollipops!" "Whistles and whirligigs!"

Weak Moment: When he made fun of the Bulgy Bears.

Greatest Moment: When Aslan playfully picks him up with his mouth and tosses him in the air and catches him.

Prize Awarded: A golden hearing aid for his old age.

Honorable Mentions: Trufflehunter the Badger, Roonwit the Centaur, Glimfeather the Owl, Jewel the Unicorn, Rumblebuffin the Giant.

Creature Hall of Shame
JEERS!

Maugrim the Wolf

Despicable Crimes: Captain of the White Witch's secret police, he destroyed Tumnus's home and attacked Susan.

Fate: Killed by Peter in his first battle.

Shift the Ape

Despicable Crimes: Dressed up Puzzle as a lion and deceived many; pronounced blasphemies and treated Narnians cruelly in Aslan's name.

Fate: Thrown into the stable and destroyed by the god Tash.

Ginger the Cat

Despicable Crimes: Conspired with the evil Prince Rishda to enslave Narnia.

Fate: Turned into a dumb beast.

Tirian had never dreamed that one of the results of an Ape's setting up a false Aslan would be to stop people from believing in the real one.

MAINLY ABOUT DWARFS

The Story ✦ Freeing the Dwarfs from a life in the salt-mines proves quick business. But freeing them from doubts about the real Aslan proves impossible, even after they see the fake one (Puzzle). Only one dwarf, Poggin, returns to pledge his allegiance and bring news from behind enemy lines.

Belike
Probably

Churl
A rude person

"Faugh!"
An exclamation of disgust

Manikin
A little man

Miscreant
An evildoer; a villain

Moke
Slang for donkey

Sagacious
Wise

Grown-up Thoughts

With this heartbreaking scene, Lewis paints a picture of the damage that can be done to the faith of believers by false prophets. Second Peter 2:1–3 echoes what is happening in Narnia: "They will secretly introduce destructive heresies…and will bring the way of truth into disrepute. In their greed these teachers will exploit you with stories they have made up." Having suffered in "Aslan's" name because of a false prophet, it is difficult for the Dwarfs to put their faith in him again. Something similar happens every time a Christian's words or actions cause others to see God in a false light.

Though you have not seen him, you love him; and even though you do not see him now, you believe in him and are filled with an inexpressible and glorious joy, for you are receiving the goal of your faith, the salvation of your souls.

1 PETER 1:8–9

LET'S TALK ABOUT IT

Disillusioned

Why do the Dwarfs no longer believe in Aslan? Do you understand their feelings?

———

"I See Jesus in You"

Lots of people decide whether to believe in Jesus based on how His followers act. What would people believe about Jesus by watching your family?

———

Who's a Puppet Now?

Shift used Puzzle like a puppet for a time, but now who is the puppet and doesn't even know it?

———

Truth & Lies

What truth did Tirian speak about Aslan that now sounds hollow to the Dwarfs?

———

"I'm For Me!"

"The Dwarfs are for the Dwarfs" sounds smart and safe. But what might be some problems with that kind of thinking?

———

FAST FACT

———

Early Christians were willing to be torn apart by lions for their faith.

Look It Up, #1

More Valuable than Gold

The Dwarfs make fun of Tirian's faith in Aslan—"Show him to us!" they sneer. People demanded that Jesus perform miracles, too, so they would know He was God. But Jesus asked His followers to have faith in Him. Faith means you believe even if you don't have proof. Is faith *foolish*? Actually, the Bible says your faith is *priceless*—more precious than _____! (See 1 Peter 1:6–9.)

Look It Up, #2

Thankful

Only one Dwarf, Poggin, was grateful to be set free. When Jesus healed ten lepers, how many returned to say thank you? (See Luke 17:11–19.)

Uncle Jack Says

"A man can no more diminish God's glory by refusing to worship Him than a lunatic can put out the sun by scribbling the word 'darkness' on the walls of his cell."

Answer on page 436

CHAPTER 8

"People shouldn't call for demons unless they really mean what they say."
—*Poggin*

WHAT NEWS THE EAGLE BROUGHT

The Story Things get worse, then worser. The foul-smelling god Tash is loosed in Narnia. Then the eagle Farsight drops out of the sky with unimaginable news: Cair Paravel is filled with dead Narnians and live Calormenes, and the Centaur Roonwit has been killed.

League
A unit of distance equal to 3 miles or 4.8 kilometers

Grown-up Thoughts

A sad but inspiring chapter. Think of it as snapshot of life for first-century Christians. "You will be handed over to be persecuted and put to death," Jesus predicted (Matthew 24:9). But He said more: "He who stands firm to the end will be saved" (v. 13). Roonwit speaks for Christian martyrs in all ages: "Noble death is a treasure which no one is too poor to buy."

"Don't be afraid of what you are going to suffer.... Be faithful, even if it means you must die. Then I will give you a crown. The crown is life itself."

REVELATION 2:10, NIRV

Big Stink

Tash is so evil and wicked he even *smells* bad! Who does he remind you of?

———

Careful!

The Ape and the others didn't take the evil god Tash seriously. How should we treat the powers of evil?

———

I Think I Love You

Jill had "quite fallen in love" with the Unicorn. Who is your favorite Narnian character so far?

———

World's End

Are you ready for Narnia to end? Talk about your feelings.

———

A Good Death

Roonwit called a noble death a treasure. What do you think he meant by that?

———

LET'S
TALK
ABOUT
IT

"If Aslan gave me my choice I would choose no other life than the life I have had and no other death than the one we go to."
—Jewel

THE GREAT MEETING ON
STABLE HILL

The Story ● Back at the hated Hill, Tirian's group hides, ready to show Puzzle to the oppressed Narnians. Then they hear the Ape announce that a donkey is wandering about dressed up in a lion-skin, and that Tashlan is furious at such a wicked deception.

Bath-chair
Wheelchair

Got the wind up
Slang meaning to become frightened

Grown-up Thoughts
A sense of doom descends, and the end seems near. Still, the children insist on staying with Tirian. Says Jill, "I'd rather be killed fighting for Narnia than grow old and stupid at home and perhaps go about in a bath-chair." Not many of us have to face death for our faith, yet the end could come at any time. Family test: *Would an observer say we're giving our whole lives to Christ's work on earth or simply waiting around for old age?*

Precious in the sight of the LORD is the death of his saints.
PSALM 116:15

If I Should Die

What do you think will happen if the children die in Narnia? a) They'll die in Narnia but *not* in England; b) They'll die in Narnia *and* in England; c) They won't actually die in *either* place.

_____

Old Folks

Jill doesn't like the idea of growing old. How do you feel about it?

_____

Half Truth, Double Damage

Why do you think that half-truths are sometimes more powerful than outright lies?

_____

No Other Life

Jewel would choose no other life than the one he's had. Do you feel the same way, or do you wish your life was very different?

_____

Next Thing You Know

What do you think will happen next? What do you *want* to happen next?

_____

LET'S
TALK
ABOUT
IT

WISDOM
for
NARNIACS

___

A noble death
is a treasure
no one is too
poor to buy.

Kiss me, Jewel, it's time for…

Narniac Attack | No. 21

[Test your knowledge on chapters 5–9]

1. Why did the children *not* use the Rings to come to Narnia?

a) *The backyard where they were buried was paved over.*

b) *They never got the chance before magically appearing here off a train.*

c) *They decided to come through the wardrobe instead.*

2. What did Jill do that Eustace declared "perfectly gorgeous"?

a) *She went off by herself and blubbed.*

b) *She went off by herself and phoned home.*

c) *She went off by herself and rescued Puzzle.*

3. How tall are Narnian Dwarfs generally?

a) *Less than three feet high*

b) *Less than two feet high*

c) *Less than four feet high*

4. Who has taken to drinking?

a) *The Ape, Shift*

b) *The Calormene Rishda*

c) *The Dwarf Poggin*

5. According to Lewis, one always feels better when one has…

a) *had tea and crumpets.*

b) *got one's own way.*

c) *made up one's mind.*

"Courage, child:
we are all between
the paws of the
true Aslan."
—Tirian

WHO WILL GO
INTO THE STABLE?

The Story The Ape says Tashlan is in the Stable, and anyone brave enough can go in. Ginger the Cat coolly volunteers. Bad idea! Out he streaks, terrified and struck dumb. Then Emeth, an earnest young Calormene, strides in. Moments later, a dead Calormene tumbles out. Tirian decides to act.

Caterwaul
A cry or screech like
a cat would make

Pert
Sassy or bold;
overly self-confident

Grown-up Thoughts

Tirian tells Jill, "Courage, child: we are all between the paws of the true Aslan." Now there's a declaration for your Narniac to remember! Yes, God holds us in His mighty hands—no matter what. Paul wrote: "For I am convinced that neither death nor life, neither angels nor demons, neither the present nor the future, nor any powers…will be able to separate us from the love of God that is in Christ Jesus our Lord" (Romans 8:38–40).

Let us then approach the throne
of grace with confidence, so that we
may receive mercy and find grace
to help us in our time of need.

HEBREWS 4:16

Fear Factor

The Narnians were eager to see Aslan until the Ape made them feel afraid.
Why can we come to God without fear? (See 1 John 4:18.)

———

Best Guess

What do you think really *is* inside that stable?
Would you go in?

———

LET'S
TALK
ABOUT
IT

"Courage, Child"

What would it feel like to be between Aslan's paws?

———

Brave Boy

Emeth believes in Tash, not Aslan. But what do you think Aslan will say to Emeth when they meet? (And they will!)

———

Mum's the Meow

Ginger, a Talking Cat of Narnia, was so terrified by what he saw in the Stable that he turned back into an ordinary cat. What do you think he saw?

———

Eustace stood with his heart beating terribly, hoping and hoping that he would be brave.

The PACE QUICKENS

The Story ❧ The fighting begins. Right off, Tirian tosses the Ape into the Stable to meet his fate (probably awful). After the first wave of attacks, the Narnians still have hope. But then the Dwarfs shoot down all the Talking Horses, and Calormene reinforcements arrive.

Bethink
Remember

Miscreant
An evildoer; a villain

Grown-up Thoughts

Terrible violence overtakes the story, and death for Aslan's followers seems certain. Can the Great Lion still be in control? Those who know Aslan trust that he is, and that even his apparent absence is part of his good plan. Brutal events here will trouble many readers. But Lewis wanted children to see the connection between important truths: life is violent, God is stronger than any fear, and for followers of Christ, even death isn't tragic. "For me, to live is Christ," wrote Paul, "and to die is gain" (Philippians 1:21).

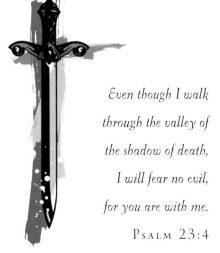

Even though I walk through the valley of the shadow of death, I will fear no evil, for you are with me.

PSALM 23:4

Wages of War

How do you feel when you read about men killing each other in battle? Why do you think we have wars in this world?

"Will I Be Brave?"

Have you ever wondered, like Eustace did, if you would be brave enough to face a frightening challenge? Talk about it.

No Kitchen-Girls Allowed

How does Tirian think a true warrior should behave?

After Death

How can knowing about heaven change how you feel about dying?

The End of the Story

Even though we are told there will be terrible times in the last days on earth, that's not the end of the story. Do you know what is? (See Revelation 7:14–17.)

LET'S TALK ABOUT IT

Fast Fact

Lewis admired dogs and once called them "honest, humble persons."

The Meaning of Everything

Is War Always Wrong?

Some Christians are pacifists—they believe that all wars do more harm than good. Pacifists point to Jesus' teaching to turn the other cheek (Matthew 5:39). C. S. Lewis hated war, but he was not a pacifist. Jesus was talking about how to get along with difficult people, Lewis said, not how nations should defend themselves. He agreed with Augustine, a fifth-century theologian, who taught that a "just war" might be necessary to restrain a greater evil or to defend the helpless. Lewis knew the horrors of battle first-hand. In World War I, he was wounded in three places by an explosion that killed the sergeant standing next to him. His injuries—one in his writing hand—bothered him for the rest of his life. For more on violence in the Chronicles, see page 356.

CHAPTER 12

THROUGH THE STABLE DOOR

The Story ❖ A Calormene throws Eustace into the Stable while a tearful Jill fights on. Then Tirian, in a last sacrifice, pulls Prince Rishda into the Stable with him. Tash (the Big Stink) carries the terrified Rishda away, but not Tirian. Instead, he's welcomed by the Seven Kings and Queens of Narnia!

Blub
Cry

Scimitar
A curved sword

Shrine
A place to worship a sacred thing or person

Grown-up Thoughts

Here comes the happy ending we've been hoping for. Only Jewel seemed to see it coming when he suggested that the terrible Stable door may actually be for them "the door to Aslan's country and we shall sup at his table tonight." Jesus told the thief on the cross, "Today you'll be with me in paradise." For believers, Jesus promised that the door of death will usher us into His very presence. (See John 14:1–4; I John 3:1–3.)

You are all sons of the light and sons of the day. We do not belong to the night or to the darkness.

1 THESSALONIANS 5:5

The Dwarfs' Mistake

The Dwarfs thought it was smarter to not be loyal to *either* side—to only care about themselves. Why didn't their plan work out?

———

Legal Munchies

Why do you think the Tarkaan was Tash's "lawful" victim?

———

Door Prize

Who predicted that loyal Narnians might find something good on the other side of the Stable door?

———

Big Bad Bird

Do you think a huge, black, man-eating bird might be especially scary? What kind of evil monster would be most scary for you?

———

Oh, Grow Up!

Why does Polly think it's a silly waste for anyone to be in a rush to grow up? Are you in a rush to be older? How old do you want to be and why?

———

LET'S TALK ABOUT IT

Ear Exam

———

What did the Calormenes plan to do with Jewel?

Answer on page 436

The Meaning of Everything #1

Where Did Susan Go?

What! No Susan in Narnia? If you were surprised—maybe even upset—you aren't alone. Many readers have been disappointed by this turn in the story. Is Lewis saying that Susan won't get into heaven because she behaves too much like, well, a normal teenager? Maybe it's just a matter of timing. Lewis once wrote to an American boy: "There is plenty of time for Susan to mend, and perhaps she will get to Aslan's country in the end—in her own way."

The Meaning of Everything #2

Was Lewis a Racist?

If you stumbled over the word "Darkies" in this chapter, you're not alone. In fact, this derogatory reference along with the role he gives the dark-faced, turbaned Calormenes have led some modern critics to accuse Lewis of being racist. It's more likely that readers now are reinterpreting the Chronicles through the lens of our own troubled times. Before you rush to judgment about Lewis, be sure to read the article, "Color & Culture in Narnia" on page 366. In the meantime, your family might want to skip over certain words or passages that could be offensive.

CHAPTER 13

> "Their prison is only
> in their own minds,
> yet they are in that
> prison; and so afraid
> of being taken in
> that they cannot
> be taken out."
> —Aslan

How the DWARFS REFUSED TO BE TAKEN IN

The Story ❧ After eating the magical fruit, the friends tell how they arrived on this side of the Stable door. Then it's time to help the Dwarfs. Or try to. They're in the same lovely place, but won't see or believe it. Even mighty Aslan can't break through their foolish "cunning."

Baccy
Tobacco

Poky
Small and cramped

Rugger
Rugby, a game similar to football

Sauce
Boldly offensive speech or behavior

Trifle
A cake soaked in sherry or brandy

Grown-up Thoughts

The Dwarfs sitting in a circle of self-imposed darkness is an unforgettable picture of the power of unbelief. Know anyone stuck in that prison? When Jesus was on earth, many refused to believe He was God's Son even when faced with abundant proof. He quoted Isaiah to describe their sad plight: "This people's heart has become calloused.… Otherwise they might see with their eyes, hear with their ears, understand with their hearts and turn, and I would heal them" (Matthew 13:15).

We have not received the spirit of the world but the Spirit who is from God, that we may understand what God has freely given us.

1 CORINTHIANS 2:12

It's All Good

Peter says he has a feeling they've got to the country where "everything is allowed." What do you think that could mean? Will heaven be like that?

————

Small Stable, Big Savior

What do you think Lucy meant by a stable in our world holding something bigger than the whole world? (See Luke 2:10–12.)

————

Heart's Desire

Tirian refers to Aslan as his heart's desire—even though he'd never seen him until now. Is that possible? Talk about it.

————

Only Believe

The Dwarfs pride themselves on not "being taken in." What does that keep them from being able to do?

————

Silly or Sad

Did you feel sorry for the Dwarfs, or did you laugh at them?

————

LET'S
TALK
ABOUT
IT

WISDOM
for
NARNIACS

———

Don't try
to be so smart
that you risk
being stupid.

Answers on page 436

Narniac Attack | No. 22

[Test your knowledge on chapters 10–13]

1. What idea terrified the Talking animals most of all?

a) *Being thrown into the Stable*
b) *Being turned into a "dumb" animal*
c) *Becoming Calormene slaves again*

2. Who went right while Jill went left in the first wave of attack on the Calormenes?

a) *Jewel, the Unicorn*
b) *A Boar*
c) *Farsight the Eagle*

3. How did Peter the High King welcome Tirian?

a) *Kissed him on both cheeks*
b) *Gave him a high five*
c) *Asked him to wait while he finished his tea*

4. Which of these would you never find in Narnian clothing?

a) *Buttons*
b) *Elastic*
c) *Pockets*

5. Who interrupts Lucy while she's telling her story to Tirian?

a) *Edmund*
b) *Poggin*
c) *Eustace*

But the others looked in the face of Aslan and loved him, though some of them were very frightened at the same time.

NIGHT FALLS on NARNIA

The Story ✹ Narnia's end is as spectacular as its birth, but sadder. The friends of Narnia witness the stars falling, the world flooding, and the sun dying. Even Father Time gets a new name. When all the creatures of Narnia are summoned, some pass into the darkness, others through Aslan's Door.

Blown
Out of breath

Grown-up Thoughts

Notice how, while his magical world is collapsing into darkness, Lewis stays close to the reader, talks in a comforting voice, and gives permission to cry—just what kids want in a storytelling Uncle! Even the "last judgment" isn't some awful calamity that comes from outside, but a mutual acknowledgment of what is already in each creature's heart. Do they know Aslan, and want to be with him, or not? One look into the Lion's face will tell.

"Heaven and earth will pass away, but my words will never pass away."

JESUS, IN MATTHEW 24:35

New Name

What do you think Father Time's new name will be, now that time in Narnia is over?

_____

Door = _____?

In the New Testament, who said He was the Door? Did this chapter help you to understand better what He might have meant?

_____

Great Divide

The creatures who swerved to the left and those who went through the Door were different. How?

_____

Kids Watching

How did you feel while Narnia was ending?

_____

Key

Peter had the key to Aslan's Door. Do you remember who Jesus told, "I will give you the keys of the kingdom of heaven"? (See Matthew 16:18–19.)

_____

LET'S TALK ABOUT IT

CHAPTER 15

*"I have been
wandering to find
him and my
happiness is so great
that it even weakens
me like a wound."*
—Emeth

FURTHER UP *and*
FURTHER IN

The Story ❦ This new place looks a lot like the old Narnia, only better. Every rock and flower and blade of grass means more. Emeth tells his moving story. Happy reunions lead to a final, joyful run, and no one gets "hot or tired or out of breath," not even fat little Puzzle.

Hovel
*A small,
crude shelter*

Plato
A Greek philosopher

Grown-up Thoughts

What do you make of Emeth and of the space Lewis gives to his testimony? You might be reminded of the surprises that faced early Christians as they took their "Jewish" faith to the ends of the earth. Old prejudices had to fall away. Kosher disciple Peter realized that "God accepts men from any nation who fear him and do what is right" (Acts 10:34–35). Emeth suggests that anyone who truly seeks the truth is seeking Jesus, who *is* the Truth.

*"You will seek me and find me when
you seek me with all your heart."*
JEREMIAH 29:13

More, Better

Do you think heaven will be a lot like the new Narnia?

———————

Seekers

Were you glad that Emeth made it into the new Narnia? What does Jesus say about those who seek? (See Matthew 7:7.)

———————

Jitters

Puzzle is worried about meeting Aslan face-to-face. What do you think Aslan will say to him?

———————

Dog Talk

When their puppies aren't behaving, dogs call them _____ or _____. (*S-s-sh!* That's not nice!)

———————

So Good It Hurts

Emeth said his happiness at finding Aslan was so great it almost hurt. Have you ever felt that happy or cried for pure joy?

———————

LET'S
TALK
ABOUT
IT

Kid Test

Here Comes the Lion!

Emeth says: Aslan's speed was like the _____, his size was like an _____, his hair was like pure _____, and the brightness of his eyes like _____ that is liquid in the _____.

Look It Up

Seek & Find

Is God hard to find? Sometimes you have to look and look…and keep looking. But He promises that you *will* find Him. The story of Emeth is similar to two stories in the New Testament:

> An African government official (Acts 8:26–39)
> A Roman military commander (Acts 10)

Uncle Jack Says

"If we really think that home is elsewhere and that this life is a 'wandering to find home,' why should we not look forward to the arrival?"

Fast Fact
———
"Emeth" is the Hebrew word for "truth."

Answers on page 436

Now at last they were beginning Chapter One of the Great Story which no one on earth has read: which goes on forever: in which every chapter is better than the one before.

F A R E W E L L

T O   S H A D O W L A N D S

The Story ⬩ The friends romp higher up and further in to Narnia. First Mouse Reepicheep welcomes them into the garden, which is larger inside than outside. Then Aslan tells them they have died and the Shadowlands are forever behind. Onward to the Great Story!

Cataract
A great downpour or waterfall

Grown-up Thoughts

Your family may be delighted that the friends of Narnia never have to leave again. Or they might be alarmed at the deaths of favorite characters. "Did Aslan cause the crash?" they might wonder. Or "Why did they have to die?" But death is part of life and reading about it in a positive light can help allay fears. Keith Webb, host of a wonderful Narnia site, puts it this way: "The children do not die for a purpose, they are resurrected in Narnia for a purpose: to quell the fear of death by eliminating the mystery behind it."

No longer will there be any curse.... There will be no more night. They will not need the light of a lamp or the light of the sun, for the Lord God will give them light. And they will reign for ever and ever.

REVELATION 22:3, 5

LET'S TALK ABOUT IT

Lion Whispers

What do you think Aslan said to Puzzle?

_____

No Tears

Why do you suppose the children are *not* upset to discover they died?

_____

Friends in Heaven

Do you look forward to seeing any particular person when you get to heaven? If so, who and why?

_____

Something's Missing

In the new Narnia, do you think there will be evil people, violence, pain, lies, or homework? Why?

_____

Surprised?

Think back: How did you think the last Chronicle story would end?

_____

Come Back Soon

Are you sad to say good-bye to Narnia? How long do you think it will be until you start over again with the first book?!

_____

WISDOM *for* NARNIACS

___

Death just turns the page to the best story of all.

Kid Test

"If I could do ANY-thing"

In the new Narnia, kids can see like a telescope, swim *up* waterfalls, and run forever without getting tired. If heaven is like that, how would you like to be different than you are now? For example:

> Your memory
>
> Your senses
>
> Your need for sleep
>
> Your emotions
>
> Your looks
>
> Your strength
>
> Your intelligence

Did You Know?

Face-to-Face with Jesus

The Bible says, "No eye has seen, no ear has heard, no mind has conceived what God has prepared for those who love him" (1 Corinthians 2:9). That means no one can know *exactly* what heaven is like. Except this: We will be with Jesus, and He will be shining so bright that we won't even need a light! (See Revelation 22:4–5.)

PART THREE

Final Exams for Narniacs

Your wish has come true!

It's time to take courage, brandish your rapier, and follow the White Stag to the...

NARNIAC
FINAL EXAM

THE NARNIAC FINAL EXAM is intended for the passionate and careful reader, whether child or adult. *Younger readers may prefer the Narniac Final Exam for Little Ones, page 317.* Both tests cover all seven Chronicles.

Here are your instructions:

1. Please, no blubbing.
2. Do not write in your copy of *Roar!*—you or someone else may want to take the same test later. Instead, download a copy of the Exam from RoarofNarnia.com. You could also make a photocopy of these pages, or simply write your answers on a separate sheet.
3. Open book, or closed—your choice.
4. For extra help without opening a Chronicle, you may "Blow the Horn" by turning to the end of the test for hints. (Parts 1, 4, 6, and 8 come with hints.)
5. When you're finished, see p. 436 for the answers. Then add up your score to discover which level of Narnian honors you have won (see p. 315).

Read the quotation and write down who spoke these words. (Blow the Horn for help—see page 322.)

1. "Aslan's instructions always work: there are no exceptions."

2. "Where I come from, they don't think much of men who are bossed about by their wives."

3. "Who said anything about safe? 'Course he isn't safe. But he's good."

4. "The help will come. It may be even now at the door."

5. "If you had felt yourself sufficient, it would have been a proof that you were not."

6. "You've no idea what an appetite it gives one, being executed."

7. "It must be exciting to live on a thing like a ball. Have you ever been to the parts where people walk about upside-down?"

8. "Minions!"

9. "In a civilized country like where I come from, the ships are so big that when you're inside you wouldn't know you were at sea at all."

10. "If she was a boy, she'd be whipped for disobeying orders."

11. "There's no point in having a new dress on if one's to go about shut up like this."

12. "I've brought you the apple you wanted, sir."

13. "It isn't Narnia, you know. It's *you*. We shan't meet *you* there. And how can we live, never meeting you?"

14. "We don't know when he will act. In his time, no doubt, not ours. In the meantime he would like us to do what we can on our own."

15. "I'd rather be killed fighting for Narnia than grow old and stupid at home and perhaps go about in a bath-chair and then die in the end just the same."

16. "It may be for us the door to Aslan's country and we shall sup at his table tonight."

17. "Pooh! Who's afraid of Aslan?"

18. "Are you going to tolerate this mutiny, this poltroonery? This is a panic, this is a rout."

19. "I'd sooner be eaten by you than fed by anyone else."

20. "Doubtless this signifies that Aslan will be our good lord, whether he means us to live or die."

Part 2. Can You Ruminate in Riddles?

Read all the clues, then guess which character they describe.

1. Who...

   _ is likely to give you jewelry?

   _ looks a little like a tree?

   _ should wear a smaller hat?

   _ is the enemy of rodents everywhere?

2. Who...

   _ could use some sun?

   _ would be great at a Halloween party?

   _ could satisfy your sweet tooth?

   _ decorates her home with statues?

3. Who...

   _ likes attention but hates to pay attention?

   _ would be first in line at a fashion show?

   _ doesn't carry her own weight
     when traveling?

   _ loves a secret but can barely keep one?

4. Who...

   _ is scary in battle but hard to see?

   _ should probably keep a spare tail?

   _ is a much-beloved chief?

   _ never died but went to heaven?

5. Who...

   _ would make great bath toys?

   _ are difficult to argue with?

   _ might point out that lunchtime is a good
     time to have lunch?

   _ could have a hard time riding a bike?

6. Who...

   _ could be a good friend to Winnie-the-Pooh?

   _ would make a terrible weather man (*Rainy
     and cloudy again?!*)?

   _ could help you see the worst in a bad situation?

   _ might turn into a prince if you kissed him?

7. Who...

   _ can be dangerous when he uses his head?

   _ won't take you for a ride?

   _ is a king's best friend?

   _ is blue and white?

8. Who...

   _ walks into the dark with "Frog-face"?

   _ gets spanked by Reepicheep?

   _ should have read different books in school?

   _ has strong opinions about civilization?

9. Who...

   _ wants to be a man but he's not?

   _ likes to play dress up?

   _ should give up politics?

   _ must have slipped on one too many
     banana peels?

10. Who...

   _ has a problem with shoplifting?

   _ needs an anger management class?

   _ knows the power of a word?

   _ has been called a "dem fine woman"?

PART 3. THE HONEST TRUTH ABOUT GIRLS AND BOYS

To defend your honor and your gender, you must choose the correct answer.

1. According to Edmund, the worst thing about girls is that they:

    a. never want to eat Turkish Delight.

    b. never have a thought in their heads.

    c. never carry a map in their heads.

    d. never think boys are smart and brave.

2. In the chronology of Narnia, the correct order of character's appearance and events is as follows (pick one):

    a. First Cor and Corin, then Erlian and Tirian

    b. First Eustace, then Edmund

    c. First Polly gets blown off the cliff, then she starts to blub behind the gymnasium

    d. First Jill is brave in the dark (Underworld), then Lucy (Dark Island)

3. Aravis was about to be unhappily married off to:

    a. King Miraz

    b. Prince Rabadash

    c. Rishda Tarkaan

    d. Ahoshta Tarkaan

4. In *The Last Battle*, these two English children are sent to the aid of Tirian:

    a. Eustace and Jill

    b. Polly and Digory

    c. Lucy and Edmund

    d. Peter and Polly

5. Which of these couples was a friend to children?

    a. Aravis and Cor

    b. Mr. and Mrs. Beaver

    c. The King and Queen of Harfang

    d. Mr. and Mrs. Hermit of the Southern March

6. Aravis and Cor, when they were King and Queen of Archenland, had a child who grew up to become:

    a. Ramses the Great

    b. Rumi the Poet

    c. Roonwit the Centaur

    d. Ram the Great

7. In *Prince Caspian*, Aslan set students free in two different classrooms where:

    a. The girls were looking at the boys and the boys were fast asleep.

    b. The girls were tickling pigs and the boys looked very much like sausages.

    c. The girls wore tickly stockings and the boys looked very much like pigs.

    d. All the boys and the girls were too interested in their history lesson to notice that there was a lion outside the window.

8. Digory told Polly that girls never want to know anything but:

    a. "silly rumors about boys and kissing."

    b. "cooking and sewing and entertaining."

    c. "gossip and rot about people getting engaged."

    d. "how to brush their hair and put on makeup."

9. Who wanted to dissolve an enchantment so he could "kiss the Princess"?

a. Caspian

b. Nikabrik

c. Prince Rilian

d. Rabadash

10. Who said, "My sister is no longer a friend of Narnia," and what was the sister's name?

a. King Miraz said it about Queen Punaprismia.

b. Peter said it about Susan.

c. Reepicheep said it about Peepiceek.

d. Rumblebuffin said it about Rinelda.

PART 4. DETAILS, DETAILS

Were you listening carefully or nodding off? These questions test your knowledge of fun facts you might have missed. (Blow the Horn for help—see page 323.)

1. Who was the lone sailor who stayed behind on the island of Ramandu?

2. What famous boxer went thirty-three rounds with the Lapsed Bear of Stormness?

3. What was Digory's mother's name?

4. How many sons did the Centaur Glenstorm have?

5. What was the chessman Susan found in the ancient courtyard made of?

6. When the kids found Tumnus's house in ruins, whose picture was slashed into shreds?

7. Trumpkin's pipe was as long as his _____.

8. How many steps were there on the staircase to the treasure chamber at Cair Paravel?

9. What color was the sail on the *Dawn Treader*?

10. What shape was the sail on the *Dawn Treader*?

Part 5. Animals, Creatures, & Vegetables

Narnia is full of unusual living things. Do you remember the answer to these questions?

1. When the children say "D.L.F.," they mean...
   a. Dear Little Friend.
   b. Dear Little Faun.
   c. Do Let's be Friends!
   d. Don't Look, Fledge!

2. When beings like Bacchus, Selenus, and other strange creatures in Narnia have a romp, they're likely to start yodeling with cries of:
   a. Yodel-ee, Yodel-oh, Yodel-ooo!
   b. Euan, Euan, eu-oi-oi-oi!
   c. Tweedle-dee, Tweedle-dum, Tweedle-dooo!
   d. For he's a jolly good fellow!

3. The Bulgy Bear can be marshal of the lists, says Peter, but he must remember to not:
   a. step on the mice.
   b. scare the bunnies.
   c. ask for honey.
   d. suck his paws.

4. At the creation of Narnia, the iron bar that Jadis threw hit Aslan on the head, then:
   a. fell into the grass and grew into a lamp-post.
   b. stuck in the mud and grew into the Tree of protection.
   c. splashed into the river and turned into a rock.
   d. struck a rock and turned into a sword named Rhindon.

5. Caspian's horse bolts during a thunderstorm and returns to the castle from which the Prince is fleeing. The horse's name is:
   a. Bree.
   b. Coalblack.
   c. Destrier.
   d. Snowflake.

6. In Underland, the gnomes (also called Earthmen) all carry:
   a. one-edged swords.
   b. two-bulbed lamps.
   c. three-pronged spears.
   d. four-sided lunch boxes.

7. In Narnia, the trees aren't just trees:
   a. The beeches are boys, and the birches are girls.
   b. The oaks are blokes, and the beeches are leeches.
   c. The willows are witches, and the pines are Poggins.
   d. The birches and beeches are girls, and the oaks are men.

8. Inside Aslan's How you'll find:
   a. gnomes digging upwards toward Narnia.
   b. gnomes digging downward toward Bism.
   c. Clodsley Shovel the Mole digging just for fun.
   d. tunnels and strange writing.

9. All Dwarfs:

   a. swear.

   b. snore.

   c. snivel.

   d. snoop.

10. Digory said afterward, "It just shows that you can't be too careful in these magical places." He was referring to being watched by:

    a. a beaver in a house by a pond.

    b. a serpent on a chair in a castle.

    c. a bird in a tree in a garden.

    d. a dragon in a cave on an island.

Part 6. Stumpers for Smarty-Pants

Few mice and fewer men have finished this section with nerves unrattled. But, please, do press on! (Blow the Horn for help—see page 323.)

1. Which animal in Narnia was apparently capable of writing a letter?

2. Who received the first "Lion's kiss" from Aslan?

3. Who is the only person Aslan pronounced a lioness?

4. Who is the only person Aslan referred to as a sinner?

5. What two characters were directly healed by Aslan?

6. What gifts, if any, did Father Christmas give to Mr. and Mrs. Beaver?

7. Who grew into a tall woman with black hair that fell almost to her feet?

8. Whose absence in Narnia prompted search parties and the posting of a reward?

9. What two characters (besides Dwarfs) knew how to sew?

10. Besides Mr. and Mrs. Beaver, what other two talking animals are mentioned as having gotten married (but not to each other)?

11. Who was most frequently scolded by Aslan?

12. On what two occasions did Aslan cry?

13. When did Lucy use the dagger that Father Christmas gave her?

14. Besides Susan and Lucy, who else rode on Aslan's back?

15. What two animals were knighted?

Part 7. The Profile of Evil

Ahh! Finally some relief! Only two choices are possible here—true or false.

1. The evil Queen in *The Magician's Nephew* is also known as Your Deplorable Highness.

2. Turkish Delight, as we all know, grows on the Toffee Tree.

3. Uncle Andrew, as we all know, gets quite a bang out of his guinea pigs.

4. When the Black Knight (later revealed to be Prince Rilian) suffered from attacks of a "strange affliction," he was tied to a silver chair. Good thing, because during the attacks he did *not* understand the truth about his circumstances!

5. In the garden, the Witch accused Digory of only pretending to love his father.

6. It was so-o-o nice of the Ape to make a lion suit for Puzzle.

7. During the battle at Anvard, Prince Rabadash shouted, "The bolt of Tash falls from above!" right before he got his hauberk hung up on a hook.

8. The god Tash smelled like petunias.

9. The White Witch was right: Because of Edmund's betrayal, his blood was her property.

10. The White Witch was wrong: There is a deeper magic from before the dawn of time that she didn't know about.

PART 8. WHAT ASLAN SAID

One voice in Narnia matters more than all the others.

Did you listen carefully to him? (Blow the Horn for help—see page 324.)

1. "Evil will come of that _____, but it is still a long way off, and I will see to it that the worst falls upon _____."

2. "I call all times _____."

3. "Things never happen the _____ way _____."

4. "I will not always be _____."

5. "Come further _____! Come further _____!"

6. "There is no other _____."

7. "They have chosen cunning instead of _____."

8. "_____, dear heart."

9. "Let us be _____ to one another."

10. "I am sad and _____. Lay your hands on my _____ so that I can feel you are there and let us _____ like that."

11. "There will always be a _____ through."

12. "All get what they want; they do not always _____ it."

13. "You would not have _____ to me unless I had been calling to you."

14. "If you had felt yourself sufficient, it would have been a _____ that you were not."

15. "The term is over: the _____ have begun. The dream is ended: this is the morning."

PART 9. WHAT THE STORYTELLER SAID

The voice of author C. S. Lewis offers strong opinions, wise explanations, and—when things get too scary—words of comfort. Do you remember what he said? Pick the ending that correctly completes the storyteller's words.

1. **What you see and hear depends a good deal on where you are standing: it also depends on**
   a. what you ate for breakfast.
   b. what sort of person you are.
   c. what sort of hat you're wearing.

2. **The trouble about trying to make yourself stupider than you really are is that you very often**
   a. just make more trouble.
   b. fail.
   c. succeed.

3. There's nothing that spoils the taste of good ordinary food half so much as the memory of
   a. bad magic food.
   b. good fairy food.
   c. wretched school food.

4. If one is nervous there's nothing like having your face toward the danger and having something warm and solid
   a. in your pocket.
   b. under your feet.
   c. at your back.

5. One of the worst results of being a slave and being forced to do things is that when there is no one to force you any more you find you have almost
   a. forgotten how to call home.
   b. lost the power of forcing yourself.
   c. no brains left to figure things out.

6. Giants of any sort are now so rare in England and so few giants are good-tempered that
   a. ten to one you have never seen a giant when his face is beaming.
   b. five to one you'll never see a giant playing in Piccadilly.
   c. you should think twice before you ask one for a bite of his fish and chips.

7. There are dozens of ways to give people a bad time if you are in your own home and they
   a. don't know all your tricks.
   b. don't like your mother's food.
   c. are only visitors.

8. Crying is all right in its way while it lasts. But you have to stop sooner or later, and then
   a. you still have to decide what to do.
   b. you still feel bad.
   c. you still have to blow your nose.

9. The more enchanted you get, the more you feel
   a. that you might be a magician.
   b. that you'll never find your way home.
   c. that you are not enchanted at all.

10. One always feels better when one has
    a. scolded a cat.
    b. made up one's mind.
    c. made one's bed.

PART 10. BIG IDEAS FOR NARNIACS

The Chronicles of Narnia are full of important truths for everyday life.

Pick the answer that is most correct in the following questions:

1. **The older you get**
   a. the easier it is to get into Narnia.
   b. the bigger Aslan becomes.
   c. the more you like boring history lessons.

2. **The more you know Aslan in Narnia**
   a. the more likely you are to go to church at a zoo.
   b. the better you know Jesus on earth.
   c. the more you want to eat Turkish Delight.

3. **The gifts that the children found in the ruins of Cair Paravel could teach us a lot about our God-given interests and abilities. For example that:**
   a. God blesses us with special abilities to help us succeed at what He wants us to do for Him.
   b. The interests and abilities we get from God are like toys—they can keep us from getting bored when we have nothing else to do.
   c. Obviously the other kids should have been upset because they all didn't get Lucy's bottle of cordial.

4. **The most important lesson from Aslan's death on the Stone Table is:**
   a. Never let a witch's friends get near your hair.
   b. As you'd expect, God does *not* love greedy, lying boys and girls.
   c. Like Aslan, Jesus paid the price for our sins by dying in our place.

5. **What happened to Uncle Andrew should make you realize that:**
   a. If you're smart enough, you can play safely with evil powers.
   b. Pride can get you in a lot of trouble.
   c. Brandy is a good solution for the trouble your pride can get you into.

6. **Remember the *Dawn Treader*'s adventure in the Dark Island? Think about that a little and you'll see that:**
   a. Only wimps are afraid of the dark.
   b. When it doesn't look like God is near, He probably isn't.
   c. Most of us experience times when God seems far away, but He's always as close as a prayer.

7. **No one is ever told**
   a. how to get to the Sunless Sea.
   b. what's inside the Stable.
   c. what would have happened.

8. **If you do one good deed because you love Jesus, don't be surprised if your reward is:**
   a. to do another, harder, even more important deed for Him.
   b. all the Turkish Delight you can eat.
   c. to be given dinner with all the nice parts left out and sent to bed early.

9. The long journey of Shasta and Aravis illustrates that all through the journey of our lives:

a. God will take care of us if we're rich and important.

b. God will want us to follow Him if our parents did.

c. God will always take care of us, even when we're not thinking about Him.

10. Like the Narnians who followed Aslan, we don't have to be afraid to die because:

a. Death is real, but for everyone who puts their trust in Jesus, death is just the beginning of a wonderful life with Him in heaven.

b. Death is real, but after we die, we won't feel anything.

c. Death isn't real.

HONORS *for* NARNIACS WHO HAVE STOOD THE TEST

Using the answer table starting on page 436, mark your answers. Then carefully add up your total points, scoring one point for each correct answer. Total points possible = 120. When you are finished, please approach the throne at Cair Paravel to claim your honors.

The Jewel Medallion, 97-120 points

You are pure brilliance, a myth in your own time, and a champion in battle.

The Reepicheep Reward, 73-96 points

You are courageous, honorable, large for a rodent, and annoyingly smart.

The Puddleglum Prize, 49-72 points

You are certainly smarter than you look and fearless in the heat of battle (is that your foot burning?).

The Bulgy Bear Badge, 25-48 points

Of course you had every right to take this test. Of course you'll do better next time. Of course you deserve some honey.

The Wimbleweather Consolation, 1-24 points

So you're not too clever, at least not yet. But you're likable, and for a small-ish giant, you have potential.

Feels like always winter but never Christmas at your house?

Then it's time for you to follow the Red Robin through the woods to your very own...

NARNIAC
FINAL EXAM
FOR LITTLE ONES

How to Take this Test

1. Miss Prizzle says: "Class, this exam covers all seven Chronicles. Sit up straight, think hard, and do not blub. You may, however, suck your paw."

2. Dr. Cornelius says: "Do not write in this book for the simple reason that you or someone else might want to take the same test later. Instead, you should download a copy from RoarofNarnia.com. Or you could make a photocopy of these pages or simply write your answers on a separate sheet."

3. Pattertwig says: "Look! Look! You can look in the books for help as you go! If you want!"

4. Glimfeather the Owl says, "Whoo, whoo, wh-when you're done, find the correct answers starting on page 439. Then add up your total score and claim your honors (see end of this test)!"

5. Aslan says, "I love you, little one. Have fun!"

Part 1. Animal Alphabet

Fill in the blank with the correct name.

My Name Begins With...

1. R and I am a Mouse _____
2. P and I am a Marsh-wiggle _____
3. J and I am a Unicorn _____
4. P and I am a donkey _____
5. M and I am a Wolf _____

6. T and I am a Dwarf _____
7. B and I am a Horse _____
8. F and I am a flying horse _____
9. R and I am a giant _____
10. G and I am an Owl _____

Part 2. Beautiful but Very Bad

Remember the wicked witches of Narnia? Choose the correct answer to the following questions:

1. **What did Queen Jadis do to Aunt Letty?**

   a. She stole her necklace.

   b. She took her to a movie.

   c. She threw her across the room.

2. **Who did Queen Jadis blame for making her speak the Deplorable Word?**

   a. Polly

   b. Her sister

   c. Mother Goose

3. **What did the Queen of Underland, also called the Green Witch, like to wear?**

   a. Pink underpants

   b. Polka-dot pajamas

   c. A green skirt

4. **What did the White Witch offer Edmund to eat?**

   a. Chocolate Turtles

   b. Turkish Delight

   c. Gummy Bears

5. **Why was the Queen of the Underworld digging a tunnel under Narnia?**

   a. She wanted to be part of the Snow Dance.

   b. She wanted to conquer Narnia.

   c. She was half witch and half mole.

PART 3. WHAT'S WRONG WITH THIS STORY?

If you listened carefully to the Chronicles, you know that something's wrong with the stories below.
Can you pick the right story?

1. **After grumpy Eustace turned into a giant Sea Serpent, he realized he wanted to change. So Aslan stripped off his scales and turned him back into a boy.**

   Why, you've got a frightfully bad memory!

   a. It was Edmund who turned into a Sea Serpent after he ate the Turkish Delight.

   b. Eustace turned back into a girl, not a boy.

   c. Eustace turned into a dragon, not a Sea Serpent.

2. **The first time Lucy went through the Wardrobe to Narnia she met a mouse named Tumnus.**

   Oh come now, don't be silly!

   a. She met a Witch named Queen Jadis.

   b. She met a Faun named Tumnus.

   c. She met a beagle named Snoopy.

3. **Puddleglum helped Jill and Eustace save Puzzle the donkey from the Queen of Underland.**

   Oh, bother! You've muffed the whole idea.

   a. Puddleglum helped the children save a prince, not Puzzle.

   b. Puddleglum helped the donkey save Jill and Eustace.

   c. Puzzle helped the children blow bubble gum.

4. **Shasta and his Talking Horse Aravis traveled with Hwin and her Talking Horse Bree.**

   Why, you've definitely been reading all the wrong books!

   a. Shasta's talking horse was named Hwin; Aravis's talking horse was named the Black Stallion.

   b. Shasta and Aravis talked a lot on their way to Narnia, but they didn't ride horses. They took a bus.

   c. Shasta and Aravis were friends who traveled together. Shasta's horse was named Bree, and Aravis's horse was named Hwin.

5. **Uncle Andrew was a sweet old man who took good care of children and pets.**

   Whistles and whirligigs!
   What are you thinking? The truth is…

   a. Uncle Andrew was a fat old man who wanted to marry Aravis.

   b. Uncle Andrew was a mean old man who did not take good care of children or pets.

   c. Uncle Andrew was a wicked old king who tried to steal the throne from Prince Caspian.

PART 4. BRAVO FOR THE BRAVE!

Do you remember the heroes of Narnia? Fill in the blank with the correct answer.

1. Who fought in battle so hard that he lost his tail? _____

2. Who rescued Puzzle from the Stable all by herself? _____

3. Who followed Polly into another World in order to bring her back safely? _____

4. Who stamped out the Queen of Underworld's magic fire with his bare feet? _____

5. Who was King Tirian's best friend and had already saved his life once? _____

6. Who offered to fight King Miraz all by himself in a sword fight? _____

7. Who ran away from a mean fisherman in order to travel to Narnia and find who he really was? _____

8. Who was willing to follow Aslan even if her brothers and sister couldn't see him and wouldn't come with her? _____

9. Who took a dangerous journey in order to bring an apple to Aslan? _____

10. Who was willing to die in order to save Edmund? _____

PART 5. ALL ABOUT ASLAN

The most important person to remember from Narnia is the Great Lion, Aslan. Choose the correct answer:

1. **Aslan is a huge lion who created Narnia while he:**

    a. sang.

    b. licked his paws.

    c. ate a cheeseburger.

2. **Aslan, Lord of Narnia, is good but he's not:**

    a. strong.

    b. safe.

    c. sweet.

3. **The children in Narnia like to ride on Aslan's back and put their faces in his:**

    a. window.

    b. whiskers.

    c. mane.

4. **After Aslan died for Edmund, he defeated the wicked Witch by:**

    a. rising from the dead.

    b. sending someone else to rescue Narnia.

    c. making sure Edmund died for his own sins.

5. Aslan's Country, where there's no more
   death or sadness, is a picture of:
   a. Disney World.
   b. Heaven.
   c. Oklahoma.

IN HONOR *of* YOU, WORTHY NARNIAC!

Contratulations, little one! You have proved your mastery in a test of Narnian knowledge. Using the answer table starting on page 438, mark your answers. Then add up your total points, scoring one point for each correct answer. Total points possible = 35. When you are ready, please come to a royal romp in your honor at Cair Paravel. There you will receive your awards:

The Jewel Medallion, 28-35 points

The Reepicheep Reward, 21-27 points

The Puddleglum Prize, 14-20 points

The Bulgy Bear Badge, 7-13 points

The Wimbleweather Consolation, 1-6 points

Blow the Horn *for* Help

Hints for Narnia Final Exam, Parts 1, 4, 6, and 8

PART 1. Who Said That?

1. Hint: *Silver Chair*, He's sounding surprisingly optimistic.
2. Hint: *Silver Chair*, You can tell she doesn't think much of the Knight.
3. Hint: *Lion*, big front teeth
4. Hint: *Prince Caspian*, This talking animal has stubborn faith in Aslan.
5. Hint: *Prince Caspian*, Only one King is sufficient.
6. Hint: *Prince Caspian*, He's relieved that Susan excels at archery.
7. Hint: *Voyage*, He's a king, but not in England.
8. Hint: *Magician*, She is fond of big, bad words.
9. Hint: *Voyage*, "record stinker"
10. Hint: *Last Battle*, the last of his line
11. Hint: *Horse*, party girl in garlic-and-onion town
12. Hint: *Magician*, Could we forget about the little problem at the bell now?
13. Hint: *Voyage*, She doesn't like to say good-bye to Aslan.
14. Hint: *Prince Caspian*, P. P.
15. Hint: *Last Battle*, She's a talented pathfinder.
16. Hint: *Last Battle*, Both this character and Susan have a horn.
17. Hint: *Lion*, He's not afraid of the Witch either—at first.
18. Hint: *Voyage*, He never backs down from a challenge.
19. Hint: *Horse*, Afterward, she walks toward Anvard in a happy dream.
20. Hint: *Silver Chair*, His shield is much improved.

PART 4. Details, Details

1. Hint: *Voyage*, rhymes with kitten cream

2. Hint: *Horse*, ____ and lightning

3. Hint: *Magician*, rhymes with table

4. Hint: *Prince Caspian*, Think mice with vision problems.

5. Hint: *Prince Caspian*, Remember the dead lord in the bottom of the lake?

6. Hint: *Lion*, not his mother's

7. Hint: *Prince Caspian*, This (not to be missed) / is the dangling appendage / 'twixt shoulder and wrist.

8. Hint: *Prince Caspian*, John 3:__

9. Hint: *Voyage*, royalty

10. Hint: *Voyage*, Times or Trafalgar

PART 6. Stumpers for Smarty-Pants

1. Hint: *Lion*, howl

2. Hint: *Magician*, He grew up to have a house in the country.

3. Hint: *Prince Caspian*, She could see the Lion when others couldn't.

4. Hint: *Magician*, Maybe the only object that didn't grow when it was planted in Narnia!

5. Hint: *Prince Caspian*, One took care of a Prince, one fought for him.

6. Hint: *Lion*, So much water and sew many things to do.

7. Hint: *Lion*, gentle

8. Hint: *Silver Chair*, He took a serious view of life.

9. Hint: *Lion* and *Last Battle*, She took care of others, he took advantage of others.

10. Hint: *Horse*, not *Propputty-propputty* on a hard road, but *Thubbudy-thubbudy* on the dry sand

11. Hint: *Lion*, *Prince Caspian*, *Voyage*, baby sis

12. Hint: *Magician* and *Silver Chair*, Mother is ill, king has died.

13. Hint: Never say ____.

14. Hint: *Prince Caspian*, "I've been waiting for this all my life," she said. "Have you come to take me away?"

15. Hint: *Prince Caspian*, Prince Caspian bestowed this honor on them at the same time, along with Trumpkin.

PART 8. What Aslan Said

1. Hint: *Magician*, said of Digory's actions

2. Hint: *Voyage*, said to a distraught Lucy in the Magician's house

3. Hint: *Prince Caspian*, said to Lucy in the woods

4. Hint: *Silver Chair*, said to an ashamed Jill

5. Hint: *Last Battle*, said to his followers at Narnia's end

6. Hint: *Silver Chair*, said to Jill when she was afraid to drink

7. Hint: *Last Battle*, said of the Dwarfs' decision to watch out only for themselves

8. Hint: *Voyage*, said to Lucy in the Dark Island

9. Hint: *Magician*, said to Digory about sharing grief

10. Hint: *Lion*, said to Susan and Lucy as he went to die

11. Hint: *Magician*, said to Polly, Digory, and Fledge before their flight to find the Garden

12. Hint: *Magician*, said to Polly and Digory about the Witch

13. Hint: *Silver Chair*, said to Jill about her and Eustace

14. Hint: *Prince Caspian*, said to Caspian regarding his readiness to be king

15. Hint: *Last Battle*, said to the children about the railway accident

PART FOUR

Leading the Way into Narnia

HELP & INSPIRATION *for* PARENTS

What C. S. Lewis Really Believed

Again and again, the Oxford professor wrote about One Great Story.

By Marcus Brotherton

If you're a Narnia fan and want to find out what C. S. Lewis really believed, the best place for you to look might not be in textbooks or doctrinal statements, but in color, action, character…in Story. Open up almost any page of the Chronicles of Narnia and Professor Lewis's beliefs tumble out.

For example, Narnia introduces us to unforgettable people and places:

* Boys and girls who are courageous, noble, honorable, and true. (You'll also find some who are proud, depraved, foolish, and unkind.)

* A journey to a new and amazing land— a real country where people can sprint for miles without getting tired, swim up waterfalls, hug loved ones not seen in years, and

Open up any of the Chronicles of Narnia and Professor Lewis's beliefs tumble out.

begin a new, everlasting adventure where each chapter is better than the one before.

❋ A joyful, romping supernatural Being—untamed yet good, wild yet tender, wonderful and terrible at the same time. This Being makes no noise when mocked, muzzled, and crucified; yet he conquers the grave to live again. He quenches thirst, spreads out feasts, welcomes, protects, heals, calms, confronts, and calls….

And what, you might ask, do people and places have to do with belief? Just this: that in every character, scene, and plot twist, you can hear, if you listen closely, the kind voice of the Professor spinning his tale and winking in our direction as if to say, "Now do you see the Truth? Now do you know Him better? Now will you believe?"

In some ways, discussing what Lewis believed isn't as important as knowing who he believed in. Again and again through his writings, we encounter the goodness and majesty of our heavenly Father, the redeeming love of His Son, Jesus Christ, and the surprising, ever-present power of the Holy Spirit.

All that certainly makes him sound like a theologian. And C. S. Lewis has been called the most influential Christian apologist of the twentieth century. Still, he might prefer to be

remembered as a good conversationalist—a well-read friend with an appreciation for fine literature, an unshakable confidence that all truth is God's truth, and a tender spot for ordinary people. Lewis was a scholar of formidable training and intellect, yet he understood what every master storyteller knows: that for most people, real learning starts in the imagination and in the heart.

Pilgrimage of the Heart

It was the death of his mother, coupled with the religious hypocrisy he endured throughout his school years, that caused Lewis to turn away from any faith he might have learned when young. For years, he considered himself an atheist.

His journey back to Christianity began with a sense of inconsolable longing. He called it *Sehnsucht*—a sense that there had to be more than the here and now, and that there must exist something that he had first sensed as a boy. He referred to this longing as his quest for joy.

In *Surprised by Joy*, he wrote: "In a sense the central story of my life is about nothing else…it is that of an unsatisfied desire which is itself more desirable than any other satisfaction. I call it Joy, which is here a technical term and must be sharply distinguished both from Happiness and from Pleasure. Joy (in my sense) has indeed one characteristic…in common with them: the fact that anyone who has experienced it will want it again." And then, later in the book, "It [the quest for Joy] was valuable only as a pointer to something other and outer."

His quest for joy directed much of his reading, and as a young man, the stories and poems of Milton, Chesterton, MacDonald, and Spenser first answered that call. The books caused Lewis at first not to believe or repent, but to approach the Lord with an honest heart. It was through books that Lewis first converted from atheism to theism—a belief in God's existence; and then later to Christianity—the belief that Jesus Christ is God and offers the pathway to salvation.

rate music." Later he came to realize that people were singing with devotion and that he had been a bit stuck-up, and so he went to church.

Lewis fellowshipped in the Church of England (Anglican) but believed that people could affiliate with many other churches and still be true believers. Once, he gave portions of his book *Mere Christianity* to "an Anglican, a Methodist, a Presbyterian, and a Roman Catholic for their criticism and discovered only minor differences from his own view." He subscribed to the major doctrines of historic Christianity as set forth in the Nicene, Athanasian, and Apostles' Creeds (which describe the existence and nature of the Trinity,

Discussing what Lewis believed isn't as important as knowing who he believed in.

"To accept the Incarnation was a further step," he wrote in *Surprised by Joy*. "I know very well when, but hardly how, the final step was taken. I was driven to Whipsnade one sunny morning. When we set out I did not believe that Jesus Christ is the Son of God, and when we reached the zoo I did."

A Profile of Belief

At first Lewis struggled with church attendance. He thought he could grow in his faith on his own and he disliked very much church music, which he considered to be "fifth-rate poems set to sixth-

the need and necessity of salvation through Christ alone, and the reality of the resurrection and the life to come). Most everything else he considered minor.

About church, Lewis wrote: "It is easy to think that the Church has a lot of different objects—education, building, missions, holding services…. [But really,] the Church exists for nothing else but to draw men into Christ…. If they are not doing that, all the cathedrals, clergy, missions, sermons, even the Bible itself, are simply a waste of time" (*Mere Christianity*).

Living as a Christian was something Lewis

thought about a lot. He believed that a Christian's primary calling is to love Christ, that a Christian is not called to religion or even good works primarily, but to holiness before God.

He believed prayer must include confession and penitence, adoration and fellowship with God as well as petition. He held that conversion is necessary, and heaven and hell are real and final. He believed in the reality of the devil, of angels, in miracles, and that the Bible teaches clearly the second coming of Christ.

THE ONE THEME

Yet it is the Person and work of Jesus Christ that is the central belief statement of Lewis's writings. "The Christian story is precisely the story of one grand miracle," Lewis wrote, "that what is beyond all space and time, what is uncreated, eternal, came into…human nature, descended into His own universe, and rose again" (*God in the Dock*).

Certainly in the Chronicles Christ is the one pervasive presence. Lewis portrays Him as Aslan, the Lion, Son of the Emperor over the Sea. The other story characters—human, animal, and parts of each—come and go, but Lord Aslan remains. Jesus is the story.

Have you met this Jesus yet? He's the One who:

❋ sings the world into existence. He's the First Voice, so beautiful you could hardly

bear it, the deep one, louder and more triumphant, that changes the eastern sky from white to pink and from pink to gold, and as it rises, all the air shakes with it. (*The Magician's Nephew*)

❋ conquers death as a willing victim, who leaps and laughs and roars so the earth shakes after He's come alive again. (*The Lion, the Witch and the Wardrobe*)

❋ is the quiet, patient guide. He's the One who arranges events so perfectly, so continuously, so miraculously that we want to "fall out of the saddle and worship at His feet." (*The Horse and His Boy*)

❋ shows us courage instead of fear, and faith instead of fright. He's the One who "every year you grow, you will find bigger." (*Prince Caspian*)

❋ peels off the outer layers of our dragonish exteriors, dressing us with new clothes and transforming us into different people. (*The Voyage of the* Dawn Treader)

❋ calls us to obedience—to "remember the signs. Say them to yourself when you wake in the morning and when you lie down at night, and when you wake in the middle of the night. And whatever strange things may happen to you, let nothing turn your mind from following the signs." He asks us to be intimately acquainted with His Word, and to feast on His Word on a continual basis. *(The Silver Chair)*

❉ brings those who love and follow Him to a place where things happen "so great and beautiful that I cannot write them." *(The Last Battle)*

Jesus Christ is the Untamed Lion whom Lewis devoted his life to. Perhaps one of Lewis's most quoted writings is a passage from *Mere Christianity* commonly referred to as "Liar, Lunatic, Lord." Lewis lays out clear reasoning for believing in Jesus: "A man who was merely a man and said the sort of things Jesus said would not be a great moral teacher. He would either be a lunatic—on a level with the man who says he is a poached egg—or else he would be the Devil of Hell…. [Jesus] told people that their sins were forgiven…. This makes sense only if He really was…God."

"By Knowing Me Here"

What is one way of knowing Jesus Christ better? Lewis writes about this in the last chapter of *Voyage*. After the children have sailed to the End of the World, they meet a Lamb on a beach who cooks them breakfast over an open fire. The Lamb transforms from snowy white to tawny gold and his size changes, and the children realize the Lamb is now Aslan himself, towering above them, light scattering from his mane.

Aslan tells the children they are to go back to their own country now, but he is in that country, too. There, he is known by "another Name"—and they must learn to know him by that Name as well.

"This was the very reason why you were brought to Narnia," Aslan says to the children, "that by knowing me here for a little, you may know me better there."

THE LITERARY BLOKE

What extraordinary appeal has made C. S. Lewis the bestselling Christian apologist of the past fifty years? J. I. Packer—like Lewis, a preeminent popular theologian—shows you why you need more than just Narnia on your bookshelf.

BY J. I. PACKER

Among today's Christians, Clive Staples Lewis of Ulster (born in Belfast, 1898), of Oxford (fellow of Magdalen College 1925–54), and of Cambridge (professor of Medieval and Renaissance Literature 1954–63) is a household name.

Countless copies of his *Mere Christianity* and *Screwtape Letters* have resourced the past half-century's evangelism and nurture; countless copies of *A Grief Observed* have helped bereaved believers; and countless copies of his Narnia stories have enriched half a century's children. Conservative Christians everywhere—both centrists and mainliners, as I would call them—see Lewis as one of God's best gifts to our era of anxiety, misbelief, and moral and spiritual drift.

Lewis was one of God's best gifts to our era of anxiety, misbelief, and moral and spiritual drift.

PUNDIT AND PAL

"He's a literary bloke, isn't he?" said a clergy friend to me years ago about one of his own peers. His phrase, which conjoined fellow-feeling and admiring wonder, fits many people's attitude toward Lewis: They hail him as a pundit while thinking of him as, in effect, a pal. Nor is this presumptuous. The "pal" feeling flows directly from the frank and intimate way Lewis presents the thoughts and visions that give him pundit rank. As a friendly, accessible exponent of Christian truth and wisdom for the twentieth century (and, I guess, the twenty-first too), Lewis stands as "literary bloke" number one—the most effective as well as the most widely read.

Learned, brilliant, and lively, Lewis was always an artist with words, whether as a professional academic writing for colleagues in his own field; as an author of novels, fantasies, and tales for children; or as a composer of didactic expositions, apologetic discussions, and journal and newspaper articles by the bushel, all seeking to commend and consolidate Christian faith.

He was fastidious and fair-minded (while sometimes satirical), probing and thoughtful, logical and magisterial, orthodox and arresting, and clear and compelling. He was clever at finding the best literary forms for what he had to say, and rich in analogies that are both arguments and illustrations in one. In short, he was never less than a first-class read. That is a main reason why, unlike many writers of the past and against his own expectations, his reputation and sales have soared sky-high during the years since his death.

ICON AND MISFIT

To evangelicals, particularly, Lewis has become a kind of icon. That is, despite his smoking and drinking; his belief in purgatory and, it seems, baptismal regeneration; his use of the confessional; his non-inerrantist view of biblical authority; and his unwillingness to affirm penal substitution and justification by faith only when speaking of salvation in Christ. He saw himself as a nonparty traditional Anglican, but was more of an Anglo-Catholic than perhaps he realized.

What evangelicals love in Lewis is Aslan, the Christlike lion of Narnia; and his strong defense of biblical supernaturalism, personal new birth, Christ's return to judgment, and the reality of Satan, hell, and heaven. They love his squelching of secular modernity and the "Christianity-and-water" religion of self-styled liberals; his stress on self-humbling repentance and submission to the living Christ as the heart of real Christianity; his open talk about his conversion from atheism, and his evident wish

What evangelicals love in Lewis is Aslan, the Christlike lion of Narnia.

to help others make the same journey; plus the playfulness of his gravity, with its schoolboyish wit and humor. Tuning in with enthusiasm to all of this, evangelicals claim Lewis as 'one of us'; and who should want to stop them doing that?

INTELLECTUAL AND IMAGINATIVE

Lewis saw himself as one who, having traded the faith of his childhood for a mess of skeptical pottage, recovered it as an Oxford don through a process of intellectual exploration, struggle, and conviction that left him certain not only of God in Christ but also of Christianity's rational superiority to all other views of reality. He tells the story straightforwardly in *Surprised by Joy* and allegorizes it, along with much else, in *The Pilgrim's Regress*. Having returned to faith by this route, and being a teacher into the bargain, he naturally became a passionate philosophical apologist. "Ever since I became a Christian," he wrote in 1952, "I have thought that the best, perhaps the only service I could do for my unbelieving neighbors was to explain and defend the belief that has been common to nearly all Christians at all times." *The Pilgrim's Regress, The Problem of Pain, Mere Christianity,* and *Miracles* are the books written directly to this agenda.

But there was always more to Lewis than this, and increasingly he concentrated on imaginative presentations of the Christian life, centered upon the spirituality quest for communion with God rather than the apologetic quest for rational demonstrations of him. The Narnia books, *Perelandra, The Great Divorce, Reflections on the Psalms, The Four Loves,* and *Letters to Malcolm: Chiefly on Prayer* are the main items here.

The two lobes of our brain, left for the logical and linear and right for the romantic and imaginative, were both thoroughly developed in Lewis, so that he was as strong in fantasy and fiction as he was in analysis and argument. There is always a didactic dimension to his spiritual-life writing, just as there is always a visionary dimension to his apologetics. The combination made him in his day, and makes him still, a powerful and haunting communicator in both departments.

THEORY AND PRACTICE

Nor was Lewis's intellectual belief mere theory, or his imaginative belief mere imagination. As those who knew him best always declared, he lived his beliefs most faithfully. Here *Shadowlands* in both its British versions (the television feature and the West End play), as also in its Hollywood dress, did Lewis a disservice. They present him as a teacher about pain who did not know what pain was, or what life was about generally, till the revelatory happiness of his three-year marriage ended in his wife's death from cancer, whereupon his professed faith, temporarily at any rate, fell to pieces. When the movie announces itself at the outset as "based on a true story," it must regretfully be convicted of bearing a good deal of false witness against its leading character.

The facts are that, first, from the time his dearly loved mother died when he was nine, Lewis knew much pain of many kinds, more I guess than most of us; and second, though grief at losing his beloved Joy laid him low emotionally for many months, his faith stayed steady. *A Grief Observed*, written out of his bereavement experience, is actually a witness to that, and any who invoke sentences from it as evidence to the contrary show that, like the German gospel critics Lewis pillories, they just do not know how to read a book. As a practicing Christian, prayerful, patient, and persistent in well-doing, Lewis was beyond question the genuine article.

His beliefs were in no way original. He aimed only to state standard Christianity, the Christianity of the Bible and the creeds and the historic mainline church, in its most universal form. Yet his presentations of it, read and reread, always seem fresh and enlivening. Why is this? It is partly because of Lewis's personal writing style, and partly because of three strands of thought that he regularly works into his reflections on "the old, old story of Jesus and His love." I label them (1) joy and conversion, (2) the Tao and formation, and (3) myth and persuasion.

Joy and Conversion

Lewis defined joy in a narrow, deep sense as a recurring stab of longing that nothing in this world will satisfy. It is a desire for God and

Lewis defined joy in a narrow, deep sense as a recurring stab of longing.

heaven that God Himself has built into the human race, though many of us in our fallenness fail to focus it and grasp its message. Lewis called it "joy" because in the longing itself there is greater delight than in any of this world's pleasures. It calls us to seek God and keep seeking till God Himself, through making us inwardly real, honest, humble, consciously chastened, and radically penitent, leads us to find Him in Christ. Lewis sought to show how discipleship to Jesus Christ leads to the fullness of joy as defined. Hence his pervasive orientation to God and heaven, and his recurring raptures of rhetoric whereby, calculating his effect as writers do, he seeks to make us feel the reality and to desire the enjoyment of both. His strategies for evoking, reinforcing, and exegeting joy give his treatments of the event and life of conversion a unique and charming flavor.

THE TAO AND FORMATION

The Tao (Tao means "way") is Lewis's name for the natural law that all persons, nations, and religions know, more or less, through what theologians call general revelation (see Romans 1–2). Lewis believed, first, that where its precepts (loyalty, honesty, courage, respect for authority, and so on) are ignored, blind and tyrannical self-preservation will take over with calamitous results. (He thinks of Nietzsche and the Nazis.) Second, he believed that inculcating appropriate responses to the values of the Tao is basic to character formation, whether in children, in Christians, or in anyone else.

One purpose of all Lewis's fiction, Narnia included, is to illustrate and model what he calls 'stock responses' to the classic trinity of values, truth, goodness, and beauty, all of which reflect God. His didactic writings about new life in Christ show the same nurturing concern, within the same moral framework. This also gives his work a unique and charming flavor.

MYTH AND PERSUASION

Myth, for Lewis, meant a story, or a figure within a story, that "grabs" us, as we say, with a sense of significance, and thus draws us to identify in some way with what it shows us. Lewis loved the god-stories of Norse and Greek mythology, and the thought that did most to bring him back to Christianity was that, in Christ, a myth found worldwide, the myth of a dying and rising deity through whose ordeal good comes to others, has become space-time fact. Then he found that what he now knew as the fact of Christ, set forth in the Scriptures, was evoking in his imagination new myths of evangelical shape—stories picturing divine mercy in worlds other than ours, past, present, and future. The space trilogy (*Out of the Silent Planet, Perelandra,* and *That Hideous Strength*), the seven Narnia books, and *Till We Have Faces* were the result.

Lewis saw these myths, and many pre-Christian pagan myths with them, as "good dreams" that can have real significance in the evangelistic process. They can project visions of wholeness restored through divine action. They can make honest hearts wish that something of this sort might be true in our world, and so prepare them to discover that something of this

Those who get most from Lewis's writing are those who commit themselves to serve Lewis's God.

sort is true, as a matter of fact. This crafting of myth as evangelistic persuasion is a third unique excellence in Lewis's work.

"If you want to learn how to do Christianity, read C. S. Lewis, and he'll tell you." So said Douglas Gresham, Lewis's stepson, and he is right. All Lewis's writing has a practical thrust, and those who get most from it are those who commit themselves to serve Lewis's God and so to travel with him to the celestial city.

Lewis never claimed to be infallible, nor is he, but he is a wise and life-enhancing guide on that journey. If you have no C. S. Lewis on your bookshelf, take it from me: You are missing a lot.

The Meaning of Magic in Narnia

Why does Lewis use the dark side of the imagination so much to bring us to the light?

By Marcus Brotherton

Sometimes C. S. Lewis seems bent on making readers squirm, but—in a sort of reverse kindness—only if we share his spiritual convictions.

Case in point: When we read through *The Chronicles of Narnia* we're faced with witches, werewolves, and wraiths. We meet magicians casting spells and civilizations doomed by hellish enchantments. While many readers won't think twice about the dark supernatural goings-on, many Christians will react with caution or concern.

Which leads us to a question: Why would a Christ-follower like Uncle Jack assemble such a supernatural cast of sorcerers and spell-casters to spin his stories for our children?

It's a valid concern for believers. In Deuteronomy 18:9–15 the Israelites were called to separate themselves from the witchcraft practiced by the nations around them. "Let no one be found among you who…practices divination or sorcery, interprets omens, engages in witchcraft, or casts spells, or who is a medium or spiritist or who consults the dead. Anyone who does these things is detestable to the Lord" (vv. 10–12).

Satan is alive and real on Planet Earth. No wonder the Bible forbids dabbling in his evil underworld.

But literature invites another question. Is writing about evil spiritual powers in a way that shows their evilness and the ultimate triumph of

In a book, we travel to these worlds through words. Off the page, they don't exist. (Ask for a bus ticket to Narnia at your local travel agency and see what reaction you get.)

Recognizing Narnia as both fiction and fantasy can help Christian moms and dads get through the squirmy material. We can affirm that the Bible condemns sorcery and black magic in our world because they *do exist* as tools of a *real* devil on a *real* Planet Earth. But we can also know—and help our children know if they ever doubt—that Narnia is in a different category. It's real only like Mickey Mouse is

Literature creates imaginary worlds in miniature—they are self-contained, fictional, and bound within the confines of a story.

God over them also prohibited? Or is it something else entirely—something that can actually accomplish great good?

The distinction matters a lot if we're to understand what Lewis is up to in the Chronicles.

LEARNING FROM "IMAGINE IF…"
Literature creates imaginary worlds in miniature; that is, they are self-contained, fictional, and bound within the confines of a story. Fantasy stories take things even further, creating worlds that may obey rules quite different from ours. These worlds are real only in the sense that a song is real while you're singing or listening to it.

real. For the same reason, Narnian magic, which is made-up, is different from earthly black magic, which is often real.

The marvel of fiction, as every bookworm knows, is that it can convey huge truths in ways we never forget. And the fact is that some of our most enduring literature has powerfully portrayed the reality of evil spiritual forces: Dante's *Inferno*, for example, or John Bunyan's evangelistic *Pilgrim's Progress*. In our time, we could point to Frank Peretti's writings, beginning with *This Present Darkness*. Works like these have been instrumental in bringing millions to a saving knowledge of Christ.

The "imagine if" of other worlds—including fantasy ones where characters have otherworldly powers—allows us to see elements of our own world that we might not see otherwise. Yes, we need to keep ourselves and our children away from any reading material that dabbles in evil and dishonors God. But tales that use magic where, for example, the evil is not commended and where pretend is not confused with real can stimulate our imaginations to see what might happen *if*, and what must happen *finally,* when the forces of supernatural good and evil clash. (Read the chapter entitled

forever and ever—a world that could only be reached by Magic."

Enter "Magic." It is Lewis's way of spotlighting a central theme of the Chronicles—we live in a world where places, forces, and beings exist beyond the here and now. Or think of magic as Lewis's language for discussing spirituality.

Uncle Andrew soon shows his spinelessness—he's simply a sniveling magician who sends children into unknown lands because he's too cowardly to go himself. Uncle Andrew dabbles in something he does not understand.

Think of magic as Lewis's language for discussing spirituality.

"Seeing Through the Mist" by Erin Healy, page 346, for more on fantasy in Christian literature.)

Tracing the Dark Thread

Magic is first introduced in *The Magician's Nephew* through the character of Uncle Andrew. He's a slippery customer who cares little for children and much for his bottle of brandy. Mostly he engages in crude scientific experiments, but he also succeeds in laying his hands on a box of fine, dry dust from another world—"another Nature—another universe—somewhere you would never reach even if you traveled through the space of this universe

Later, the Witch Jadis tells him, "There is no real Magic in your blood." She, on the other hand, has tapped into the full depths of dark power. Jadis is a cruel tyrant, able to destroy worlds for the sake of her pride as well as bring evil to the Lion's beautiful creation. She tempts Digory to ignore the commands of Aslan by eating an apple intended for someone else, and she becomes the White Witch seen in later books who holds Narnia captive by endless winter.

This is Lewis's "magic" world then, a place where good and evil are given characters, names, and faces so they are easier for children to understand. It's all allegorical—magic in Narnia has meaning that transcends its literal sense.

In *The Silver Chair*, something akin to the Witch has returned to Narnia in the form of the Queen of Underland. She inflicts a power over young Prince Rilian through a magic chair that binds him to her service. His spell is described as a "heavy, tangled, cold, clammy web of evil magic"—something that can be conquered only if the young protagonist Jill remembers the Word of Aslan. With this story, Lewis aptly gives voice and character to a truth we tangle with in real life. In a land of fiction, an

Aslan is allegorical for Christ, and the Emperor-beyond-the-Sea is God the Father. Aslan governs Narnia, yet evil has entered this world through the White Witch. Only through Aslan's work at the Stone Table is evil defeated. Aslan does this work because he has access to "a deeper magic" than the White Witch. This doesn't mean Aslan and the Witch are tapping into the same source—a type of neutral power up for grabs to the highest bidder. It means that Aslan has greater authority over things unseen. Christ conquers evil—period.

Magic is likewise the metaphor Lewis uses to show that things exist beyond what we can

By using the power entrusted to us (prayer) by the Ultimate Servant of Good (Christ), we are able to have power beyond ourselves over forces we do not see.

evil power exists that can be bested by a good power only if characters remember to heed the good. In real life, we sit on the couch reading *Silver Chair* with our kids, and we nod. Yes, heeding and obeying the Lord in this world *is* necessary if He is to prevail over evil in and through us.

Lewis wrings all he can from this device. Magic is the primary tool he uses to dramatize the great truths of the Christian faith. Nowhere is this seen more clearly than in *The Lion, the Witch and the Wardrobe*. Atonement, resurrection, repentance, faith, justification, sanctification, and redemption are all shown in this book.

experience with our five senses. In *Prince Caspian*, Doctor Cornelius gains access to Queen Susan's long lost horn by enduring many terrors and uttering many spells when he was young. It's a good horn, one that brings help, and Cornelius is able to find it when he uses a source from beyond himself. In *The Voyage of the* Dawn Treader, Lucy is able to understand the plight of the Dufflepuds by a book of spells she finds in the house of Coriakin the Magician. Coriakin is a good magician and in the service of Aslan. By using the spells, or power, entrusted to her by a servant of good, Lucy is able to have supernatural power over natural forces.

Royal Kids in a Right-Side-Up World

Should Lewis's use of magic alarm us? To the contrary, Christianity has room for both the natural and the supernatural, for the ordinary and the miraculous, and certainly room for healthy imagination. Lucy is an everyday schoolgirl in London, but she is also a Queen in Narnia. As royalty, she is able to access unseen truths of goodness and beauty. In this other world that Lewis shows us, Lucy engages in battles between unseen forces of darkness and light. We're able to identify with Lucy through Lewis's use of magic. We are ordinary humans, yet we're also royalty, a holy nation, a people belonging to God (1 Peter 2:9).

By using the power entrusted to us (prayer) by the Ultimate Servant of Good (Christ), we are able to have power beyond ourselves over forces we do not see. "For our struggle is not against flesh and blood, but against the rulers, against the authorities, against the powers of this dark world and against the spiritual forces of evil in the heavenly realms" (Ephesians 6:12).

Being able to tell the difference between fantasy and reality is an essential life skill. (We call people who can't tell the difference "insane.") But we also like to make sense of life, and a good read allows us this opportunity. Circumstances and choices have causes and effects. To have that reaffirmed, even in a story, gives us satisfaction. We leave the last page with hope that God will prevail and our personal puzzles will fall into place. We sigh in relief: It's a right-side-up world after all.

That's what Lucy and the friends of Narnia learn by the end of *The Last Battle*. And that's what the stories can accomplish memorably for our children as well.

WHO SAID ANYTHING ABOUT SAFE?

He shows up in people's lives, usually unannounced,
and not to bargain or to plead.
He swallows families whole.
He's wild, you know.

BY MARK BUCHANAN

I first met Aslan when I was eight. My grade three teacher read *The Lion, the Witch and the Wardrobe* to our class, in a voice smooth and dulcet as wind, and we all sat very still and very quiet, afraid to miss a word. That teacher's voice could have made cursing seem like benediction. But at some point the story separated from her speaking it, unfolded out of her words like trees appear from seeds, and became a living thing, huge and vivid and wondrous.

There was the White Witch, pale as death, icy with contempt. There was Mr. Tumnus, skittish with dread and remorse, sworn to a terrible pact. Mr. and Mrs. Beaver's modesty and about, went for drives in the country. The last thing that crossed our minds was to go to church. So if I understood then that Aslan represented Christ, it was at a subterranean depth I could not plumb. It was an instinct I could in no manner articulate.

Aslan was captivating, terrible and wonderful, all on his own. I knew this apart from any allegorical connection I might have made. His presence sent shivers through me. His death, the cruelty and mockery and injustice of it, made me weep bitterly. His surprising reappearance was the best news I ever imagined. His triumph over the Witch and her dark domain gave me

He walks past and, turning abruptly, issues a stark command: Follow Me.

industry settled me down as it did Peter and Susan and Lucy, gave me a sense of order and protection. Edmund's treachery, his skulking off to betray flesh and blood, irked me all day long, troubled my mind when I should have been working on long division or identifying countries in Africa. *How could he do such a thing?*

I knew in my bones that this was no ordinary story. It was make-believe, no question there, but also deeply true, true in a way many factual stories are not. And its truth had mostly to do with Aslan. In those days, I was completely ignorant of the Gospels. On Sundays our family slept in, watched television, puttered

my first taste of what, much later, I learned to call *shalom*.

Aslan prepared me to meet Jesus. Maybe that's getting the order of things backward, but that's how it was. Aslan struck me, at age eight, with a longing that was only satisfied when I met, at age twenty-one, the Lion of Judah, Jesus of Galilee. There was, in that encounter, the thrill of recognition, the sense that I had seen and known Him long beforehand, only disguised.

Now He came to me unveiled.

The order of things might be backward, but it gave me, I think, this great advantage: I have never been much inclined to see Jesus as meek and mild. I think He is many things, but *nice* isn't one. From the start, I realized the futility of trying to domesticate Him. You can no more do that than make Aslan into a house pet. He's good, yes, but safe, no. He has, as Aslan tells Jill in *The Silver Chair*, "swallowed up girls and boys, kings and emperors, cities and realms."

Who Said Anything About Safe?

My wife and I and our son, then two, were in Calgary some years ago, and spent a day at the zoo. We saw camels, shaggy and morose, and

spliced together two sections of the tall fence that closed in the zoo's pair of tigers. Inside were two cages with concrete floors and thick iron bars. A chute opened out the back of each, into the large, dense forest where the tigers roamed. At the front of the cages were two barred doors, each knotted with chain and lock, and beside this a slotted drawer like a safety-deposit box.

The zoo warden had a single condition for those present: Stay back from the cage. Well back. Five feet back.

I knew in my bones that this was no ordinary story. It was make-believe, no question there, but also deeply true.

giraffes, sprawling their spindly legs and dipping their long necks down to drink in the muddy water hole of their pen. We laughed at the antics of the chimpanzees, who simultaneously ignored and basked in the crowd's attention. We watched, with queasiness, various snakes—fat and drooping, slender and coiling, fingerlike and dart-quick—lounge in their glass houses.

We'd seen almost everything and were preparing to leave when an announcement came over the PA system: The Bengal tigers were about to be fed. The public was invited to watch.

We hurried down and, with about a dozen others, crowded into a small building which

She opened the chute at the rear of the cage closest to us, and in came, stealthy and quick, one of the tigers, the male. We all gasped. He walked a slow circle around the small floor and then lay down and stretched out against the back wall. The warden put a hunk of raw meat in the chute, shut it, and pulled a lever: the meat tumbled out on the floor and rolled to a few inches of the tiger's paw.

The tiger never even looked. He lay there, imperious and aloof, seemingly oblivious to the crowd, the warden, the food. We all waited. After a few minutes, he began to flick two claws at the meat, turning it over, indifferent.

"How long have you been caring for these

animals?" I asked the warden.

"Almost fifteen years," she said.

"They know you, then?"

"Yes, of course. If I was visiting here on my day off and just walked by the yard, they would smell me and come over to the fence to greet me."

"What if you went inside the yard?" I asked. "What would they do?"

"Eat me," she said.

Then she looked at me as though I was very thick, very slow, and she spoke with emphasis: "They're wild, you know?"

And right then, the male tiger proved it. A little boy—not my own, but another about his age—had wandered over to the cage while the warden and I were talking. When the boy was mere inches from the cage, the tiger sprang and in one seamless motion leapt the full length of the floor and pressed his massive face against the bars. One paw, glinting claws curving out, wedged between the metal. He growled, low and angry. The boy fell back, terrified. His even more terrified mother swooped in to snatch him.

The warden, stern but with measured calmness, said: "*I told you:* Stay back from the cage."

Narnia taught me early that of all the things we might accuse Jesus of, meekness and mildness are not among them. Of all the responses we might make toward Him, trying to tame Him is among the more foolhardy.

Jesus shows up in people's lives—Matthew's, John's, Zacchaeus's, Paul's, yours, mine—usually unannounced, and not to bargain or to plead. He nowhere asks us to invite Him, pretty please, into our hearts. He walks past and, turning abruptly, cryptic or gruff, issues a stark command: *Follow Me. Come down from there. Leave all you have. Go wherever I tell you.*

He swallows up girls and boys, moms and dads. Who said anything about safe?

He's wild, you know.

Seeing Through the Mist

How the make-believe of Christian fantasy can draw us closer to the truth.

By Erin Healy

When our daughter turned seven, my husband and I planned to give our little audiobook lover the dramatized recordings of *The Chronicles of Narnia*. We were both older than she when we first encountered the books, so, dutiful-parent style, we previewed the recordings—a top-notch production from the radio-drama experts at Focus on the Family.

Without question, the Chronicles are tales we're going to have to help our daughter sort out. Each book contains enough mythology, witchcraft, occult allusions, and other elements to worry Christian parents. Aslan calls forth river gods, satyrs, dwarfs, and goddesses of the woods to serve him. Centaurs and unicorns make regular appearances. Dryads are murdered. Humans marry nymphs and practice magic.

*More than any other genre, fantasy with spiritual dimensions
presses Christian parents' worry buttons.*

When our daughter was a preschooler, the sorting was simpler: "That's real, and this is make-believe" or "This is good, and that is bad" worked most of the time as we tried to guide her budding awareness of the world. Now that she's older, the sorting requires more clarification. At present, my husband and I don't object to Barbie Fairytopia dolls or unicorn toys or classic fairy tales. But we've chosen to say no to Pokémon cards and fantasy video games and ghost stories. As she matures, it's our job as her parents to be able to explain—and maybe even reevaluate—our reasoning in play and movies and books alike.

Perhaps more than any other genre, fantasy with spiritual dimensions includes elements that press Christian parents' worry buttons. The Narnia series is no exception. But does that mean we should treat it just like those secular fantasy children's books we won't let in the door? Yes and no, but mostly no, in my opinion. Here's why.

Is Fantasy Okay?

As far as I can tell, the question never occurred to C. S. Lewis, steeped as he was in medieval literary traditions, or even to his critics, who hated his work for other reasons. They accused the fantasy genre of being childish, of being deceitful, of scaring children, and of promoting escapism. Lewis had little patience for this kind of condemnation. "About once every hundred years some wiseacre gets up and tries to banish the fairy tale," he wrote, as if irritated that this kind of argument against "the kind [of story] I know and love best" would keep rearing its head.

University of Edinburgh lecturer Colin Manlove, who specializes in works of fantasy, explains the most common complaint against Christian writers of the genre: "The imagination is often attacked as free and self-indulgent…. [Its practitioners] know the dangers of invention: they know that new images may divert the mind from the truth contained in them. But they believe also that through such new images the faith can be revitalized; and that the very act of 'going away' from truth may bring one nearer to it."

C. S. Lewis, for one, considered fantasy invaluable in helping to shape a child's blossoming Christian worldview.

Fantasy That Clears the Mist

Rather than promoting escapism, Lewis argued, fantasy accomplished the exact opposite and was exceptionally good at bringing us nearer to Truth. Readers could be drawn closer to

God if the limitations of our human understanding were broken down and exposed to truths that only the freshness of fantasy could powerfully portray. "It would be much truer to say that fairyland arouses a longing [in the reader] for he knows not what," Lewis wrote. "It stirs and troubles him (to his lifelong enrichment) with the dim sense of something beyond his reach and, far from dulling or emptying the actual world, gives it a new dimension of depth….

"I thought I saw how stories of this kind could steal past a certain inhibition which had paralyzed much of my own religion in childhood," Lewis explained. "Why did one find it so hard to feel as one was told one ought to feel about God or about the sufferings of Christ? I think the chief reason was that one was told one ought to. An obligation to feel can freeze feelings…. But supposing that by casting all these things into an imaginary world, stripping them of their stained-glass and Sunday school associations, one could make them for the first time appear in their real potency? Could one not thus steal past those watchful dragons? I thought one could."

In stealing past the watchful dragons, Lewis cast readers into an imaginary world he created using classic literary devices—mythology and symbolism, for example—and writing in a Christian tradition that included such greats as Dante, Milton, and Bunyan. Efficiency and brevity were important to Lewis, an apologist and essayist who made every effort to subdue his "expository demon" while telling stories. He chose nonhuman character types (elf, fairy, sprite, witch, talking beasts) for their effectiveness in portraying essential human qualities quickly and without the need for extensive characterization. ("The imagined beings have their insides on the outside; they are visible souls.")

"We're squinting in a fog, peering through a mist," says Paul in *The Message* translation of 1 Corinthians 13:12. Lewis believed that in its purest form, fantasy cleared a little mist in a way that realism couldn't. And children, Lewis observed wryly, always seem to do better than adults at seeing through it. His *Letters to Children* bears out his affection for them and his shared delight in their discoveries. How many of us who read the Narnia series as children have a stunted Christian worldview today that we can blame on Lewis or his fantasy elements? I'd guess that the opposite is more often true.

Rather than promoting escapism, Lewis argued, fantasy accomplished the exact opposite.

FANTASY THAT MUDDIES THE TRUTH

Does that mean all fantasy is worth our children's time? Of course not. As with any other genre, there's probably more trash than treasure out there. And if your child is like mine—still young enough to confuse the two—it's a tricky distinction to make. When the time comes for us to introduce our daughter to the Narnia stories, we'll use questions like these to help her process them:

1. *What does the Holy Spirit speak to your heart as the events of the story unfold?* Children who haven't invited Christ to be their Lord will be at a disadvantage here. Others, though, can expect the Spirit to be an active participant in their lives and to "take you by the hand and guide you into all the truth there is" (John 16:13, *The Message*). I remember being deeply impressed as a ten-year-old by the magnitude of Aslan's gentle love toward Lucy and his gracious forgiveness of Edmund's betrayal. Some readers might process the Spirit's voice more consciously by keeping a reflective journal as they read.

2. *When you set the book aside and your mind returns to the story, where do your thoughts take you?* To what is "true, noble, reputable, authentic, compelling, gracious—the best, not the worst; the beautiful, not the ugly; things to praise, not things to curse" (Philippians 4:8, *The Message*)? To this day, what has stayed with me

from these stories is the magnificence of Aslan, his sacrificial redemption of the world and creatures he spoke into being, and his guiding presence throughout Narnia's history.

3. *Which does the story portray as more powerful and attractive: good or evil?* In Lewis's fantasies, what a character is—mythical, magical, monstrous—is less important than what he represents. And so, in Narnia's case, evil is horribly personified and any creature or magic or invention or idea not subservient to Aslan is thwarted.

Explaining his approach, Lewis wrote: "Let there be wicked kings and beheadings, battles

version to the crazed mob of ogres and wraiths and hags and evil spirits and all variety of monsters goading the White Witch to plunge her knife into the great lion's heart, we looked at each other, wide-eyed, and decided that perhaps our young daughter could wait a year or so for this literary adventure. Still, when the time is right, the truth of that powerful scene is one we won't want her to miss. Evil, no matter how attractive or compelling it appears at the start, is always ultimately ugly—and through Christ it *will* be defeated by good.

4. *What does the story make you wish for?* Can you identify that "longing" that Lewis

He believed that fantasy, in its purest form, cleared a little mist in a way that realism couldn't.

and dungeons, giants and dragons, *and let the villains be soundly killed at the end of the book.* I think it possible that by confining your child to blameless stories of life in which nothing at all alarming ever happens, you would fail to banish the terrors, and would succeed in banishing all that can ennoble them or make them endurable (emphasis added).

Of course, evil horribly personified still leaves parents to deal with the issue of timing. My husband and I were particularly concerned about the violence in *The Lion, the Witch and the Wardrobe*. Take the slaughter of Aslan, for example. When we listened on our audio

says good fantasy should awaken? How does that longing line up with what the Bible says we should desire as Christians? (See, for starters, Isaiah 55:2, Matthew 5:6, and 1 John 2:16.) After reading *The Lion, the Witch and the Wardrobe* as a child, I longed for Turkish Delight—an unknown treat that surely tasted as wonderful as it sounded. (I was later grossly disappointed.) But more important, I also longed for a romp on Aslan's back, and for a chance to wear Susan's crown. In the case of the latter two, I would see as an adult that they symbolized something very close to what God has promised us in our future home with Him.

By far the strongest appeal of Lewis's fantasy is Aslan himself. His mighty presence, strong and good, seems to stride across every page. What do most children wish for when they close a Chronicle? Aslan. To meet him, to press their faces into his mane, to take a wild ride with him through his kingdom. Lucy said it for all of us at the end of *The Voyage of the* Dawn Treader, when she told Aslan what she was already missing:

"It isn't Narnia, you know," sobbed Lucy. "It's you. We shan't meet you there. And how can we live, never meeting you?"

As the foremost heroic figure of the books, Aslan also represents the greatest virtues: sacrificial love, a passion for justice, faithfulness and trustworthiness, obedience to his father, a surprising tenderness toward failures and fools, and many more qualities. By loving and wishing for Aslan, readers are drawn more truly toward God and what He wants for us.

5. How do you think God would judge the story's heroes/heroines? In the Narnia stories, we have overt answers to this question in the way Aslan judges his characters. In *The Magician's Nephew,* consider what different sentences he hands down to Jadis (and ultimately the White Witch), Uncle Andrew, and Digory.

This question will make most fantasy authors bristle: *Look,* they'll say, *our characters don't abide by the rules of this world at all, let*

alone your uptight religious codes. As a student of literature I must agree. But as a mom concerned with the moral training of my daughter, I'll let the question stand. After all, we're reading the story in this world, and fantasy heroes are models here.

6. *Are you glad you spent your time with those characters, in their world, with their practices and rules and truths?* An honest answer—especially if it's no—will be useful in heightening our awareness of the Holy Spirit's voice the next time we need to hear it. Chances are He gave us fair warning before we reached the end of the tale.

it's fair to say that their version of "truth" has the opposite effect, and muddies the truth of Scripture.

Even so, I don't think it's especially helpful to label books "bad" or "good." The pessimism of A Series of Unfortunate Events might completely undo one child while compelling another to share his hope in Christ with any hopeless people he befriends. Pullman's series might strip one child of her faith while preparing another for a future as a Christian apologist. And so I suggest a different approach, which might not be earth-shattering: Know your kids and guide them

It's possible that Christian fantasy as a genre is dying, and the books we have from Lewis and Tolkien are among the last of a tradition.

These same questions can be used to evaluate the relative worth of any story, fantasy or otherwise. Today, between Harry Potter releases, kids are captivated by best-selling books like Lemony Snicket's Series of Unfortunate Events (which the author wrote to challenge readers' expectations of happy endings in stories and in life), Philip Pullman's *His Dark Materials* trilogy (which is overtly anti-Christian), and other eyebrow-raisers. While these authors use fantasy for the same reason Lewis did—to bring readers closer to the truth they hold dear—I think

into maturity. Read what they're reading. Then talk about it. Questions like those above can do the double duty of pointing kids back to biblical truth and sharpening critical-thinking skills.

A Thickening Mist

I'm saddened by the possibility that Christian children of overzealous "fantasy is bad" parents might eventually be conditioned to reject Lewis's imaginative traditions rather than to embrace and continue them. "The people who spend the most time with the Bible are in large numbers the foes of art and the sworn foes of imagination," wrote Clyde Kilby in an article titled "The Aesthetic Poverty of Evangelism." "How can it be that with a God who created birds and the blue of the sky and who before the foundation of the world wrought out a salvation more romantic than Cinderella, with a Christ who encompasses the highest heaven and deepest hell, with the very hairs of our heads numbered, with God closer than hands and feet, Christians often turn out to have an unenviable corner on the unimaginative and the commonplace?… The symbol, the figure, the image, the parable—in short, the artistic method—so pungent in the Lord's teaching and acting, are often noteworthy for their absence in ours."

It's possible that Christian fantasy as a genre is dying, and the books we have from Lewis and Tolkien are among the last of a tradition that Dante helped set in motion. Colin Manlove says that Christian fantasy "is now often seen as quaint and peripheral" as the church's authority and influence wanes. If this is true, the loss is immeasurable. If this tradition is lost (or worse, commandeered by authors who champion unbiblical claims), what will replace it to help *our* children see through the mist and steal past the dragons?

C. S. Lewis often encouraged his young readers to keep Narnia alive in literature after he had done all he could with it. "Write stories…to fill up the gaps in Narnian history," he urged. "I've left you plenty of hints." Maybe someday I'll share this encouragement with my daughter. She'll eventually be old enough for the Chronicles, and I'll wait until the right time to introduce her. But I won't wait too long, lest her imagination succumb to adult worries or grow too old to run through the mist toward the truth.

Unicorns, Myth & Mystery

Is the Legendary Creature a Childish Imagining, Cult Fantasy, or Christian Icon?

In *The Last Battle,* Jill Pole's affections toward her unicorn friend Jewel rival my daughter's for her unicorn toy named Violet. "She thought…that he was the shiningest, delicatest, most graceful animal she had ever met." My daughter's obsession with the mythical creatures emerged inexplicably when she was five. I dragged myself reluctantly into this passion of hers. Unicorns, in my mind, were the stuff of sorcery and cultish fantasy and tacky, New Age poster art. But how to explain this to a five-year-old? I decided to investigate, and turned up a pleasant surprise

Although the unicorn has roots in pagan myth, the animal was "adopted" by the medieval church as a central symbol of Christ. The power of the image in the Christian imagination became so strong that it pervaded the religious arts for nearly a thousand years. Lewis wove this thread of religious literary tradition through his Chronicles, ultimately giving a prominent role to Jewel in *The Last Battle.*

The Christian spin on the unicorn legend is overtly allegorical, if occasionally muddy. But the most popular story follows a line like this: A great king (God) had a son (Adam, representing mankind) who was near death. The king ordered a hunt for the elusive unicorn (Christ), whose ivory horn has magical healing powers. Because unicorns cannot be captured by anyone except a virgin maiden (Mary), the hunters drove the unicorn into her waiting arms. He was seized and slaughtered, and his horn was crushed to powder and used to revive the son. This version of the story is recounted most famously in the *Hunt of the Unicorn* tapestries, which also show the unicorn resurrected in the final panel.

Generally speaking, the unicorn-as-Christ is fierce, courageous, gentle, holy, loyal, constant, powerful, majestic, and valiant. His small stature represents his humility; his single horn, unity with God. He cannot be subdued against his will, but

> The unicorn-as-Christ is fierce, courageous, gentle, holy, loyal, constant, powerful, majestic, and valiant.

he gives his life in love for his maiden. In myth he represents purity, everlasting life and immortality, power and majesty, and the loving union between a bride and groom. His horn, hide, and even liver heal the sick and wounded. He is a champion for the weak. He protects other animals from the serpent, who poisons the waters where they come to drink and then lies in wait to kill them. The unicorn, however, purifies the water by dipping his horn in it, making it safe for all.

As my daughter gets older, I'll need to help her develop a discerning mind and heart (to help her sort out, say, the intent of the Christian stories from the intent of the tacky poster art). I'll have to go with her as teacher into this world where most things— from history to myth to reality to tradition—are growing murkier rather than clearer. But at this stage, the unicorn is a creature I don't at all mind my daughter knowing.

—ERIN HEALY

Just Say "Boo!"

Courage, Mom! Lewis believed that a little fright with you in sight may be just what your child needs to grow up right.

By Laurie Winslow Sargent *with* David Kopp

Don't let the description "Christian children's classic" lull you into thoughts of cozy comfort on every page—Narnia is *not* a place for the faint of heart.

Yes, Lewis conjures up a world of wonder and delight where God's love reigns supreme. But terrors lurk there too. Ghouls, witches, ogres, an island of nightmares, bloody battles, heads rolling (literally), a stone knife through the heart of Aslan…

And then there's the fate of all but one of those charming English schoolchildren: They die.

Some parental reflection is definitely in order. For example, you may want to consider whether Lewis's masterpieces are appropriate bedtime fare for your younger ones. If your children are older and will be reading the Chronicles on their own, you may need reassurance that Uncle Jack really has their best in mind. And whatever the age of your kids, you'll want to know how to talk with them about the fears and other intense emotions the stories might evoke.

Even more important, though, is to get a clear grasp of what real-life prize waits for your children on the other side of the Chronicles' paper dragons.

Children as Moral Beings

The truth is, C. S. Lewis was anything but careless or insensitive as he fashioned his stories. He grew up as a wildly imaginative and sensitive boy, often lonely, who suffered from recurring night fears. He even rewrote the Dark Island chapter in *The Voyage of the* Dawn Treader for later editions because he decided the original version didn't show enough respect for a child's experience of night terrors.

In addition to his own temperament and boyhood, Lewis's view of children's literature greatly shaped his storytelling. Actually, Lewis never liked the distinction "*children's* literature." He thought it should simply be good literature that children like to read. "Most of the great fantasies and fairy tales were not addressed to children at all, but to everyone," he wrote. And "No book is really worth reading at the age of ten which is not equally (and often far more) worth reading at the age of fifty—except, of course, books of information."

As you'd expect, this view affected how he approached the scary stuff. Lewis believed that protecting a child from the dark realities of life was a disservice. In his essay "On Three Ways of Writing for Children," he wrote: "Those who say that children must not be frightened mean two things. They may mean (1) that we must not do anything likely to give the child those haunting, disabling, pathological fears against which ordinary courage is helpless…. Or they may mean (2) that we must try to keep out of his mind the knowledge that he is born into a world of death, violence, wounds, adventure, heroism and cowardice, good and evil. If they mean the first I agree with them, but not if they mean the second."

Lewis is not alone in this thinking. Laura Miller, an editor of Salon.com, explains the context in which Lewis wrote, and the potential for good that comes from it: "The British children's writers think children are important enough to be treated as moral beings…. Lewis's depiction of what it means to be tempted by evil, as Edmund is by the White Witch…made a tremendous impression on me as a child. It communicated that, faced with often deceptive and even self-destructive emotions and impulses, I had choices to make in my life, choices that *mattered*."

Why Narnia Isn't Too Scary for Most

In the case of the Chronicles, most children old enough and interested enough to follow the stories are also old enough to handle the frightening parts. Here's why:

The child is in charge. Even the violent scenes are not overly graphic—no more graphic than many classic fairy tales at least. When only a few

SOMETHING SCARY THIS WAY COMES

With a little forethought, you can be prepared to guide your children safely through the scary parts of the Chronicles. Read ahead if you have concerns. Be ready to skip or paraphrase a particularly troublesome scene. And if your child does get frightened, resolve not to make him or her feel silly or ashamed. ❊ To help you read wisely, scan this book-by-book list of the most potentially frightening or violent scenes in the Chronicles:

Book 1. The Magician's Nephew

A funny, fast-action book without many frights—unless you count exploding guinea pigs!

Book 2. The Lion, the Witch and the Wardrobe

High drama that may shake you and move you to tears, but powerfully redemptive. Scary: The Witch's demonic rabble, chapters 14–15; Aslan's death, chapter 14.

Book 3. The Horse and His Boy

A travel adventure with no scenes of supernatural evil. Violence: A lion chases and scratches Aravis, chapter 10; fierce battle at Anvard, chapter 13.

Book 4. Prince Caspian

A sense of threat hangs over the book until the forces of good prevail. Violence: A Hag, a Wer-Wolf, and Nikabrik the Dwarf are killed, chapter 12; the battle between Miraz and Peter, chapter 14.

Book 5. The Voyage of the Dawn Treader

High adventure at sea, but dragons and a Sea Serpent will evoke more fascination than dread. Scary: Sailing into darkness and nightmares at the Dark Island, chapter 12 (could be skipped with little interruption to the story).

Book 6. The Silver Chair

Two English kids and Puddleglum have plenty of adventures (including almost getting eaten by Giants), but the Marsh-wiggle is a steadying presence. Violence: The Green Witch loses her head, chapter 12.

Book 7. The Last Battle

Ultimately triumphant and unforgettably hope-filled, this book is also the darkest and most violent. Cautions: Tirian and Jewel attack and kill unarmed Calormenes, chapter 2; Tash, terrifying god of the Calormenes, chapters 8 & 12; final battle scenes—the Dwarfs kill the Talking Horses, Jewel the Unicorn tosses men like hay, key characters get thrown through the Stable Door where Tash awaits, chapters 11–12.

details are provided, as is nearly always the case with the more alarming creatures and events in Narnia, children will tend to conjure up only as scary an image as they can handle. Take a centaur, for example. In Lewis's text, this wondrous creature—half man, half horse—is left to have exactly the face the child imagines.

The narrator is present as an adult who understands the child's world. Lewis constantly interjects his voice and comforting presence into the story, affirming a child's feelings, and reminding the reader when necessary that this is, after all, only a tale. For example, in *Lion,* in the middle of his description of the horrible creatures who accompany the Witch, Lewis adds with a wink, "…and other creatures whom I won't describe here because if I did the grown-ups would probably not let you read the book."

The narrator guides the experience. Lewis is likewise especially sensitive when a character we care about is meeting his death. For example, when it comes time for the Witch to stab Aslan, Lewis mercifully spares us the details by making Susan and Lucy unable to watch.

The story is ultimately redemptive. Finally, the dread, fear, or grief we feel in the Chronicles are not manufactured or gratuitous (as, say, in a ghost story, melodrama, or teen horror movie). They're for a purpose, and they're attached to human experiences we recognize as significant. It helps, too, that in the end justice is done. Good wins out. And when it does—for example, when Aslan rises again—we don't merely feel relief that he's alive. We realize (even if only later) that we now know something of what Mary Magdalene must have felt when she first saw Christ, whose death she had mourned, standing alive before her and calling her by name.

The Readiness Test

If you're wondering if your child is ready for the Narnia experience, ask yourself some key questions that other parents have found helpful:

Can my child separate reality from fantasy? In other words, is he or she old enough to realize for certain that the White Witch won't be visiting your house tonight? If not, then they're not ready to climb through that wardrobe.

Is my child reading independently, or with a parent? What might seem terrifying when the child is alone in bed won't be so daunting when the story is unfolding on or near your lap.

Does my child already have a tendency toward fear, bad dreams, or being haunted by boogeymen? If so, wait longer than you might otherwise. And when you do read, give extra attention to reading and talking through the experience together.

What else is going on in my child's life? If your child is going through an anxious or stressful season—a recent divorce, a seriously ill sibling, a move—any fears he or she already feels are likely to get amplified by a fictional fright. Again, extra empathy and wisdom are in order.

What is my child's temperament? Keep in mind

your child's emotional and creative makeup. Some children feel things deeply but are quick to talk things through with a parent. Some are more sensitive to emotional issues in stories than they are to violence. The variations are endless. But each child deserves what you can do best—observe, care, love, protect, pray, and then parent with discretion.

Facing the Fears, Keeping the Faith
As you think through the parenting choices related to fears and frights in the Chronicles, don't lose sight of the big picture: Good literature prepares us for better living, and the frights of the Chronicles can teach our children a priceless lesson—how to live with courage.

The characters in Narnia must face and overcome enormous obstacles in order to grow, or maintain their integrity, or follow where Aslan leads. Life is like that. Often the greatest obstacles the Narnians must face are their own fears. Life is like that too! We know that adults who want to live responsible, productive, godly lives need courage every day to face their fears and make the right choices.

The Narnia stories can help our children grow in the same ways.

Which brings us to the single greatest "fright" in Narnia—the world-shaking roar of Aslan! It stands for lordship, righteousness, power, and judgment over all of creation. But the children come to know this: if Aslan is for them, *nothing* real or imagined can be against them.

Like Jill, our children can learn to face anything life brings with God's help—"Courage, child: We are all between the paws of the true Aslan."

Like Eustace before the Stable Door, our children *will* come to a defining crisis when they stand there trembling, "heart beating terribly, hoping and hoping that [they] will be brave."

Like Susan, who gave up hope that Aslan would ever come to the rescue, our children can live bravely in the knowledge that with God on their side, fear *is* the only enemy. From *Prince Caspian:*

> Then, after an awful pause, the deep voice said, "Susan." Susan made no answer but the others thought she was crying. "You have listened to fears, child," said Aslan. "Come. Let me breathe on you. Forget them. Are you brave again?"
>
> "A little, Aslan," said Susan.

Think of all the fears and frights of Narnia as kind Uncle Jack's unforgettable attempt to pass on to your children the real prize: courage. And think of *courage* in children's literature as another word for faith. The Bible says that with just a little faith, not a thing in the world—no matter how scary—can stop us.

MERCY! HOW THE WINE DOTH FLOW IN NARNIA!

What was our beloved children's author thinking? And how should Christian parents respond?

BY LAURIE WINSLOW SARGENT WITH DAVID KOPP

Nestled in with all the imaginative delights and spiritual surprises of the Chronicles is a not-so-convenient reality: recurring alcohol consumption by creatures large and small. The story strand of imbibing will be entirely missed by plenty of readers, your kids perhaps among them. But it is a point of concern to many parents.

Actually, once you start noticing it, the drinking is hard to miss. Pints pour and corks pop all over the place. Turn a page and you're likely to meet:

- ❋ a brew-loving beaver

- ❋ sea-soaked English kids getting revived with a stiff shot of spirits

- a very drunk Marsh-wiggle

- Aslan and a Wood full of beings romping with Bacchus, Roman god of revelry

- banquets where wine is common dinner-table fare for all

If the presence of any alcohol in a children's story is unacceptable to you, the Chronicles might not be right for you and your family. But assuming you're not inclined to toss out the books with the bubbly, a little clear thinking can go a long way.

First off, we should remember that C. S. Lewis intended the Chronicles to be literature with a Christian message, not a Christian message with literary trappings, and certainly not a Sunday school lesson. Second, as any seasoned Bible reader knows, recording a behavior or choice is not the same thing as saying God recommends it. This is especially true when any negative consequences associated with those behaviors and choices are also recorded. And third, reading a story that references beer or wine just isn't likely to lead a child to get drunk on Friday night, especially when there's a loving, open, ready-to-talk parent reading alongside.

In fact, you may have already discovered that the beverage issues in Lewis's books can easily be turned to important family conversations. But before we suggest ways to do that, we might as well ask the obvious question: What *was* Uncle Jack thinking?

Back at the Eagle and Child

Well, he might have been thinking of toddling down to the pub. Actually, a lot of everyday business gets taken care of in English pubs (often with children and dogs running about underfoot). Every Tuesday for years, Lewis and his writing friends (including J. R. R. Tolkien) met in an Oxford pub called the Eagle and Child. There they discussed religion, mythology, morality, and literature, including their own works in progress.

It's well known that Lewis prized a good pint. That, along with his use of tobacco, sets him up to be a rather awkward flag bearer for contemporary conservative North American Christians. While Lewis was orthodox and evangelical in his faith, he remained a lifelong member of the Anglican church, a mainline denomination that condones moderate alcohol consumption by adults.

Lewis watched his brother Warnie struggle with alcoholism for years.
And the plotlines of the Chronicles clearly show his concern.

An inebriated Puddleglum ends up stammering about respect while he's busy not earning any.

On the subject of temperance, Lewis wrote in *Mere Christianity:*

> *Temperance is, unfortunately, one of those words that has changed its meaning.... Temperance referred not specially to drink, but to all pleasures; and it meant not abstaining, but going the right length and no further.... An individual Christian may see fit to give up all sorts of things for special reasons— marriage, or meat, or beer, or the cinema; but the moment he starts saying the things are bad in themselves, or looking down his nose at other people who do use them, he has taken the wrong turning.*

Lewis believed that all true pleasures, including food and drink, are gifts from God to be enjoyed. Still, he was not glib about the potential for abuse. He watched his brother Warnie struggle with alcoholism for years. And the plotlines of the Chronicles clearly show his concern. But more on that in a minute.

FURTHER BACK IN THE MIDDLE AGES

In addition to Lewis's own views on drinking, his stories reflect the times in which they are set—approximately the Middle Ages. As a specialist in medieval literature, Lewis was familiar with the prevalence of and attitudes toward wine and beer consumption in that era. It certainly wasn't the flash-point issue that it is today in post-Prohibition, post–M.A.D.D. middle America. Back then, wine was considered a food staple, and safer to drink than the often bacteria-laden water. Beverages brewed from grains were thick and relatively nutritious, and their alcohol content tended to be lower. Mead, a mildly alcoholic brew made from honey, was distributed liberally to all ages. (Distilled alcohol came along hundreds of years later.)

As in many times and cultures, including our own, alcohol then was supposed to have medicinal qualities. On board the *Dawn Treader*, Prince Caspian pulls the children from cold seas, then offers them hot spiced wine as a warmer (Eustace grumbles that he'd rather have a vitamin preparation). Think of this kind of imbibing as the cough syrup, or hot tea with whiskey and honey, of the day.

LESSONS IN A BOTTLE

Probably more important than listing how the beverages are used in the Chronicles is looking at what lessons the stories themselves can convey to your children. Here are five:

1. Alcoholic beverages have been a part of adult social gatherings and celebrations for many centuries.

From the wedding at Cana to champagne toasts for winners today, wines and beers go with special festivities. You'll notice, though, that at Narnian celebrations, drinking is portrayed as moderate, sociable, and responsible, with no references to drunkenness.

In all seven Chronicles, wine or beer are included nonjudgmentally in lists of food and drink items present at meals or celebrations. Sometimes the story makes it clear that the drink is only for adults. In other passages it's not clear who drank what, but in no instances are the children described as intoxicated.

Some parents may find certain "romps" disturbing—for example, when Bacchus, the mythological god of wine, shows up with his friends for a party in *Prince Caspian*. Most children will not read anything alarming into these festivities. But if you're uncomfortable about these scenes or are reading with small children, you might want to skip these parts.

2. You might feel smarter or stronger on too much alcohol, but what you'll be is a bumbling fool.

Take in a little too much alcohol and you'll believe what the giants at Harfang told Puddleglum: "The more you drink, the bigger a man you are." It's a line most kids these days have to deal with by the sixth grade, if not before.

The bumbling happens to both good guys and bad, since alcohol is no respecter of persons. For example, an inebriated Puddleglum ends up stammering about respect while he's busy not earning any. And then there's Uncle Andrew. He says rules don't apply to "profound students and great thinkers and sages…men like me who possess common wisdom." But his weakness for brandy proves his foolishness to all. After several pulls on the bottle, he gets lost in imagining that the heartless Queen Jadis will fall for him. He can't recognize his own vanity or the Queen's danger. But don't worry, your kids will.

There's probably never been a generation more aware of the dangers of addiction than the one coming of age today.

3. You might think you can hide the negative consequences of too much alcohol, but you only risk being the last to know.

You might point out, if your family hasn't already noticed, that the hard liquor mentioned in *The Magician's Nephew* is always shown as imbibed in secret, at irrational times, and in excess. Uncle Andrew hides his flask of brandy in his wardrobe, away from Aunt

Letty, who disapproves of his drinking. (This contrasts to the social drinking at meals and special occasions described elsewhere.) But no matter how much Andrew tries to be sly, the negative consequences of his drinking habit reveal themselves, and even if he doesn't seem to notice, everyone else gets a laugh and a lesson at his expense.

In *The Silver Chair*, Puddleglum hides his "nasty stuff" in a black, square bottle. The giant at Harfang Castle who poured Puddleglum large quantities from his own black bottle cautioned him not to tell anyone (after cheering him on to drink in excess). The secret use/public shame theme can prompt helpful conversations with your kids about conscience, living in denial, the power of reputation, bringing honor or dishonor to God's name, and natural consequences.

4. You might think alcohol (or any addictive substance) puts you in control, but the truth is you're at risk of becoming its slave.

There's probably never been a generation more aware of the dangers of addiction than the one coming of age today. Sadly, most families have a loved one who's struggled with a dependency on drugs or alcohol, and perhaps lost. The good news here is that you're not likely to have to deliver much parenting advice. Just let the story dramatize the issues! Whereas an earlier generation may have seen more humor in Edmund's greed for Turkish Delight, most kids today will quickly see the sadness and feel the awful tyranny of it. Same goes for watching the Ape in *The Last Battle* become a stooge for an evil power completely beyond his ability to escape or even comprehend.

5. Abstinence is a wise choice.

Sure, this is never an explicit message from Lewis. But you can make a powerful case for it from the Chronicles if you want. The deepest, most exhilarating, most enduring pleasure we find there isn't from any drink but from the nearness of Aslan himself. All the real romps in life—no negative consequences to follow—start with him!

Color & Culture in Narnia

When it's a story about fair-skinned good guys versus dark-skinned bad guys (and the author is white), do we have a problem?

By Marcus Brotherton

What a closed mind that C. S. Lewis had—imagine creating a country that's an Irishman's paradise. Of all the nerve. Narnia is full of heather, moss, and forests— "Narnia and the North!" is a rallying cry. Narnians themselves are fair, noble, and free. They swing their arms when they walk, chatting and laughing in a friendly manner. What a tidy utopia for Lewis to dream up.

He also dreamt up those sneaky Calormene infidels. They're a turbaned, dark-skinned people who wear pointed shoes. They're not like the Narnians. They reek of onions and garlic, and use oil on their bread instead of butter. A proud and cruel race, they're the epitome of all that's wrong in the series. "An hour's life in Narnia is better than a thousand years in Calormen," sighs Bree, the Talking Horse.

What could Lewis possibly be thinking?

Narnia: white…fair…free…superior…
Britain, of course.

And Calormen: dark…turbaned…
sneaky…stinky… Well, that must mean…

Was C. S. Lewis a Racist?

The answer is "Of course not!" Or maybe it is "Obviously, yes!" It all depends on whom you ask.

Some modern critics accuse the Chronicles of being anti-Arab, anti-Muslim, racist, sexist, imperialist, antiliberal, antiprogressive—just about anything a literary critic can think of.

Have you heard anything about these debates? They've been going on for several years, and continue today. Let's examine the foundations of the racism issue for a moment from a critic's point of view.

But first, let's talk about why this debate matters to you (maybe more than you think).

Why It Matters

It's true: The Chronicles indeed contain some race references that don't sit well with modern ears. "Had enough, Darkies?" the wicked Dwarfs jeer to the Calormenes. Whoa, careful now. Parents reading to children may want to make some on-the-fly word changes. It's valid for parents not to want some words echoing through their children's minds.

And the issue as a whole is one that can't be ignored. There are good people with important concerns on all sides of this debate, and the concern over racism in the Chronicles deserves thoughtful acknowledgement, especially for Christian parents.

So was Lewis merely creating a bunch of entreating children's stories, or was there a subtle and insidious racial bias to the books he wrote? That's the question.

Here are a few reasons why Christian readers should wrestle with this:

❋ Christians may encounter friends and neighbors who chastise the books, and will want to know how to intelligently grapple with these issues.

❋ We live in a world right now where "white and Christian" is portrayed as being at war against "brown and Muslim." It's the consuming conflict of our times. The risk of slipping into categorical prejudice is great for any of us.

❋ Troubling but true: America doesn't have the best track record with every minority group it's encountered in its history—Native Americans and African Americans, to name two. This is an issue we can't afford to dismiss.

We want our kids to grow up with a healthy view of the *real* gospel, not some "us" versus "them" gospel where the developed world is pitted against the undeveloped, or where pale is pitted against dark. The true gospel is about reconciling mankind to God through the work of Christ on the cross, not about conquering other races in the name of religion.

And, as is the point of this book, we want to be able to talk to our kids about these issues as the opportunity arises in the reading of the Chronicles.

When Things Weren't as PC

Remember when the Chronicles were written? Literature in the 1950s was cut from a different cloth than today. Lewis wrote from the standpoint of a world that had just been through two horrific world wars. Themes of nationalism and colonialism were still prevalent in people's minds. Countries, battles, enemies—these all held different shades of meaning than they do in 2006.

Consider the challenges the Chronicles are up against in this politically correct, twenty-first-century global village. It's harder for us to identify "enemies" than ever before. It used to be that a group of people could be portrayed as evil in literature or film without raising eye-

brows. "Good" cowboys used to fight "bad" Indians. Noble Briton James Bond used to battle devilish Russians. Caricaturizing people groups was once a common literary device, shorthand for "who we're against." We still create enemies today in our works of fiction, but our antagonists are much more non-specific now. They're terrorists or governments, ideologies or technologies.

Probably Lewis was just creating convenient antagonists when he dreamed up the race known as the Calormenes. His protagonists are mostly London schoolchildren, which Lewis portrayed as himself or as what he guessed most of his readers would identify with—fair-skinned Britons, pasty even (in the case of Eustace Scrubb), and yes, white. It's logical progression to assume that Lewis created enemies who appeared the opposite of London schoolchildren—in this case of Calormen, dark. Pale versus dark. A conflict doesn't get any more classic than that. The creators of *Star Wars* recognized it; they just came along thirty-five years after Lewis and had the politically-correct fortitude to reverse-color their Storm Troopers.

But did Lewis hate "brown"? It doesn't seem that way. He also makes green Bad Guys, as in the Lady of the Green Kirtle, and white Bad Guys, as in the White Witch. Color, sometimes in the form of a country, is

We still create enemies today in our works of fiction, but our antagonists are much more nonspecific now.

just the team uniform Lewis put on his characters. It lets the readers know whom the protagonists are up against. And using such a literary device wouldn't have caused a stir in Lewis's day.

It's a Closer World Now

The challenge of literature is that our shorthand for "enemy" changes over time. Shades of similarity can be found between Calormen and the Arab world, sure, but there wasn't a war in Iraq as there is today, with all the sensitivities that brings, when Lewis wrote the Chronicles.

In fact, with the advent of the Internet, widespread air travel, and global communication devices, it's a completely different world today than it was in 1950. Today, there's someone of Middle Eastern descent sitting at the cubicle next to us at work, whose wife is in the PTA and whose kids play soccer with ours. In this century, "right next to us" includes the entire planet. Even if North Americans never leave Kankanee, Walla Walla, Toronto, Poughkeepsie—wherever we're from—we're directly connected to the rest of the world, hardwired to each other for better or worse.

Lewis would have probably fit in just fine if he were alive today in such a global village. He tended to resist the "Rule Britannia" mindset that was still voiced in his day—the thought that the entire world should be under British influence. He was more into letting others be themselves, a very twenty-first-century concept for a man of the 1950s. Elsewhere he writes of his respect for other countries:

> *In any mind which has a pennyworth of imagination it produces a good attitude towards foreigners. How can I love my home without coming to realise that other men, no less rightly, love theirs? Once you have realized that the Frenchmen like café complet just as we like bacon and eggs— why, good luck to them and let them have it. That last thing we want is to make everywhere else just like our own home.*

But hang on, back to the whole Darkies issue. How does using a word like that jibe with Lewis's nationally sensitive comments about bacon and eggs and all that?

Could it be, simply, because *Lewis* didn't actually say Darkies? It was the Dwarfs, remember? When an author creates slanderous characters, he will portray the characters as doing slanderous things. One may conclude that the *Dwarfs* were racist—and they may indeed have been; they certainly showed no love for the Calormenes. But the Dwarfs are not Lewis. Simply because an author creates characters that do racist things doesn't mean the author is racist himself.

In fact, strong character development is central to every book in the Chronicles. In *The Last Battle*, for example, Tirian, Jill, and Eustace find it distasteful when they have to darken their skin to disguise themselves as Calormenes. When Tirian removes the coloring he says, "That is better. I feel a true man again."

But did Tirian say this because he is a racist king, or because Tirian (or Lewis, for that matter) hates all dark-skinned people?

Consider the context of the story. Tirian is in the midst of a difficult battle against his opponents, the Calormenes, who have come to viciously overthrow his country and his kingship. Probably Tirian says what he does because he's been disguised as his enemy, and he, the last noble king of Narnia, is not one for disguises.

Tirian says he feels like "a true *man* again" because he's no longer hiding—he's no longer doing something he believes is questionable for a man of valor such as himself. He's relieved because he's now distinguishable from his enemy—not because he's back to being Caucasian.

Take Us to Another Place

Let's say for a moment that Calormen was indeed created to characterize Arab culture. Would that have been equal to saying the Arabs are the enemy—or could Lewis have been saying something else? A careful study of the Chronicles will show that Lewis often actually spoke favorably about his created race, even longingly; not against it. He certainly prizes Aravis's fine Calormene storytelling ability in *The Horse and His Boy*.

One of the central characteristics of the Chronicles is excitement—take London schoolchildren out of their normal environment, Lewis is asking, and what wonderful things might they encounter? His answer is that components of Calormen are really cool. Children read the Chronicles for the same reasons they've been reading *One Thousand and One Arabian Nights* for years. The components that make these books exciting are new worlds and magic carpets and strange customs they've never encountered before.

Probably, Lewis sets much of *Horse* in Calormen simply because it's an exciting land to describe. Its customs and flavorings are exotic, intelligent, and captivating, even though many of its values run contrary to Narnia values. *Horse* is not a horror story because it's set in Calormen; it's a story of intrigue and adventure, where home seems an impossibly long way off.

When Shasta enters the Calormene capital of Tashbaan for the first time (a city Lewis describes as "one of the wonders of the world"), he is awed and exclaims: "This is a wonderful place." Aravis, a Calormene through and through, eventually becomes the Queen of Archenland and the mother of Ram the Great, the "most famous of all the kings of Archenland."

Aravis, in fact, is a good example of the individuality of Lewis's characters—and this may be the central counterpoint to any cry that Lewis is racist. Though Aravis is from a country Lewis often positions counter to Narnia, she still grows as a person. Aravis evolves from being a prideful and vain princess to a noble and grateful worshiper. It's the person that's important, Lewis is saying. There are good Calormenes, capable of change and redemption—Aravis, for example, or Emeth in *The Last Battle*—much the same as there are bad Narnians—Nikabrik, for example, or Edmund at his worst.

If Lewis Could Speak

Dead authors, of course, are inconvenienced when it comes to speaking up in their own defense. Time passes and issues change, but their words in print don't. Their voice is stuck in a time and place that recedes further and further from our own. What readers are left with, increasingly, are their own interpretations.

But if Lewis could return to clear things up—well, just imagine the scene…

There he stands in the country lane on a perfect English morning, hat and walking stick in hand, a twinkle in his eye, and apparently a readiness to chat—with you! You're simply too enchanted to be shocked. You exchange pleasantries, but almost immediately begin to fear that he'll disappear any second. So, rather too soon for comfort, you hit him with the whole unpleasant race case against him.

"Aah, I see! Oh my!" he says, clearly taken aback. But hardly hesitating, he clears his throat, and with the authority of one who's just vacationed in Al Khurma, declares, "That's not what I meant *at all!*"

Then back on goes his hat. "You simply *must* come along with me to the Kilns—right this very minute," he says, the twinkle back too. "We shall have some garlic and onions together and come up with a *much* better enemy. And first, a nice cup of *café complet*—I've really developed a taste for it lately."

Riding the Light

What great business of life does a child's journey through make-believe accomplish?
Can a fairy tale ring so perfectly true that it prepares us to meet the Truth in person?

By Kristen Johnson Ingram

When I was small, we didn't have a big wooden wardrobe where I could push through to another world. But when the late afternoon sun gleamed through our lace curtains, I traveled to places where Zeus was king or where my dolls came alive. The key to my imaginary kingdom was the music; the door was under the instrument.

I sat underneath our grand piano, listening, while my mother gave piano lessons. I learned with her pupils the amazing names of lines in the treble and spaces in the bass, learned how to count time by fours and threes and twos. But when the last pupil left, I lingered between the ordinary and the magical and held my breath, hoping my mother would play.

On most days, she just got up from the piano and walked into another room. But once in a while, when the students were gone and my father was not yet home, she would play "Liebestraum," "The Minute Waltz," "Clair de Lune," or "Prelude in C-sharp Minor." Her small, slender fingers flew across the keys. In my place below the sound, if I put my hands up on my "roof" (the piano's wooden sounding board), I could feel the vibration of the brass strings.

I flew out on those brass-colored shafts of light, flew over our red Arizona desert where saguaro cactus grew to forty feet. Sometimes I soared over the ocean that was hundreds of miles to the west, and finally above places I had never seen, where forests stood thick and green, and great limpid lakes were full of dolphins and seals. In most of those places, animals talked with humans. Sometimes my dog went with me, and then he could talk too. I rode the light into a make-believe land where little girls didn't have asthma or ear infections, and where a dinosaur or a fairy's wand could really exist.

My afternoon soaring always ended abruptly, and too soon. My mother would stop playing and put the wing down on the piano, and then we had dinner. But when nobody else was around, my dog could still talk, and did. He talked at night before one of my parents would chase him off my bed and

escort him to the basement. He and our cat played an amazing game: the cat would stand on a living room chair and the dog would race through the house in a circle. When he came around, the cat would leap onto his back and ride him around. I am certain I heard the cat talking to him.

I did not have Aslan yet, because I was born before he was written. But I read *The Wildling Princess* and *At the Back of the North Wind*, where I learned about God's participation in our lives. I read *Tanglewood Tales* by Nathaniel Hawthorne, in which Baucis and old Philemon, an aging couple in northern Greece, unknowingly entertained Quicksilver and Zeus with such great hospitality that the gods blessed them. It is a Lewis-like story about something done to the least of these being done to Christ. And just about my favorite book in the whole world was my eighth-birthday gift from my godmother, *The Book of Live Dolls* by Josephine Scribner Gates. It begins with a fairy princess who rides in a tiny coach pulled by white kittens and who tosses out flyers saying that on the next day all the dolls in that city will come alive—and they do. The book was a reprint of one my godmother had read when she was a child, and that brought me closer to her, as well as awakening my own imagination.

If I hadn't read and reread the stories of live dolls and sleeping princesses who were wakened by a kiss, I might not have been ready for the facts of the Bible.

I had enchantment every day: the music that made me able to ride a shaft of sunlight, the books that carried me into other times and places, my dog and cat, and a godmother who took our relationship seriously and offered me the magic that made my life, with its ear infections and coughing and chronic tonsillitis, more bearable. Stories about such enchantments made my experience at Sunday school better too, because I had taught my mind to believe that anything was possible. Even though I knew the live dolls were fantasy while the miracles Jesus performed were real, fantasy showed me how to believe the impossible.

What all the books held within their pages, the theme suspended unspoken within the stories, was resurrection. Ugly ducklings, pecked and abused by their foster siblings, turned into beautiful white swans. Feckless, despised boys became kings (or at least mayors). Girls who swept cinders turned into beautiful princesses. And when you kissed them, amphibians changed into handsome princes. Even as a child, I recognized Type, and when I was eight, I announced to my Sunday school teacher that the earthly life of Jesus was like an enchantment by a bad wizard, and that Easter was His—and our—

victory over the evil sorcerer. She was shocked.

But was I wrong? J. R. R. Tolkien, author of *The Fellowship of the Ring,* said that true fairy tales contained four biblical principles: fantasy, recovery, escape, and consolation. Fantasy helps us suspend disbelief. Recovery, which may include physical or spiritual danger, is seeing things as we are meant to see them. Escape reveals an alternative to the enchantment. And consolation shows us the happy ending, the living forever after resurrection.

Every *real* story, from the Brothers Grimm to Tom Clancy, contains those four traits. They all offer death and resurrection as opposing themes. And since every real story contains these elements, then they must each reflect a real, larger story and a larger Truth. Imagining my way along the trail of real stories led me straight to the Bible and Jesus Christ.

Looking back at my childhood, I realize that my experience as an only child—beset by both frequent illness (before antibiotics) and my mother's chronic anger—could have been a harder life than it was. God lifted me out of physical and emotional pain to ride the light. Imagination and fantasy and music taught me how to relate to the seen *and* the unseen, to rip through the membrane that separated me from Christ Himself so I could live His story or at least let Him live it in me. If I hadn't sat under the piano and soared on "Liebestraum," if I hadn't read and reread the stories of live dolls and sleeping princesses who were wakened by a kiss, I might not have been ready for the facts of the Bible.

By the time I had children, psychiatrists had decided that realistic stories of modern-day boys and girls were better sources of fiction. But nothing doing! If all my children's generation had read were those kinds of books, they would all have become dwarves with hobnail boots, marching through the streets. Instead we proved the doctors wrong by making *The Cat in the Hat* a classic and by clamoring for Aslan stories, which I first benefited from by reading them aloud to my kids.

How perfect a lion is, to stand for Christ! C. S. Lewis knew that Christ is called the lion of Judah in Revelation, even though He is most often portrayed as a lamb. You can pick up a lamb and kiss its nose and walk away when you please. But a lion requires more—especially one who talks and even gives commands. Especially a lion who is willing to be killed at the Stone Table for a child's offenses.

Of all the Narnia books, my favorite is *The Magician's Nephew*, because I saw and heard God create the heavens and the earth.

Well, at least God's double, Aslan. He stood somewhere on nothing, and he *sang* everything into being. He sang to make stars and planets, sang to make a world, and in that world, a country called Narnia, where the trees talk and a mouse named Reepicheep could row his boat through the lilies and straight into heaven where Aslan was waiting. Aslan didn't hurl lightning bolts that exploded into comets, or roll balls of mud to make planets. He sang, and there was light. He sang, and he saw that it was good.

It's five in the afternoon now, and my windows face west just as they did when I was a child. I put a disc in my CD player and sit down to listen to a famous pianist play Chopin and Liszt. The late afternoon sunshine pours through the blinds and the music dances around me, begging me to come, to soar out on the light, to believe the impossible.

I forget for a while that I'm now a grandmother with bifocals and a trick knee, and feel myself hurrying through the universe to where Jesus is waiting. And now I know what this has all been about: Riding the light has prepared me to begin "the Great Story...which goes on forever: in which every chapter is better than the one before."

PART FIVE

Roar! Fact File

The Official ROAR! Guide
to What Happened When in Narnia

Book	Year in English Time	Year in Narnian Time	Who's in Narnia from England	How They Got to Narnia	Key Event
The Magician's Nephew	1900	1	Polly Plummer, 11, Digory Kirke, 12	Magic rings	Narnia is founded and the first king and queen appointed.
The Lion, the Witch and the Wardrobe	1940	1000	Pevensie children: Peter, 13, Susan, 12, Edmund, 10, Lucy, 8	Through the wardrobe	Aslan dies for Edmund and defeats the White Witch.
The Horse and His Boy	1940	1014	The Pevensie children (but Peter is off fighting giants)	Still reigning in Narnia from Lion	Shasta journeys to Narnia to find his true identity.
Prince Caspian	1941	2303	Pevensie children: Peter, 14, Susan, 13, Edmund, 11, Lucy, 9	Summoned from a train platform by Susan's horn	Caspian reclaims his kingdom and delivers Old Narnia from the Telmarines.
The Voyage of the Dawn Treader	1942	2306	Edmund Pevensie, 12, Lucy Pevensie, 10, Eustace Scrubb, 9	Through a picture	Caspian sails east in search of lost lords.
The Silver Chair	1942	2356	Eustace Scrubb, 9, Jill Pole, 9	Through a door in a wall at Experiment House	Prince Rilian is freed from the Queen of Underland's spell.
The Last Battle	1949	2555	Eustace Scrubb, 16*, Jill Pole, 16*	A railway accident	A false Aslan deceives many and Narnia comes to an end.

*An official timeline lists 1949 as the date of the railway accident. However, in The Last Battle when the kids arrive in Narnia, Eustace tells Tirian that he and Jill were here "more than a year ago by our time." In that case, the two would be ten years old. If the timeline is right, they are both sixteen.

Glossary of Difficult & Unusual Words

Addled Rotten

Aft Toward the rear (stern) of a ship

Aloft Up in the sails or rigging of a ship

Alsatian A German shepherd

Antechamber A smaller room serving as an entryway into a larger room

Anteroom An outer room that opens into another room; often a waiting room

Apophthegm A short teaching

Ark A chest

Ass Old term for donkey

Astrolabes (and other big words) Ancient instruments of navigation

Attend Pay attention

Avouch To declare openly

Baccy Tobacco

Bagged Stolen

Baited Tormented with insults

Bally Slang for *really* or *very*; similar to *bloody* or *blooming*

Balmier Crazier

Balustrade A railing to prevent people from falling

Bane A cause of harm, ruin, or death

Bastables Children in books by Edith Nesbit

Bath-chair Wheelchair

Bathe Swim

Bathing Swimming

Battledore A flat wooden paddle used in an early form of badminton

Battlement A low, notched wall running along the edge of a roof, used for defense

Batty Crazy or insane

Becalmed Made calm; still

Beggar To make a beggar of; impoverish

Belike Probably

Bellows A device that blows air onto a fire to make it burn more fiercely

Bequeath To pass something on to another; hand down

Bethink Remember

Bilge Stupid talk or nonsense

Bilious Sickly, greenish

Billy-oh A great amount

Biped An animal with two feet

Bittern A marsh bird

Bivouac A temporary camp

Bivouacked Set up a temporary camp

Blab A person who reveals secrets

Blighter A persistently annoying person

"Blimey" An exclamation of surprise

Blithering Senseless or foolish

"Blowed if I ain't" An expression of amazement

Blown Out of breath

Blub Cry

Blue-bottle A kind of housefly

Boatswain A crew member, especially one in charge of the smaller boat(s) on deck

Bobance Flashiness, boasting

Boggles and Cruels Imaginary evil beings

Boom A heavy pole attached to the bottom edge of a sail

Boon A timely blessing or benefit

Bow Front end of a ship

A bowshot The distance that an arrow can be shot

Bow-window A curved bay window

Bracken A widespread, often weedy fern

Brain-wave Smart thinking

Brick A helpful, reliable person

Buffer A foolish old man

Bulwarks The part of a ship's sides that are above the upper deck

Buskins Laced boots that come halfway to the knee

"By Jove!" An exclamation of surprise; Jove was a Roman god

Cairn A mound of stones erected as a memorial or marker

Cambric Thin white material

Canny Careful and shrewd

Canter A horse's gait between a trot and a gallop

Cantrip A magic spell; a witch's trick

Caraways Confections made from the fruit of the caraway plant

Carbuncle A red precious stone

Carrack A sturdy ship similar to a cog but with two masts, circa 1400 A.D.

Carrion Dead or decaying flesh

Cataract A great downpour or waterfall

Caterwaul To cry or screech like a cat

Centaur A mythical being that is half man and half horse

Chafe Annoy or irritate

Chamber A room in a house or castle, especially a bedroom

Chamberlain The head steward who manages a noble or royal household

Chap A man or boy

Chaplet A wreath or garland for the head

Charwoman A cleaning lady

Cheek *Noun*: Rudeness or back talk; *Verb*: Sass or back talk; *Adjective*: Rude, impolite

Chide Scold

Chivalry Ideal qualities such as bravery, courtesy, honor, and gallantry toward women

Churl A rude person

Circumspection Careful thinking

Cistern A hot water tank

Cob A short-legged, stocky horse

Cock-a-leekie A soup made with chicken broth and leeks

Cockney A person from London's East End

Cock-shies A throwing contest

Cog A sturdy single-masted ship, circa A.D. 1200

Coil A disturbance; a fuss

Coiner Someone who makes counterfeit (fake) coins

Colonnade A row of pillars

Come up to scratch Measure up

Comfit A piece of fruit, a seed, or a nut coated with sugar

Conjunction A meeting or passing of two or more celestial bodies in the same degree of the zodiac

Consorts Companions or partners

Constancy Holding firm without wavering or changing one's mind

Copse Woods, thicket

Coracle A small, rounded boat

Cordial A healing liquid

Coronet A small crown worn by princes and princesses

Corporal punishment Spanking

Counterpane A bedspread

Courtier An attendant at a royal court

Cove British slang for man

Crew Kind or type

Cricket An outdoor game played by two teams of eleven players each using bats, a ball, and two goals called wickets

Cricket pitch The field where you play cricket

Curvet A light leap by a horse, in which both hind legs leave the ground just before the forelegs are set down

Cutting A place where train tracks cut into a hillside

Dais A raised platform

Dandified Exhibiting extreme elegance in dress and manner

Dandled Bounced (as a baby on a knee)

Dastard A sneaking, malicious coward

Deck The platform that runs from one side of the ship to the other

Deucedly Devilishly, crazily

Device A graphic symbol or motto, especially in heraldry

Doddering Wobbly

Dog-fox A male fox

Dossier A collection of papers giving detailed information about a particular person or subject

Dotard Someone whose age has impaired his intellect

Dotty Mentally unbalanced; crazy

Double the cape To go round the cape in a boat or ship

"Drat!" An exclamation of annoyance

Draw lots To decide by picking straws or throwing dice

Dromond A medieval sailing galley

Dryad A mythical spirit of forests and trees; a wood nymph

Dumb Unable to talk

Efreets Demons or monsters of Mohammedan mythology

Eggs in moonshine Foolishness

Ejaculation A sudden, short exclamation

Electric torch Flashlight

Enmity Hatred; ill will

Entrenchments Earthen trenches meant to shield warriors in battle

Estre The interior of a building

Ettins Evil, vicious giants who worked for the White Witch

Fall foul To clash or have conflict with

Fall to Begin an activity energetically

"Faugh!" An exclamation of disgust

Faun A creature from Roman mythology with a man's body, horns, pointed ears, and a goat's tail

Fell Capable of destroying; lethal

Felled Cut down

Fetlock A knob and tuft of hair on the back of a horse's leg just above the hoof

"Fie" Used to express distaste or disapproval

Fief Piece of land

Fighting-top A platform on a ship near the top of the mast where archers can be posted

Firkin About nine gallons

Fjord A long, narrow, deep inlet of the sea between steep slopes

Flagon Pitcher

Fool A cold dessert made of fruit and cream

Forbear To hold back or resist

Fore Toward the front (bow) of a ship

Foreboding A sense of impending evil or misfortune

Forecastle or fo'csle The raised decking at the bow of a ship, often with cabins below for the crew

Forlorn Hopeless

"For nuts" Slang for "at all" or "no matter what"; similar to "worth beans"

Fortnight A period of fourteen days; two weeks

Fray A scuffle; a brawl

Frock-coat A man's dress coat with knee-length skirts

Frowsty Stale smelling or slovenly in appearance

Frowsy Having an unpleasant smell; musty

Funk To shrink in fright from doing something

Furlong 220 yards (201 meters)

Fusty Smelling of mildew or decay; musty

Galleon A large war or merchant ship with two to three masts, circa A.D. 1500

Galley A long, narrow ship that was powered by rowers, not sails, circa A.D. 100–1000; also a term for the cooking and eating area on board ship

"Garn!" An exclamation of disgust or aggravation

Garrison A military post

Gasometer A large, drum-shaped tank used as a storage container for fuel gas

Gassing Talking too much

Gauntlet A protective glove worn with medieval armor

"Get two dozen" Receive two dozen lashes or whippings

Ghoul A mythical demon believed to plunder graves and feed on corpses

Gibbered Talked unintelligibly or foolishly

Girdle A belt or sash worn around the waist

Girt Equipped with

Girth The strap on a saddle that goes around the horse's belly like a belt

Give over Give up, abandon

Give you good language Speak to you respectfully

Given over Given up

Got the wind up Slang from 1915 meaning to become frightened

Grog Alcoholic liquor, especially rum diluted with water

Grousing Grumbling or complaining

Grub Food

Guffaw A hearty, boisterous burst of laughter

Gum boots High boots made of rubber

"Guns be blowed" An expression of surprise

Hag A witch

Halberd An axlike weapon

Half-sovereign, half-crown Coins formerly used in Great Britain

Hamadryad A wood nymph who lives only as long as the tree she lives in

Hansom A horse-drawn carriage

Hatches On a ship, openings in the deck with covers to keep water out; it's called "battening down the hatches" when you close them up because a storm is coming

Hauberk Defensive armor of woven metal

Haversack Knapsack

Head Headmaster, principal

Helm Handle that turns the rudder and steers the ship

Heraldry Family symbol displayed on a shield

Hols Holidays, school vacation

"Honor be blowed" Slang meaning honor should be disregarded

Horrors Evil creatures who attended Aslan's murder

Hovel A small, crude shelter

Hull The outer body of a ship; the part that floats in the water

"I pledge you" "I toast you"

Impeachment Accusation against

Impertinent Bold, without good manners

Incantations Words with magical power

Incubuses Demons

Indigence Poverty or need

Inexorable Unstoppable

Inquisitive Curious

Inspector A school official

Irrefutable Beyond question

Jabber Endless talking

Jackal A wild dog similar to a coyote

Jackanape A mischievous child

Jackdaw A bird in the crow family

Jawing A lot of talking

Jerkin A short, often sleeveless coat, usually of leather

Jest An object of ridicule; a laughingstock

Jibe A taunting remark

Jiggered Surprised

Jinn A demon

Jostled Pushed or elbowed

Joust To compete against other knights on horseback

Judicious Sensible

Keel The backbone of a ship running from bow to stern along the bottom of the hull

Kettledrums Large, barrel-shaped drums

Kinsman A male relative

Knight-errant A knight in search of adventures to prove his chivalry

Kraken A sea monster in Norwegian legend

Laburnum Flowering shrubs or trees having bright yellow flowers

Languid Lacking energy or vitality; weak

Lapsed Onetime; returned to wild ways

Larder A place, such as a pantry or cellar, where food is stored

Leads A flat roof covered with sheets of lead

League A unit of distance equal to 3 miles or 4.8 kilometers

Lessoned Instructed or taught

Lie off Drop sails and wait near a particular place

Liege Lord

Lily-livered Cowardly; timid

Lineage Ancestry

Lintel Crosspiece at the top of a doorway

Listing Leaning over or to one side

Lists A place of combat; an arena for jousting tournaments or other contests

Litter A canopied couch carried by men on foot

Lodge a disposition Sue you in court

Loquacity Wordiness

Made on Moved forward

Maenad In Greek mythology a female follower of Dionysus

Mail shirt Flexible armor made of metal rings, chain, or scales

Malapert Disrespectful

Maleficence Harm, evil

Manikin A little man

Mantle A loose, sleeveless coat; cloak

March A border region used for defense

Marks Grades

Marshal of the lists A military referee who kept things organized and enforced the rules

Mast The vertical pole that supports sails and rigging on a ship

Masters Teachers

Masthead The top of a mast

Mate A deck officer on a ship

Mattock A hoe

Maxim A wise saying

Maying Going on a spring outing

Mazer A large drinking bowl or goblet made of metal or hardwood

Mead An alcoholic drink made from honey

Mettle Courage

Minaret A tower with a round top

Minions Lowly and powerless followers

Minotaur A mythical monster who was half man and half bull

Miscreant An evildoer; a villain

Moat A water-filled trench around a castle

Moke Slang for donkey

Morsel Bit of food

Moulder To crumble or turn to dust by natural decay

Mouldy Moldy

Moved Requested

Muck sweat A great amount of sweat

Muffed Botched; bungled

Mutton The flesh of fully grown sheep

"My hat, what a picnic" An exclamation of surprise over an unexpected event

Naiads Water-nymphs, offspring of the god who arose from Narnia's river; AKA the well-women

Nymph A mythical maiden who lives in nature

Oasis A place in the desert with water

Odious Hateful

Ogre A mythical giant or monster that eats humans

"Oh, dry up!" "Stop talking!"

"Oh, Lor!" Short for "Oh, Lord!"

Order-mark A demerit or penalty

Orknies & Wooses Only C. S. Lewis knows, but they don't sound nice

Out of countenance Not confident; embarrassed

Over-awed Intimidated

Overhauled Caught up with

Pajock Fool

Pannier A basket with carrying straps

Parley *Verb*: To have a discussion, especially with an enemy; *Noun*: A discussion, especially with an enemy

Parliament A gathering of leaders who make decisions

Pasty A meat-filled pastry

Pat Completely, exactly, or perfectly

Pavilion A large and often sumptuous tent

Pax Slang for calling a truce or making peace

Pay you all out Get you back

Pelt To move at a rapid pace

Peppery Sharp-tempered

Pert Sassy or bold; overly self-confident

Pewit A small, black-headed European gull

Physic Medicine

Pike A long spear

Pillar box A letter box

Pincers A tool with jaws for grasping

Pitch Motion of a boat's ends up and down, bow up/stern down, then bow down/ stern up

Plaguey Bothersome

Plato A Greek philosopher

Playbox A box for a child's toys and personal things (especially at a boarding school)

Pleasantry A humorous remark or act

Pluck Courage and determination

Poky Small and cramped

Poltroon A coward

Poltroonery Great cowardice

Pomely A dappled (spotted) horse

Poop deck The raised decking at the stern of a ship, often with cabins below for the captain

Port Left side of a ship when you're facing forward

Portcullis Protective iron bars

Postern A small rear gate

Pother A state of nervous activity; a fuss

Pound British unit of money

Precipice A steep drop-off

Pretty kettle of fish An awkward or alarming situation

Prig A conceited, annoying person

Prognostic A prediction about a future event

Prow The forward part of a ship's hull; the bow

Pump, bilge pump What you use to empty water that has leaked into a ship

Punt A boat you push with a pole

Puttees Strips of cloth wound around the legs to form leggings

Quay A wharf or reinforced bank where ships are loaded or unloaded

Queue A line of waiting people or vehicles

Quoit A flat metal ring used in a throwing game like horseshoes

Rampart A defensive fortification consisting of an embankment

Rapier A long, slender, two-edged sword

Raucous Rough-sounding and harsh

Reasons of State Politics

Reef A ridge of rock or coral just under the surface

Rigging Ropes (lines) that secure spars and sails

Rigmarole A set of confused and meaningless statements

Rive To split

Rook A bird that resembles the North American crow

Row Quarrel

Rowan An ash tree

Rugger Rugby, a game similar to football

Rum Strange or unusual

A rum go A surprising event

Rush A rapid flow or surge of water

Rushes Stiff marsh plants

Saccharine tablet A pill the size of an aspirin

Sagacious Wise

Sail A large piece of fabric that catches the wind and moves the ship forward

Salt-cellar A small dish for holding and dispensing salt

Sapient Having great wisdom and discernment

Satyr A creature from Greek mythology with a man's body, horns, pointed ears, and a goat's tail

Sauce Boldly offensive speech or behavior

Scimitar A curved sword

Score Twenty

Scullery A small room adjoining a kitchen, in which dishwashing and other kitchen chores are done

Scullion A kitchen helper

Scurvy Mean or contemptible

Seneschal The chief steward or butler of a great household

Sentinel Guard

Sentry A watch guard

Sepulcher A burial vault

Shamming Pretending

"Sharp's the word" Quickly!

Shoals Areas of shallow water

Showing the white feather Slang for acting like a coward

Shrine A place to worship a sacred thing or person

Silvan One that lives in or frequents the woods

Skirl To produce a high, shrill, wailing tone (think bagpipes)

Skulked Lurked, prowled

Slanging To use angry and abusive language

Sloth Laziness

Smite To attack or damage by hitting

Smith-craft The art of forging metals into a desired shape

Smithied Made from metal

Smithy A workplace where metal is worked by heating and hammering

Smote Rebuked or chastened

Snipe A marsh bird

"So keep your hair on" "Stay calm"

Sortie An armed attack, especially one made from a place surrounded by enemy forces

Spar A strong pole that supports sails or rigging

Specter Ghost

Spirits An alcoholic beverage, especially distilled liquor

Sprites Elves or goblins

Square Fair and just

Squib A small firecracker

Stand In nautical terms, to take or hold a particular course or direction

Starboard Right side of a ship when you're facing forward

Stern Rear end of a ship; astern is toward the stern

Stoup A beverage container; a mug

"Stow it, Guv'nor" Slang for "Shut up, fellow!"

Strait Affording little space or room; confined

Stratagem A clever or deceptive plan; a scheme

"Strike me pink" An exclamation of great surprise

Sucks An offensive experience

Swank Pretending to be brave

Taking on Showing emotion

"Tally-ho! Tantivy!" Slang for "Let's go!"

Tapir A chiefly nocturnal mammal with a heavy body, short legs, and a long, fleshy, flexible upper lip

Theorbo A seventeenth-century stringed instrument

Thrush A migratory songbird noted for a clear, melodious song

Tick An annoying bug that sucks blood

Tig A game among children

Tiller Handle that turns the rudder and steers the ship

Tilt To charge an opponent; attack

Tinder-box A box of flammable contents used to kindle a fire

Tinker A traveling mender of metal household utensils

Trams Streetcars

Tribute Taxes

Trice An instant

Trifle A cake soaked in sherry or brandy

Trippers Tourists

Truant Playing hooky; missing

"Turn and turn about" "Let's take equal turns"

Turret A small tower extending above a building

Tussock A clump of growing grass

Twopence A British coin worth two pennies

An ugly furrow to plow An unpleasant job

Uncover Bare the head in respect

Usurper One who seizes another's place, authority, or possession wrongfully

Venison Deer meat

Vermilions Vivid red colors

Vermin A person considered loathsome or highly offensive

Victuals Food

Vixen A female fox

The War of the Roses A thirty-year-long civil war in England.

'Ware Short for beware

Water-butt A large, open-headed container for water

Wheedling To urge through teasing or flattery; insincere

Whipcord A strong twisted or braided cord sometimes used in making whips

Wireless A radio

Wolds Unforested rolling plains

Wraiths Spirits that can be seen

Yard The spar that hangs from the mast and supports the top of a sail

Yeomanry A cavalry force that became part of the British Territorial Army

"You make very free" You make a big claim

Index of Characters & Creatures

(And Creatures Who Are Characters!)

Alberta Scrubb

Mother of Eustace; a subscriber to modern trends who was a vegetarian, refused alcohol and cigarettes, and barely furnished her house (*Voyage*)

Albatross

Unnamed bird who spoke to Lucy with Aslan's voice and led the *Dawn Treader* out of the terrifying blackness of the Dark Island (*Voyage*)

Adela Pennyfather

One of the nasty bullying gang at Experiment House, the school Jill Pole and Eustace Scrubb attended (*Silver Chair*)

Ahoshta Tarkaan

Man to whom Aravis was unhappily betrothed; toadying Grand Vizier of Tashbaan (*Horse*)

Alambil

The Lady of Peace planet in Narnia's night sky (*Prince Caspian*)

Alimash

Captain of the chariots in a battle in Calormen; cousin to Aravis (*Horse*)

Andrew Ketterley

A dangerously ambitious but uninformed magician; self-important, but stupid; brother to Letitia, whose money he'd squandered (*Magician*)

Anne Featherstone

Nasty schoolmate whose conversation Lucy heard via a spell (*Voyage*)

Anradin

Red-bearded Tarkaan lord who purchased Shasta from his guardian, Arsheesh, in Calormen; Bree's former master (*Horse*)

Aravir

The morning star of Narnia (*Prince Caspian*)

Aravis Tarkheena

Young Calormene noblewoman "as true as steel"; later married Corin (Shasta) and became Queen of Archenland; mother of Ram the Great (*Horse*)

Ardeeb Tisroc

Great-great-great-grandfather of Aravis (*Horse*)

Argoz

One of the seven noble lords driven from Narnia by evil King Miraz; rescued on the Island of the Star (*Voyage*)

Arlian

Telmarine lord under Caspian IX; executed for treason on a false charge under Miraz (*Prince Caspian*)

Arsheesh

A poor fisherman in Calormen; cruel guardian of Shasta (*Horse*)

Aslan

The enormous Lion creator/ruler of Narnia: "Nobody saw anything more terrible or beautiful"; AKA the Singer, the High King above all high kings, son of Emperor-beyond-the-Sea, Lord of the whole wood, the King of Beasts, the great Lion

Axartha Tarkaan

Grand Vizier of Tashbaan before Ahoshta (*Horse*)

Azaroth

A god of the Calormenes (*Horse*)

Azrooh

Calormene lord in the army of Prince Rabadash slain by King Lune (*Horse*)

Bacchus

Greek god of wine and celebration; AKA Bromios, Bassareus, the Ram (*Lion/Prince Caspian*)

Bannister

Student at Experiment House, the school Jill Pole and Eustace Scrubb attended (*Silver Chair*)

Bar

Embezzling lord dismissed by King Lune; kidnapper of Shasta (Prince Cor) (*Horse*)

Mr. and Mrs. Beaver

Talking beavers who sheltered and guided the Pevensie children as they sought Aslan's help against the White Witch (*Lion*)

Belisar

Great lord of King Caspian IX, killed by Miraz's men on a hunting party (*Prince Caspian*)

Bern

Lord driven from Narnia by evil King Miraz; made Duke of the Lone Islands by King Caspian (*Voyage*)

Betty

Servant to Professor Digory Kirke (*Magician*)

Black Dwarfs

One of three kinds of Dwarfs; skeptical and immovable; their hair and beard are "black, and thick and hard like horsehair" (*Prince Caspian*)

Boggles

Demonic spirits who witness Aslan's murder on the Stone Table (*Lion*)

Bree

A Talking Horse, once owned by a Tarkaan warrior; he encouraged Shasta to run away from his owner in Calormen (*Horse*)

Eleanor Blakiston

One of the nasty bullying gang at Experiment House, the school Jill Pole and Eustace Scrubb attended (*Silver Chair*)

Bricklethumb

One of the Red Dwarfs who befriended Shasta on his arrival in Narnia; brother to Rogin and Duffle (*Horse*)

Buffins

Giant family in Narnia (*Lion*)

Cabby

See *Frank I*

Calormenes

Inhabitants of Calormen; wore robes and turbans

Camillo

Talking hare in Narnia; subject of Caspian; joined in the great Council (*Prince Caspian*)

Carter

Student at Experiment House, the school Jill Pole and Eustace Scrubb attended (*Silver Chair*)

Caspian I

A Telmarine king who conquered Narnia and silenced the talking beasts (*Prince Caspian*)

Caspian VIII

Telmarine king of Narnia, father of Miraz and Caspian IX (*Prince Caspian*)

Caspian IX

Telmarine king of Narnia whom Miraz murdered (*Prince Caspian*)

Caspian X

Telmarine king of Narnia; delivered Old Narnia from his usurping Uncle Miraz; sailed east on the *Dawn Treader* to seek the seven noble lords; AKA Caspian the Seafarer (*Prince Caspian/Voyage/Silver Chair/Last Battle*)

Chervy

Glorious white stag who warned King Edmund and Queen Lucy of Rabadash's attack on Archenland (*Horse*)

Chief Voice

The Dufflepuds' leader, who told their story to Lucy and the others from the *Dawn Treader* (*Voyage*)

Chlamash

Calormene lord in the army of Prince Rabadash (*Horse*)

Cholmondely Major

Student at Experiment House, the school Jill Pole and Eustace Scrubb attended (*Silver Chair*)

Clipsie

Daughter of a Dufflepud (the Chief Voice); cast the spell that made the Monopods invisible (*Voyage*)

Clodsley Shovel

Talking Mole in Narnia who led Moles to the great Council (*Prince Caspian*)

Cloudbirth

A Centaur healer who healed Puddleglum's burnt foot (*Silver Chair*)

Coalblack

Prince Rilian's horse (*Silver Chair*)

Cole

Fighter for Archenland in battle between Prince Rabadash of Calormen and King Lune of Archenland; brother to Colin (*Horse*)

Colin

Fighter for Archenland in battle between Prince Rabadash of Calormen and King Lune of Archenland; brother to Cole (*Horse*)

Cor

See *Shasta*

Coriakin

The magician/retired Star who ruled the Dufflepuds as punishment for an unnamed failing (*Voyage*)

Corin

Prince of Archenland, son of King Lune, twin brother of Shasta; AKA Corin Thunder-Fist (*Horse/Silver Chair/Last Battle*)

Corradin

Calormene lord in army of Prince Rabadash slain by King Edmund (*Horse*)

Cruels

Evil spirits who attend Aslan's murder on the Stone Table (*Lion*)

Doctor Cornelius

Caspian's tutor; taught him secretly about Old Narnia; a half-Dwarf (*Prince Caspian*)

Dar

Lord in the court of King Lune of Archenland; fighter for Archenland with King Lune in battle against Prince Rabadash of Calormen; brother to Darrin (*Horse*)

Darrin

Lord in the court of King Lune of Archenland; fighter for Archenland with King Lune in battle against Prince Rabadash of Calormen; brother to Dar (*Horse*)

Daughter of Eve

Aslan's term for female humans in Narnia; only humans could rightly rule Narnia (*Magician*)

Daughter of Ramandu

A beautiful, mysterious, unnamed young woman on Ramandu's Island; married Caspian X; mother to Prince Rilian; killed by the Queen of Underland (*Voyage/Silver Chair/Last Battle*)

Destrier

Caspian's traitorous horse (*Prince Caspian*)

Diggle

One of the rebel Dwarfs who refused to believe in or enter Aslan's country (*Last Battle*)

Digory Kirke

Nephew of Magician Andrew Ketterley; rescued Polly from being stranded in the Wood between the Worlds; woke Jadis by ringing a bell in Charn; witnessed the creation of Narnia; planted the Tree of protection; later became a professor through whose wardrobe the four Pevensie children came and went from Narnia (*Magician/Voyage/Last Battle*)

D.L.F.

Edmund's abbreviated nickname for Trumpkin, meaning "Dear Little Friend" (*Prince Caspian*)

Dragon

Unnamed creature that was sick and died soon after Eustace discovered it (*Voyage*)

Drinian

Captain of the *Dawn Treader* and a lord of Narnia; friend and servant to King Caspian and Prince Rilian (*Voyage/Silver Chair*)

Dryads

Mythical spirit of forests and trees; wood nymphs

Duffle

One of the Red Dwarfs who befriended Shasta on his arrival in Narnia; sent Chervy the Stag to Cair Paravel with news of Rabadash's coming attack on Anvard; brother to Rogin and Bricklethumb (*Horse*)

Dufflepuds

One-legged Dwarflike creatures, not bright but enthusiastic, who lived under Coriakin's rule and were invisible for a time; AKA Monopods (*Voyage*)

Dumb Beasts

The animals whom Aslan decided would not speak in Narnia (*Magician*)

Dumnus

A Faun who fought for Caspian in the War of Deliverance (*Prince Caspian*)

Dwarfs

Short, stocky, hardy humanlike folk who often dwell in caves or underground; skilled archers and metal workers; AKA sons of Earth

Earthmen

Variously shaped gnomes enslaved in Underland by the Queen; originally from Bism (*Silver Chair*)

Edith Jackle

A hanger-on of the nasty bullying gang at Experiment House, the school Jill Pole and Eustace Scrubb attended (*Silver Chair*)

Edith Winterblott
Student at Experiment House, the school Jill Pole and Eustace Scrubb attended (*Silver Chair*)

Edmund Pevensie
Second-youngest of the Pevensie children; betrayed his siblings to the White Witch; later redeemed by Aslan's sacrifice; fought to defend Anvard against Prince Rabadash; helped overturn Miraz and install Caspian X as rightful King of Narnia; journeyed with Caspian X on his eastward voyage aboard the *Dawn Treader*; AKA King Edmund the Just (*Lion/Horse/Prince Caspian/Voyage/Last Battle*)

Efreets
Demonic spirits under the rule of the White Witch (*Lion*)

Emeth
Brave young Calormene who first served Tash, then Aslan (*Last Battle*)

Emperor-beyond-the-Sea
Father of Aslan, symbol of God the Father

Erimon
Telmarine lord under Caspian IX; executed for treason on a false charge under Miraz (*Prince Caspian*)

Erlian
King of Narnia; father to Tirian, the last king (*Last Battle*)

Ettins
Evil, vicious giants who worked for the White Witch (*Lion*)

Eustace Clarence Scrubb
Cousin of the Pevensie children; journeyed with Caspian X on his eastward voyage aboard the *Dawn Treader*; restored from a dragon to a human by Aslan on Dragon Island; together with Jill Pole and Puddleglum the Marsh-wiggle rescued Prince Rilian from the Queen of Underland; fought alongside King Tirian in the Last Battle (*Voyage/Silver Chair/Last Battle*)

Farsight
Eagle who carried news of Cair Paravel's capture and Roonwit's death to King Tirian; fought in the Last Battle alongside Tirian (*Last Battle*)

Father Christmas
Large, red-robed man who marked the end of the Hundred Years of Winter by distributing presents: "He was so big, and so glad, and so real." (*Lion*)

Father Time
Larger than any giant, "noble and beautiful," he had been a king in Overland but lay asleep in the Deep Realm until the end of Narnia (*Silver Chair/Last Battle*)

Fauns

Creatures from Roman mythology with a man's body, horns, pointed ears, and a goat's tail (*Magician*)

Fenris Ulf

See *Maugrim*

Five Black Dwarfs

Dwarfs who fought for Caspian in the War of Deliverance (*Prince Caspian*)

Fledge

The Narnia name of Strawberry, the London horse Aslan transformed into a flying horse (*Magician/Last Battle*)

Frank I

The former London cabby who became the first king of Narnia (*Magician/Last Battle*)

Gale

Ninth king of Narnia, killer of the dragon of the Lone Islands (*Last Battle*)

Garrett Twins

"Loathsome" students at the Experiment House, the school Jill Pole and Eustace Scrubb attended (*Silver Chair*)

Ghouls

Mythical demons believed to plunder graves and feed on corpses; many served the White Witch (*Lion/Horse*)

Giants

Tall Narnian creatures, both good (Rumblebuffin) and bad (the giants of Harfang)

Ginger

An evil, apricot-colored tomcat who was struck dumb when he encountered Tash in the last days of Narnia (*Last Battle*)

Girbius

A Faun who fought for Caspian in the War of Deliverance (*Prince Caspian*)

Glenstorm

Yellow-bearded Centaur with three sons; "a prophet and a star-gazer"; subject of Caspian; advocated war against Miraz and joined in the great Council (*Prince Caspian/Last Battle*)

Glimfeather

Mighty white Owl who aided Jill and Eustace and suggested Puddleglum guide them to the Ruined City (*Silver Chair/Last Battle*)

Glozelle

Ambitious Telmarine lord who first served, then killed, King Miraz (*Prince Caspian*)

Golg

Earthman captured by Puddleglum, Eustace, Jill, and Rilian as they escaped Underland (*Silver Chair*)

Green Witch

See *Queen of Underland*

Griffle

Black Dwarf who led Dwarfs in revolt against both Tash and Aslan at Stable Hill (*Last Battle*)

Gumpas

The sputtering, ineffectual governer of the Lone Islands (*Voyage*)

Gwendolen

Little girl in Beruna who chose to stay with Aslan when her teacher and schoolmates fled (*Prince Caspian*)

Hag

Hideous, aged witches who served the White Witch by helping to tie Aslan to the Stone Table; later one Hag served as accomplice to Nikabrik in a plot to call up the White Witch (*Lion/Prince Caspian*)

Hamadryads

A wood nymph who lives only as long as the tree she lives in (*Magician/Prince Caspian*)

Hardbiters

Three badgers who attended Caspian's great Council, where he planned the War of Deliverance (*Prince Caspian*)

Harold Scrubb

Father of Eustace; lived in Cambridge (*Voyage*)

Harpha Tarkaan

Father of Emeth, Calormene in Aslan's country (*Last Battle*)

Helen

Wife of the cabby, Frank, of London; the first queen of Narnia; mother to kings of Narnia and Archenland (*Magician/Last Battle*)

Hermit of the Southern March

A wise and elderly (109 years old) man who lived on the southernmost border of Archenland; had a magic pool; treated Aravis's ten scratches from Aslan (*Horse*)

Hogglestock

A Talking hedgehog; subject of Caspian; joined in the great Council (*Prince Caspian*)

Horrors

Evil creatures who attended Aslan's murder (*Lion*)

Hwin

Talking mare, a former slave of Calormen who accompanied Aravis in her escape from Calormen to Narnia (*Horse*)

Ilgamuth

Calormene lord in the army of Prince Rabadash; had a "twisted lip" (*Horse*)

Ilsombreh Tisroc

King of Calormen; great-great-grandfather of Aravis (*Horse*)

Incubuses

Demons who attended Aslan's murder (*Lion*)

Ivy

Servant to Professor Digory Kirke (*Lion*)

Jackdaw

Small bird related to crows; source of the "first joke" in Narnia (*Magician*)

Jadis

The seven-foot-tall, dazzlingly beautiful, evil empress of Charn; followed Digory and Polly into our world and then into Narnia, where she was the first evil in that world; stole and ate a magic apple that gave her endless life; AKA the White Witch, the White Lady (*Magician/Lion/Prince Caspian*)

Jewel

Beloved Unicorn with a white body and blue horn; best friend of Tirian, the last king of Narnia; fought alongside Tirian in the Last Battle (*Last Battle*)

Jill Pole

Schoolmate of Eustace Scrubb; together with Eustace Scrubb and Puddleglum the Marsh-wiggle rescued Prince Rilian from the Queen of Underland; rescued Puzzle the donkey from Shift the Ape and so revealed the false Aslan; fought alongside King Tirian in the Last Battle (*Silver Chair/Last Battle*)

Kidrash Tarkaan

Lord of the province of Calavar who promised his daughter, Aravis, in marriage to Ahoshta Tarkaan (*Horse*)

King of Harfang

Grand-looking King of giants; had hands with "terrible pointed nails"; ate humans and Marsh-wiggles (*Silver Chair*)

Lady of the Green Kirtle

See *Queen of Underland*

Lapsed Bear of Stormness

Talking Bear turned wild who attacked those traveling by Stormness Head; reformed after a boxing match with Corin-Thunderfist (*Horse*)

Lasaraleen Tarkheena

Childhood friend of Aravis who aided in her escape from Calormen to Narnia; a flighty giggler (*Horse*)

Mrs. Lefay

Andrew Ketterley's godmother; said to have "fairy blood"; she gave a box of dust from the Wood between the Worlds to Andrew to burn after her death, which he failed to do (*Magician*)

Letitia (Letty) Ketterley

Sister to Andrew Ketterley and Mabel Kirke; a "very tough old lady" (*Magician*)

Lilith

First wife of Adam; a member of the (nonhuman) Jinn; ancestress of the White Witch (*Lion*)

Liln

Woman Olvin took as his bride after battle with the giant Pire (*Horse*)

Lilygloves

Chief Mole who helped plant the orchard at Cair Paravel (*Prince Caspian*)

Lucy Pevensie

The youngest of the four Pevensie children; the tender-hearted discoverer of the entrance to Narnia through the wardrobe; witnessed Aslan's death and resurrection at the Stone Table; rode with the archers to defend Anvard against Prince Rabadash; helped overturn Miraz and install Caspian X as rightful King of Narnia; journeyed with Caspian X on his eastward voyage aboard the *Dawn Treader*; sees Aslan more often than anyone; AKA Queen Lucy the Valiant (*Lion/Horse/Prince Caspian/Voyage/Last Battle*)

Lune

King of Archenland, father of Cor and Corin; "the jolliest, fattest, most apple-cheeked, twinkling-eyed king" (*Horse/Last Battle*)

Mabel Kirke

Sickly mother of Digory who was cured with an apple from the Tree of protection in Narnia; stayed with her brother and sister, Andrew and Letitia Ketterley, during her illness (*Magician*)

Mrs. Macready

Professor Digory Kirke's housekeeper (*Lion*)

Maenads

Female followers of Bacchus; "his fierce, madcap girls" (*Prince Caspian*)

Margaret

One of Professor Digory Kirke's three servants (*Lion*)

Marjorie Preston

Schoolmate and friend whose conversation Lucy heard via a spell (*Voyage*)

Marsh-wiggles

Tall, thin marsh-dwelling folk with green-gray hair and webbed hands and feet who ate eels, smoked strong tobacco, and maintained a generally morose disposition (*Silver Chair/Last Battle*)

Master Bowman

Unnamed crew member on the *Dawn Treader* who shot the Sea Serpent (*Voyage*)

Maugrim

Captain of the White Witch's secret police; an enormous gray wolf whom Peter slayed; AKA Fenris Ulf (*Lion*)

Mavramorn

One of the seven noble lords driven from Narnia by evil King Miraz; rescued on the Island of the Star (*Voyage*)

Mentius

A Faun who fought for Caspian in the War of Deliverance (*Prince Caspian*)

Mer-People

Sea creatures who swam close to shore and sang by Cair Paravel (*Lion/Prince Caspian/Voyage*)

Minotaurs

Massive men with bulls' heads; toadies of the White Witch (*Lion*)

Miraz

Usurping Telmarine "Lord Protector" of Narnia; uncle of Caspian X, the true king (*Prince Caspian*)

Moonwood

A legendary hare in ancient Narnia who had exquisite hearing (*Last Battle*)

Mullugutherum

Gnome in service of the Queen of Underland (*Silver Chair*)

Naiads

Water-nymphs, offspring of the god who arose from Narnia's river; AKA the well-women (*Magician/Lion/Prince Caspian*)

Nain

King of Archenland during Caspian's flight from Miraz (*Prince Caspian*)

Nancy

Wished-for woman mentioned by a sailor near the Dark Island (*Voyage*)

Nausus

A Faun who fought for Caspian in the War of Deliverance (*Prince Caspian*)

Nellie

See *Helen*

Neevil

A fictitious creature the Talking beasts searched for in early Narnia; they mistook Aslan's description of "an evil" that had landed in Narnia (*Magician*)

New Narnians

The Telmarines who ruled Old Narnia from Caspian I to Miraz; Caspian X restores Old Narnia

Nikabrik

Black Dwarf "soured by hate" who wanted to kill Caspian and call up the White Witch (*Prince Caspian*)

Nimienus

A Faun who fought for Caspian in the War of Deliverance (*Prince Caspian*)

Nurse

Unnamed, beloved caretaker of Caspian X; told him of Old Narnia; Aslan healed her from mortal illness (*Prince Caspian*)

Nymphs

Mythical maidens who live in nature
(*Magician/Lion*)

Obentius

A Faun who fought for Caspian in the War of
Deliverance (*Prince Caspian*)

Octesian

One of the seven noble lords driven from Narnia by
evil King Miraz; died on Dragon Island (*Voyage*)

Ogres

Mythical giants or monsters that eat humans; many
attended the murder of Aslan and one cut off his
mane (*Lion*)

Old Narnians

The creatures of Narnia Aslan created,
including talking and nontalking animals, Dwarfs,
and wild people

Old Raven of Ravenscaur

Raven who attended Caspian's great Council,
where he planned the War of Deliverance
(*Prince Caspian*)

Olvin

Archenland king who turned Pire the giant into
stone, thereby creating Mount Pire; married Lady
Liln (*Horse*)

Orknies

Dastardly creatures who attended Aslan's murder
at the Stone Table (*Lion*)

Orruns

Faun who fed Eustace and Jill breakfast the morning
after their escape from Underland (*Silver Chair*)

Oscuns

A faun who fought for Caspian in the War of
Deliverance (*Prince Caspian*)

Passarids

Telmarine lords who served under Caspian IX;
killed fighting giants under Miraz's orders
(*Prince Caspian*)

Pattertwig

A red squirrel; one of Caspian's subjects; took
news of the great Council to many other Old
Narnians and journeyed to Lantern Waste to meet
any help Aslan might send there (*Prince Caspian*)

Peepiceek

Mouse who served under Reepicheep and
succeeded him as head of the talking mice in
Narnia when he paddled to the End of the World
(*Prince Caspian*)

People of the Toadstools

Evil creatures the White Witch invited to Aslan's
murder at the Stone Table (*Lion*)

Peridan

Lord in the Narnian court at Cair Paravel under King Edmund and Queen Susan (*Horse*)

Mr. and Mrs. Pevensie

Parents of Peter, Susan, Edmund, and Lucy; Mr. Pevensie was a university lecturer; Mrs. Pevensie was sister to Alberta Scrubb; both parents died in a train accident (*Lion/Voyage/Last Battle*)

Peter Pevensie

The oldest of the Pevensie children; Aslan named him the High King of Narnia; fought against Miraz in single combat and helped install Caspian X as rightful King of Narnia; closed the Door when Narnia ended; AKA Sir Peter Wolf's-Bane, King Peter the Magnificent (*Lion/Prince Caspian/Last Battle*)

Phoenix

A mythological bird that was known to arise from ashes after burning itself to death; present with Digory in the garden and in Aslan's Country (*Magician/Last Battle*)

Pire

Giant whom Olvin turned into stone (*Horse*)

Pittencream

Sailor who hesitated to sail to the World's End; he was left on the Island of the Star during the *Dawn Treader's* voyage there (*Voyage*)

Poggin

The only Dwarf who left the unbelieving Dwarfs to join Tirian in the war for Narnia (*Last Battle*)

Polly Plummer

Friend of Digory Kirke; practical, loyal, and perceptive; the first human to experience the Wood between the Worlds; witnessed the creation of Narnia (*Magician/Last Battle*)

Pomona

A goddess, according to Roman mythology, of fruit trees and gardens; she put spells on the orchard outside Cair Paravel (*Prince Caspian*)

Miss Prizzle

Prickly teacher who fled from Aslan in Beruna (*Prince Caspian*)

Prunaprismia

Married to usurper Miraz; the birth of her son threatened Caspian X's existence (*Prince Caspian*)

Puddleglum

A Marsh-wiggle whose endless despair makes him the Eeyore of Narnia; led Jill Pole and Eustace Scrubb across Ettinsmoor to the ruined city of the ancient giants and together with them freed Prince Rilian from his enchantment (*Silver Chair*)

Pug

A thieving pirate who traded in slaves on the Lone Islands (*Voyage*)

Puzzle

Impressionable donkey whose failure to think for himself led to tyranny in the last days of Narnia (*Last Battle*)

Queen of Underland

Beautiful, evil Witch who killed Caspian's queen, kidnapped Prince Rilian, and plotted to rule Narnia using him as her puppet; could assume the shape of a great green serpent; AKA the Lady of the Green Kirtle, Queen of the Deep Realm, Queen of the Underworld (*Silver Chair*)

Rabadash

Prince of Tashbaan, son of the Tisroc; he wanted to capture/marry Queen Susan and conquer Narnia; a "proud, bloody, luxurious, cruel, and self-pleasing tyrant" whom Aslan turns into a donkey, AKA Rabadash the Ridiculous (*Horse*)

Ram

The son of Queen Aravis and King Cor; most famous of the Archenland kings; AKA Ram the Great (*Horse/Prince Caspian*)

Ramandu

The "retired" Star who ruled the Island of the Star (or World's End Island) (*Voyage*)

Ramandu's Daughter

See *Daughter of Ramandu.*

Red Dwarfs

Those Dwarfs with hair "rather like a Fox's" (*Lion/Prince Caspian*)

Reepicheep

A "gay and martial mouse"; "the most valiant of all the Talking Beasts"; the Chief Mouse who carried a sword and fought for Caspian in the war between the Telmarines and the Old Narnians; explorer of the World's End; always ready to fight for a good cause (*Prince Caspian/Voyage/Last Battle*)

Restimar

One of the seven noble lords driven from Narnia by evil King Miraz; died when the lake at Deathwater Island turned him to gold (*Voyage*)

Revilian

One of the seven noble lords driven from Narnia by evil King Miraz; rescued on Island of the Star (*Voyage*)

Rhince

First mate on the *Dawn Treader* (*Voyage*)

Rhindon

Peter's sword, a gift from Father Christmas, with which Peter killed Maugrim, the Wolf Captain of the White Witch's secret police (*Lion/Prince Caspian*)

Rhoop

One of the seven noble lords driven from Narnia by evil King Miraz; rescued from the Dark Island, where he had been driven nearly mad (*Voyage*)

Rilian

Son of Caspian X and the Daughter of Ramandu; abducted by the Queen of Underland after she killed his mother; after his escape, he ruled Narnia; AKA King Rilian the Disenchanted (*Silver Chair*)

Rishda Tarkaan

Calormene captain who allies with Shift and Ginger to try to conquer Narnia (*Last Battle*)

Rishti Tarkaan

Father of Kidrash Tarkaan, grandfather to Aravis (*Horse*)

River-god

One of the "wild people" of Narnia; rose from the Great River with his Naiad daughters; chained by the Bridge of Beruna which Bacchus destroyed under command of Aslan (*Magician/Prince Caspian*)

Robin

The bird who led the Pevensie children through the forest of Narnia to the Beaver (*Lion*)

Rogin

One of the Red Dwarfs who befriended Shasta when he arrived in Narnia; brother to Duffle and Bricklethumb (*Horse*)

Roonwit

Noble, yellow-bearded, star-reading Centaur who warned Tirian of a coming evil in Narnia; murdered by a Calormene (*Last Battle*)

Rumblebuffin

A kind giant who broke down the gates of the White Witch's castle after Aslan restored him from stone to living (*Lion*)

Rynelf

Brave, assertive sailor on the *Dawn Treader* who spoke in favor of sailing on from Ramandu's Island and against Caspian X's proposed exit to World's End (*Voyage*)

Salamanders of Bism

Dragonish creatures, small but witty and eloquent, existing in the fiery rivers of Bism (*Silver Chair*)

Sallowpad

Raven who counseled King Edmund and Queen Susan in Tashbaan (*Horse*)

Sarah

Housemaid to the Ketterleys of London (*Magician*)

Satyrs

Creature from Greek mythology with a man's body, horns, pointed ears, and a goat's tail (*Magician/Lion/Prince Caspian/Last Battle*)

Schoolmistress

Unnamed woman in unnamed town who taught mathematics to piggish boys; happily accepted Aslan's proposal that she come with him (*Prince Caspian*)

Sea People

A fierce underwater race, riders of large sea-horses, spotted in the Last Sea (*Voyage*)

Sea Serpent

Monstrous creature that ineffectively attacked the *Dawn Treader* in the Eastern Sea (*Voyage*)

Seven Brothers of the Shuddering Wood

Red Dwarfs who gave Caspian high-quality shirts, helmets, and swords; fought in the War of Deliverance (*Prince Caspian*)

Seven Friends of Narnia

Digory, Polly, Peter, Edmund, Lucy, Eustace, and Jill; Tirian called for their help when Narnia's freedom was threatened (*Last Battle*)

Seven Noble Lords

Telmarine lords loyal to King Caspian IX; dispatched by Miraz to explore the unknown Eastern Seas (*Prince Caspian/Voyage*)

Shar

Fighter for Archenland in battle between Prince Rabadash of Calormen and King Lune of Archenland (*Horse*)

Shasta

Ward of a poor, cruel fisherman in Calormen who escaped to seek Narnia; one of twin sons born to King Lune of Archenland; AKA Cor, brother to Corin (*Horse/Last Battle*)

Shift

Clever, ugly Ape who lived near Caldron Pool and who schemed to surreptitiously rule in the last days of Narnia (*Last Battle*)

Silenus

A fat old man who accompanied Bacchus, riding on a donkey (*Lion/Prince Caspian*)

Silvans

Those that live in or frequent the woods (*Magician/Prince Caspian*)

Slinkey

A fox who joined with the Calormenes in war against Narnia; killed by Eustace (*Last Battle*)

Snowflake

The Witch's horse in Underland (*Silver Chair*)

Son of Adam

Aslan's name for male humans in Narnia; only humans could rightly rule Narnia (*Magician*)

Sopespian

Ambitious, flattering, traitorous lord in the court of Miraz (*Prince Caspian*)

Spear-Head

The bright, guiding star in Narnia's night sky

Spectres

Horrifying ghosts who attended Aslan's murder at the Stone Table (*Lion*)

Spivvins

A boy Eustace defended against the bullies at Experiment House (*Silver Chair*)

"Spotty" Sorner

Student at Experiment House, the school Jill Pole and Eustace Scrubb attended (*Silver Chair*)

Sprites

Evil spirits who attended Aslan's murder at the Stone Table (*Lion*)

Stars

"Glittering people" who served Aslan (see *Coriakin* and *Ramandu*) and who fell from the sky to Aslan's Country at Narnia's final destruction (*Magician/ Lion/Voyage/Silver Chair/Last Battle*)

Stonefoot

A giant whom the Centaur Roonwit called to battle under Tirian during the last days of Narnia (*Last Battle*)

Strawberry

See *Fledge*

Susan Pevensie

Second-oldest of the Pevensie children; witnessed Aslan's death and resurrection at the Stone Table; wooed by Prince Rabadash; helped overturn Miraz and install Caspian X as rightful King of Narnia; by the time of the Last Battle, she had stopped being a friend of Narnia; AKA Queen Susan the Gentle (*Lion/Horse/Prince Caspian/Last Battle*)

Swanwhite

A Narnian queen of great beauty who lived before the Hundred Years of Winter created by the White Witch (*Last Battle*)

Tacks

Slave trader working for Pug on the Lone Islands (*Voyage*)

Talking Beasts

Those animals in Narnia to whom Aslan gave the ability to speak

Tarva

The Lord of Victory planet in Narnia's night sky (*Prince Caspian*)

Tash

A demonic god worshiped by Calormenes; a terrifying four-armed creature with the head of a vulture (*Horse/Last Battle*)

Tashlan

A name blending Tash and Aslan; the divine creature that Shift claimed occupied the shed on Stable Hill (*Last Battle*)

Telmarines

People from the land of Telmar, beyond the western mountains outside Narnia; descendants of pirates; the invaders who "silenced" the beasts, trees, and fountains and drove out the Fauns and Dwarfs (*Horse/Prince Caspian/Voyage*)

"Them"

The bullies of Experiment House, the school Jill Pole and Eustace Scrubb attended (*Silver Chair*)

Thornbut

Dwarf in the Narnian army charged with protecting Prince Corin and keeping him out of battle (*Horse*)

Three Bulgy Bears

Brown bears who honored Caspian as true king of Narnia over Miraz (*Prince Caspian*)

Three Sleepers

Three (Argoz, Revelian, Mavramorn) of the seven noble lords Miraz drove from Narnia; they fell into an enchanted sleep on the Island of the Star; rescued by Reepicheep's voyage to World's End (*Voyage*)

Tirian

The last king of Narnia, brave and faithful to Aslan although occasionally given to angry outbursts in which he acted rashly and destructively (*Last Battle*)

Tisroc

The title used by kings of Calormen (*Horse/Last Battle*)

Tom

A dead man mentioned by a sailor near the Dark Island (*Voyage*)

Tran

Fighter for Archenland in battle between Prince Rabadash of Calormen and King Lune of Archenland (*Horse*)

Tree-People

Trees which can on occasion take on a human form; silenced by the Telmarines, they woke to worship Aslan and then joined in the War of Deliverance against the Telmarines; AKA talking trees (*Magician/Prince Caspian/Last Battle*)

Trufflehunter

A kindly, loyal badger; one of the Old Narnians; friend and loyal subject to Caspian; fought in the War of Deliverance (*Prince Caspian/Voyage/ Last Battle*)

Trumpkin

Red Dwarf given to outrageous exclamations— "Lobsters and lollipops!" "Whistles and whirligigs!"—who was skeptical of Aslan until he met him face-to-face; friend and loyal subject to Caspian; fought in the War of Deliverance; acted as Regent in Caspian's absence; AKA the D.L.F. (Dear Little Friend) (*Prince Caspian/Voyage/ Silver Chair/Last Battle*)

Tumnus

A friendly, loyal Faun who refused to betray Lucy to the White Witch and became her dear friend (*Lion/Horse/Last Battle*)

Two Brothers of Beaversdam

Telmarine lords who ruled Beaversdam under Caspian IX; later imprisoned by Miraz (*Prince Caspian*)

Unicorns

Beautiful, fierce, graceful, horselike creatures having a single horn growing from the forehead (*Lion/Last Battle*)

Updwellers

Those who lived aboveground, over the Deep Realm; AKA Uplanders (*Silver Chair*)

Uplanders

Those who lived aboveground, over the Deep Realm; AKA Updwellers (*Silver Chair*)

Urnus

Faun who carried Trumpkin's ear trumpet (*Silver Chair*)

Uvilas

Great Telmarine lord under King Caspian IX; killed by Miraz's men on a hunting trip (*Prince Caspian*)

Voltinus

A Faun who fought for Caspian in the War of Deliverance (*Prince Caspian*)

Warden of the Marches of Underland

One of the Earthmen under the rule of the Queen of Underland (*Silver Chair*)

Water Rat

Talking Rat who mistakenly believed Aslan had commanded him to float a raft made of talking trees down the Great River to Calormen (*Last Battle*)

Voluns

A Faun who fought for Caspian in the War of Deliverance (*Prince Caspian*)

Wer-Wolves

Men who became wolves; they served the White Witch (*Lion/Prince Caspian*)

White Lady

See *White Witch*

White Stag

A creature whom many hunted because he granted wishes when caught (*Lion/Horse/Prince Caspian*)

White Witch

The evil Witch who ruled Narnia for one hundred years and made it always winter and never Christmas; turned her enemies into stone statues with her wand; tall, beautiful, and pale as snow; slew Aslan on the Stone Table; AKA Jadis, the White Lady (*Magician/Lion*)

Wimbleweather

A "small but genuine" giant from Deadman's Hill; brave but not bright; fought for Caspian in the War of Deliverance (*Prince Caspian*)

Wood People
Includes dryads, silvans, tree-people, hamadryads, and wood gods and goddesses (*Magician/Prince Caspian*)

Wooses
Evil spirits who attended Aslan's murder on the Stone Table (*Lion*)

Wraggle
Centaur who joined Calormenes in final war against Narnia; killed by Jill Pole (*Last Battle*)

Wraiths
Horrifying spirits who attended Aslan's murder on the Stone Table (*Lion*)

Zardeenah
Moon deity to whom Calormene maidens made sacrifices; AKA the Lady of the Night and of Maidens (*Horse*)

Index of Places in Narnia

Anvard

King Lune's castle in Archenland (*Horse*)

Archenland

Peaceful kingdom south of Narnia

Aslan's Country

The land beyond the End of the World; where no one fears, cries, or dies (*Voyage*)

Aslan's How

A huge mound Narnians raised over the Stone Table, where Aslan was slain by the White Witch (*Prince Caspian*)

Aslan's Table

A banquet table on Ramandu's Island on which a fresh feast was magically renewed each sundown (*Voyage*)

Avra

Third of the Lone Islands (*Voyage*)

Azim Balda

City of Calormen from which messengers of Tisroc rode to all parts of the empire (*Horse*)

Beaversdam

Dam built by Mr. Beaver, later a town (*Lion*)

Bernstead

Lord Bern's estate on the Lone Island of Avra (*Voyage*)

Beruna

Town in center of Narnia where the Great River and Rush River met; a center of trade (*Prince Caspian/Voyage*)

Beruna's Bridge

Bridge over the Fords of Beruna that served as chains for the river-god (*Prince Caspian/Silver Chair*)

Bism

The land a thousand fathoms beneath Underland; AKA the Really Deep Land (*Silver Chair*)

Black Woods

What the Telmarines called the Great Woods; said to be filled with ghosts (*Prince Caspian*)

Bramandin

One of the cities conquered by wicked Queen Jadis (*Magician*)

Brenn

Second of the Seven Isles which lie northeast of Narnia and northwest of the Lone Islands (*Voyage*)

Burnt Island

A low, green land where nothing but rabbits and goats lived; where Reepicheep found the coracle he used to sail to Aslan's country (*Voyage*)

Cair Paravel

Castle on the Eastern Sea from which reigned Kings Peter and Edmund and Queens Susan and Lucy

Calavar

Calormene province ruled by Kidrash Tarkaan (*Horse*)

Caldron Pool

The beginning of the Great River; a pool beneath cliffs at the western edge of Narnia (*Last Battle*)

Calormen

Southern empire separated from Archenland and Narnia by the Great Desert; a "great and cruel country" whose capital was Tashbaan (*Horse/Last Battle*)

Cambridge

Where Eustace Scrubb lived (*Voyage*)

Castle of the White Witch

Sits near the Great River; where the White Witch turned loyal Narnians to stone (*Lion*)

Castle Tormunt

City in eastern province of Calormen (*Horse*)

Charn

A dead city Polly Plummer and Digory Kirke discovered via the Wood between the Worlds; where they awakened Queen Jadis (the White Witch) (*Magician*)

Chippingford

City to which Shift sent Puzzle for food (*Last Battle*)

Dancing Lawn

Meeting and feasting place for Old Narnians before war between Caspian and Miraz (*Prince Caspian*)

Dark Island

A dark, horrifying land where one's worst nightmares came to pass; AKA the Island Where Dreams Come True (*Voyage*)

Deadman's Hill

Home of Wimbleweather the Giant (*Prince Caspian*)

Deep Realm

Underground land north of Ettinsmoor, where Earthmen worked under the rule of the Lady of the Green Kirtle; AKA Underland (*Silver Chair*)

Deathwater Island

Deadly island where Caspian and his companions found Lord Restimar at the bottom of a lake whose waters turned everything to gold (*Voyage*)

Doorn

The second nearest to Narnia and the most peopled of the Lone Islands; site of the islands' capital, Narrowhaven (*Voyage*)

Dragon Island

Discovered by Caspian X, this was where Eustace was turned into a dragon and Lord Octesian died (*Voyage*)

Ettinsmoor

The land south of the giants' Ruined City, north of the River Shribble and the marshes where Puddleglum lived (*Silver Chair/Last Battle*)

Experiment House

A coed school where children were allowed to do as they pleased; eventually Aslan cleaned house and made it a respectable place of learning (*Silver Chair*)

Felimath

Nearest to Narnia of the Lone Islands, contained only sheep and shepherds (*Voyage*)

Felinda

One of the cities conquered by wicked Queen Jadis (*Magician*)

Flaming Mountain of Langour

A beauteous, volcanic mountain in Calormen mentioned by Emeth (*Last Battle*)

Fords of Beruna

A broad, shallow area in the Great River where Peter and Edmund fought against the White Witch in the Battle of Beruna, and where the town of Beruna later grew up

Galma

Island in the Eastern Sea, where Lucy, Edmund, Susan, and Peter—and later Caspian and crew on the *Dawn Treader*—traveled (*Prince Caspian/ Voyage*)

Glasswater Creek

South of Cair Paravel, originated at the Hill of the Stone Table (*Prince Caspian/Horse*)

Goldwater Island

Where Lord Restimar of Narnia met his fate in a pool that turned everything to gold; later named Deathwater Island by Reepicheep (*Voyage*)

Great Desert

The arid land between Archenland on the north and Calormen on the south, which Shasta, Aravis, Bree, and Hwin crossed to reach Narnia (*Horse*)

Great River

Narnia's primary river, which flows eastward from Lantern Waste to Aslan's How to the Eastern Sea; site of river-god's imprisonment outside Beruna (*Silver Chair/Last Battle*)

Great Waterfall

Waterfall where the Great River flows into Narnia at the westernmost edge of the country

Great Woods

Forest that stretched from Eastern Sea to the Hill of the Stone Table; renamed the Black Woods by Telmarines who were afraid of the trees (*Prince Caspian*)

Harfang

The castle in the north where the evil human- and Marsh-wiggle-eating giants dwell (*Silver Chair*)

House of Coriakin

Gray, stone, two-story house where the Dufflepuds live (*Voyage*)

House of Professor Digory Kirke

A country house in the south of England, an intriguing home ripe for exploration when the Pevensie children visited it—and discovered a portal to Narnia (*Lion/Voyage/Last Battle*)

House of the Tisroc

A palace with many ornate gardens that stretched to the river's edge

Ilkeen

Site of Tarkaan palaces and a lake (*Horse*)

Island of the Monopods

See *Land of the Duffers, Island of Voices*

Island of the Star

Where Ramandu and his daughter lived along with three enchanted lords of Narnia; AKA World's End Island, Ramandu's Island (*Voyage/Silver Chair*)

Island of the Voices

The land where dwelled the Dufflepuds and their ruler, Coriakin (*Voyage*)

Island Where Dreams Come True

A dark, horrifying land where one's worst nightmares came to pass; AKA the Dark Island (*Voyage*)

Land of the Duffers

The estate of Coriakin and the Dufflepuds; AKA Island of the Voices (*Voyage*)

Land of Youth

The site west of Narnia where Digory retrieved an enchanted apple for Aslan (*Magician*)

Lantern Waste

The site in the Narnian forest where stood a lamp-post marking the western edge of Narnia (*Magician/Horse/Last Battle*)

Last Sea

The sea between Ramandu's Island and World's End, where Reepicheep took his leave of the *Dawn Treader;* AKA the Silver Sea (*Voyage*)

Lily Lake

See *Silver Sea*

Lone Islands

The islands Felimath, Avra, and Doorn, which lay east of Cair Paravel; Caspian and crew visited these on the *Dawn Treader*; also where elderly Caspian X sought Aslan (*Lion/Prince Caspian/ Voyage/Silver Chair/Last Battle*)

Mezreel

Calormene city where Aravis's friend Lasaraleen lived; boasts a lake and lush gardens (*Horse*)

Mount Pire

A mountain divided into two peaks at the top (*Horse*)

Muil

The westernmost island of the Seven Isles (*Voyage*)

Narnia

The magical land Aslan sang into being, which lay between Lantern Waste and the castle at Cair Paravel on the eastern sea (*Lion*)

Narrowhaven

City on the Lone Island Doorn, where Governor Gumpas reigned until Caspian declared Lord Bern a duke (*Voyage*)

Northern Frontier

Land of the northern giants (*Silver Chair*)

The Old Narnia

The actual land and creatures Aslan called into being; dragons and dinosaurs eradicated it at the end of time; AKA Shadowlands

Overland

The surface of the earth; AKA Overworld (*Silver Chair*)

Pugrahan

Salt mines in Calormen where Dwarfs and some animals were to serve as slaves (*Last Battle*)

Real Narnia

The everlasting and perfect Narnia on the other side of the Door, of which the other Narnia was only a shadow or a copy

Really Deep Land

The land a thousand fathoms beneath Underland; AKA Land of Bism (*Silver Chair*)

Redhaven

City on the isle of Brenn, where Caspian and crew traveled on the *Dawn Treader* (*Voyage/Horse*)

River Rush

Tributary that met the Great River at the Ford of Beruna (*Prince Caspian*)

River Shribble

A significant Narnian river that formed the boundary between Ettinsmoor and the marshes (*Silver Chair*)

Ruined City of the Ancient Giants

Located just outside Harfang in Ettinsmoor, a massive structure into which wandered Jill, Eustace, and Puddleglum (*Silver Chair*)

Seven Isles

Group of islands in the Eastern Sea visited by Lucy, Edmund, Susan, and Peter—and later Caspian and crew on the *Dawn Treader*; where elderly Caspian sought Aslan (*Prince Caspian/Voyage/Silver Chair*)

Shadowlands

Narnia and England when remembered from Aslan's country

Shallow Lands

The underground land ruled by the Lady of the Green Kirtle, AKA Underland (*Silver Chair*)

Shribble

River between the marshes and Ettinsmoor (*Silver Chair/Last Battle*)

Silver Sea

The end of the Last Sea; AKA Lily Lake (*Voyage*)

Somerset

Region of England where the soil is nearly pink (*Prince Caspian*)

Sorlis

One of the cities conquered by wicked Queen Jadis (*Magician*)

Spare Oom

What Mr. Tumnus misunderstood to be Lucy's home; should have been "spare room" (*Lion*)

Stable

A thatch-roofed structure where Shift claimed to house Aslan, then Tashlan (*Last Battle*)

Stable Hill

Site of the Stable, where Shift claimed to hold court with "Tashlan" (*Last Battle*)

Stormness Gap

The primary pass to Narnia from Archenland (*Horse*)

Stormness Head

Mountain between Narnia and Archenland that indicated storms coming with clouds (*Horse*)

Sunless Sea

The sea running in Underland (*Silver Chair*)

Tashbaan

The capital city of Calormen, where Tisroc the ruler lived; "one of the wonders of the world" (*Horse/Last Battle*)

Teebeth

Calormene city taken in a battle Bree fought in (*Horse*)

Tehishbaan

City in Calormen west of the desert; where Emeth lived (*Last Battle*)

Telmar

Land beyond the western mountains from which came the Telmarines, who silenced the Talking Animals and Trees and drove the kindly creatures from Narnia (*Prince Caspian*)

Terebinthia

Island east of Galma in the Eastern Sea visited by Lucy, Edmund, Susan, and Peter—and later Caspian and crew on the *Dawn Treader*, where elderly Caspian sought Aslan (*Prince Caspian/Voyage/Silver Chair*)

Tombs of the Ancient Kings

Meeting place for Shasta and Aravis north of Tashbaan, on the edge of the desert; said to be haunted (*Horse*)

Tumnus's Cave

A cave carved in reddish rock which housed a fire, two chairs, table, dresser, mantelpiece, a portrait of an old Faun, and a book called *Is Man a Myth?* (*Lion*)

Underland

The underground region north of Ettinsmoor, where Earthmen worked under the rule of the Lady of the Green Kirtle; AKA the Deep Realm (*Silver Chair*)

Valley of a Thousand Perfumes

A Calormene valley Aravis visited (*Horse*)

Western March

The boundary region of which Edmund was Count (*Prince Caspian*)

Western Wilds

An unsettled region in the western part of Narnia; a nontalking lion killed there served as Shift's tool of trickery against the Narnians (*Magician/Lion/Prince Caspian/Last Battle*)

White Witch's House

A small castle with many small towers: "They looked like huge dunces' caps or sorcerors' caps" (*Lion*)

Winding Arrow

River flowing east to west; formed the border of the Great Desert (*Horse*)

Wood Between the Worlds

A kind of stopping place between Earth and other lands, where Digory and Polly landed when they first used the magic rings; Digory called it "a *rich* place: as rich as plumcake" (*Magician*)

World's End

A flat, grassy plain that seemed to meet the sky, south of the Silver Sea (*Voyage*)

World's End Island

See *Island of the Star*

Zalindreh

Site of battle in Calormen at which Bree and Anradin made names for themselves (*Horse*)

INDEX OF BIBLE ALLUSIONS & PARALLELS

(All Scripture quotations are from the NIV unless otherwise indicated)

HOW TO USE THIS INDEX: The wealth of C. S. Lewis's biblical knowledge seems everywhere evident in the Chronicles, from the overarching ideas to the details. Still, Lewis didn't intend for his stories to be proof-texted or interpreted strictly as teaching allegories. He saw Narnia instead as a fantasy—a fairy tale, actually—that he hoped would prepare children to encounter Jesus Christ personally in later years while illustrating biblical truths now. The learned professor's stories are also packed with possible references to other cultural sources he esteemed besides the Bible—ancient Greek and Roman folklore, for example, and the mythology of the Celts and the Vikings. The list that follows is a compilation of some biblical allusions and parallels that the editors of *Roar!* and others have identified in the Chronicles. Use this index to enrich, but not limit, your literary experience.

THE MAGICIAN'S NEPHEW

Singing Stars

As Aslan sang Nothing into Narnia, the sky suddenly blazed with innumerable stars, which seemed to be singing triumphantly.

In Job 38, God spoke of Creation as a time when "the morning stars sang together and all the angels shouted for joy" (v. 7).

Two by Two

After creating the animals, Aslan went up to two at a time and touched them with his nose.

In Genesis, God instructed Noah to save two of each kind of animal to be the start of a new generation (6:19).

Breath of Life

When Aslan breathed on the animals, they were able to love, think, and speak.

Adam did not live, love, think, or speak until God "breathed into his nostrils the breath of life" (Genesis 2:7).

Creation

Aslan says, "Be walking trees. Be talking beasts. Be divine waters."

These echo God's "Let there be" statements in Genesis.

Animal Names

Aslan gave the first king and queen of Narnia the authority to name and rule over all of the land's creatures.

God gave Adam, the first man, the responsibility of naming all the creatures in Eden (Genesis 2:19–20).

Favoritism

Aslan wanted Narnia's king and queen to rule without partiality.

James forbade believers to practice favoritism (2:1).

Justice and Mercy

Aslan told the first monarchs of Narnia to "be just and merciful and brave. The blessing is upon you."

The prophet Micah told Israel, "What does the LORD require of you? To act justly and to love mercy" (6:8).

Justification

Aslan says, "Evil will come of that evil, but it is still a long way off, and I will see to it that the worst falls upon myself…. As Adam's race has done the harm, Adam's race shall help heal it."

Paul wrote, "Death came into the world because of what one man (Adam) did, and it is because of what this other man (Christ) has done that now there is the resurrection from the dead" (1 Corinthians 15:21, TLB).

Tears of Compassion

Digory learns that Aslan deeply shares his grief about his mother.

When Jesus saw Mary weeping, "he was deeply moved in spirit and troubled…[and] Jesus wept" (John 11:33, 35).

Only Ask

Fledge tells Digory that Aslan would have provided for their meals if he'd asked him to. Polly says, "Wouldn't he know without being asked?" And Fledge agrees, but adds, "I've a sort of idea he likes to be asked."

Jesus assured us, "Your Father knows what you need before you ask him" (Matthew 6:8). Matthew 7:7 says, "Ask and it will be given to you." And James put it bluntly: "You do not have, because you do not ask" (James 4:2).

First Temptation

Digory Kirke's first temptation in the new land of Narnia was to eat an apple from the tree in the center of the garden. Jadis promised him it was "the apple of youth, the apple of life…. Eat it, Boy…and you and I will both live for ever."

Eve's first temptation in the new earth was to eat fruit from the tree in the middle of the Garden of Eden. Satan promised her everlasting life (Genesis 3:4).

Well Done!

When Digory brings the apple, Aslan says, "Well done."

The master in Jesus' parable of the talents commends his servant, "Well done, good and faithful servant!" (Matthew 25:21).

Powerful Trees

Aslan's tree in the garden brings healing life.

Ezekiel wrote of heaven's trees: "Their fruit will serve for food and their leaves for healing" (Ezekiel 47:12).

The Lion, the Witch and the Wardrobe

Kingship

Aslan is "Lord of the whole wood."

Jesus is "King of kings and Lord of lords" (Revelation 19:16).

The Betrayer

Edmund betrayed his family as well as all of Narnia—and especially Aslan.

Judas betrayed his fellow disciples and especially Jesus.

Expectation and Joy at His Arrival

When Mrs. Beaver meets the children, she says, "To think that ever I should live to see this day!"

Luke recorded that Simeon responded similarly to the arrival of the infant Jesus: "Sovereign Lord, as you have promised, you now dismiss your servant in peace. For my eyes have seen your salvation" (Luke 2:29–30).

Giving of Gifts

Father Christmas gives the children gifts that are "tools not toys," which will enable them to do all Aslan requires of them.

The Holy Spirit bestows spiritual gifts so believers can do all that God calls them to do (1 Corinthians 12).

Blood Requirement

The White Witch said that the price of Narnia's freedom was blood. "[Aslan] knows that unless I have blood as the Law says, all Narnia will be overturned and perish in fire and water."

The price of humankind's freedom from sin is blood. "The law requires that nearly everything be cleansed with blood, and without the shedding of blood there is no forgiveness" (Hebrews 9:22).

The Savior's Loneliness

On the night before his execution, Aslan longed for the comfort of companionship. He said to Lucy and Susan, "I should be glad of company tonight…. I am sad and lonely."

On the night before His execution, Jesus drew away from the group to pray and clearly longed for companions and comfort. He took with him Peter, James, and John, telling them, "My soul is overwhelmed with sorrow to the point of death. Stay here and keep watch with me" (Matthew 26:38).

Mocking the Savior

Once Aslan was bound, his enemies "surged round…jeering at him."

Once Jesus was captive, the governor's soldiers gathered round "and mocked him. 'Hail, King of the Jews!' they said" (Matthew 27:29).

The Savior's Silence

As he was being prepared for execution, Aslan "made no noise, even when the enemies, straining and tugging, pulled the cords so tight that they cut into his flesh."

Jesus was also silent before His accusers. "When he was accused by the chief priests and the elders, he gave no answer…. Jesus made no reply, not even to a single charge" (Matthew 27:12, 14).

The Innocent Dies for the Sinner

Aslan explained the way of Narnia's "salvation": "When a willing victim who had committed no treachery was killed in a traitor's stead, the Table would crack and Death itself would start working backwards."

Jesus the Righteous died for the unrighteous. "For Christ died for sins once for all, the righteous for the unrighteous, to bring you to God" (1 Peter 3:18).

A Missing Body

When Lucy and Susan returned to the Stone Table, Aslan's body was gone.

When the women returned to Jesus' tomb to anoint His body, it was gone. "They found the stone rolled away from the tomb, but when they entered, they did not find the body of the Lord Jesus" (Luke 24:2–3).

Resurrection Spreads Life

The resurrected Aslan immediately traveled to the Witch's castle, where he restored life to those she had turned into stone.

Even as Jesus died, "the tombs broke open and the bodies of many holy people who had died were raised to life" (Matthew 27:52).

The Breath of Life

Aslan breathed on the stone lion and Dwarf to bring them back to life.

God brought the man made of dust, Adam, to life when He "breathed into his nostrils the breath of life, and the man became a living being" (Genesis 2:7).

Food for Thousands

On a hill, Aslan miraculously feeds an impossible number of creatures.

On a hill, Jesus fed more than five thousand people with just a bit of bread and fish (Matthew 14:15–21).

The Horse and His Boy

The Doubting Disciple

Aslan invited Bree, the "poor, proud frightened Horse" who doubted his existence, to "draw near…. Touch me. Smell me. Here are my paws, here is my tail, these are my whiskers. I am a true Beast."

Jesus invited Thomas, the insecure disciple who doubted Jesus' resurrection: "Put your finger here; see my hands. Reach out your hand and put it into my side. Stop doubting and believe" (John 20:27).

The Evil Ones Recognize Their Righteous Nemesis

" 'Demon! Demon! Demon!' shrieked the Prince. 'I know you. You are the foul fiend of Narnia. You are the enemy of the gods.' "

The demons in a possessed man recognized Jesus, saying, "What do you want with me, Jesus, Son of the Most High God?" (Mark 5:7); so did the jealous Jews, who called him "demon-possessed" (John 8:48, 52).

Justice Tempered by Mercy

Aslan decreed, "Justice shall be mixed with mercy."

James wrote, "Judgment without mercy will be shown to anyone who has not been merciful. Mercy triumphs over judgment!" (2:13).

Prince Caspian

Stones at Work

Trumpkin muses on the idea of natural things responding to events in a righteous manner: "Wouldn't it be even nicer if the stones started throwing themselves at old Miraz?"

When the Pharisees told Jesus to quiet His praising disciples, He responded, "I tell you, if they keep quiet, the stones will cry out" (Luke 19:40).

The Comfort of the Savior's Voice

When Aslan called Lucy, she "woke…with the feeling that the voice she liked best in the world had been calling her name."

Jesus said, "[My] sheep follow [me] because they know [my] voice…. My sheep listen to my voice; I know them, and they follow me" (John 10:4, 27).

The Sometimes Solitary Disciple

Aslan instructs Lucy that her obedience must not be conditioned on others' responses: "If they will not, then you at least must follow me alone."

Jesus said, "Anyone who loves his father or mother more than me is not worthy of me; anyone who loves his son or daughter more than me is not worthy of me; and anyone who does not take his cross and follow me is not worthy of me" (Matthew 10:37–38).

Watching the Savior

When others mocked her claims to have seen Aslan, "Lucy…[was] biting her lip and trying not to say all the things she thought of saying to Susan…. She forgot them when she fixed her eyes on Aslan."

The writer to the Hebrews recommended that in response to discouragement, "Let us fix our eyes on Jesus, the author and perfecter of our faith" (12:2).

A Horn of Help

Caspian uses Susan's horn to draw helpers to his cause.

"Praise be to the Lord…. He has raised up a horn of salvation for us…to rescue us from the hand of our enemies" (Luke 1:68–69, 74).

Radiant Faces

After Edmund encountered Aslan, "a kind of greatness" marked him.

Moses' encounter with God made his face so radiant, he had to wear a veil (Exodus 34:29–33). Christians today "reflect the Lord's glory" with unveiled faces. Now all believers, "with unveiled faces…reflect the Lord's glory" (2 Corinthians 3:18).

The Voyage of the Dawn Treader

Turning the Tables

Caspian responds to Gumpas's corrupt government by turning over his desk.

Jesus responded to corruption in the temple by turning over tables (Matthew 21:12–13).

What Doesn't Change

"Do you think I wouldn't obey my own rules?" says Aslan to Lucy.

Jesus said, "Do not think that I have come to abolish the Law or the Prophets; I have not come to abolish them but to fulfill them. I tell you the truth, until heaven and earth disappear, not the smallest letter, not the least stroke of a pen, will by any means disappear from the Law until everything is accomplished" (Matthew 5:17–18).

The Concept of Time

Aslan "call[s] all times soon."

Peter wrote, "With the Lord a day is like a thousand years, and a thousand years are like a day" (2 Peter 3:8).

Everlasting Symbols

The White Witch used the Stone Knife as a tool of death. Once Aslan rose from death, Narnians revered the Knife as a symbol of his sacrifice and triumph.

Jesus was tortured and killed on the cross. Since His resurrection, Christians treasure the cross as symbolic of His sacrifice and triumph.

Few Are Chosen

On the voyage to the World's End, Caspian doesn't ask for volunteers but announces he will choose from those he invites.

Jesus said in one of His parables, "Many are invited, but few are chosen" (Matthew 22:14).

The Burning Coal

On the Island of the Star, as Ramandu and his daughter sang, a bird flew to the Old Man carrying what looked like a "little live coal," something "too bright to look at": "And the bird laid it in the Old Man's mouth."

Isaiah wrote that when he "saw the Lord," he despaired of his sinfulness. Then a seraph flew to him and touched a "live coal" to Isaiah's mouth, thus purifying him (Isaiah 6:1, 7).

Breakfast with the Lamb

At the End of the World, Lucy, Edmund, and Eustace encounter "something so white on the green grass that even with their eagles' eyes they could hardly look at it. They came on and saw that it was a Lamb." In a "sweet milky voice," the Lamb bid them to "come and have breakfast." There they ate fish the Lamb had prepared for them. He then revealed himself as Aslan.

After Jesus' resurrection, He appeared to His disciples at a seashore, calling them to a breakfast of fish He prepared (John 21).

He Who Made Himself a Bridge

Aslan tells Lucy, Edmund, and Eustace that his country "lies across a river. But do not fear that, for I am the great Bridge Builder."

Jesus is "the way into the Most Holy Place," the "new and living way" to heaven (Hebrews 9:8; 10:20). When Thomas asked how he could get to where Jesus was going, Jesus declared Himself "the way and the truth and the life. No one comes to the Father except through me" (John 14:6).

THE SILVER CHAIR

Let the Thirsty Drink
Jill tells Aslan she is dying of thirst, and he invites her to drink from the stream.

And Jesus told the woman at the well, "If anyone is thirsty, let him come to me and drink" (John 7:37).

Repeating the Signs
Aslan instructs Jill to remember the signs by which he would guide her to Rilian this way: "Say them to yourself when you wake in the morning and when you lie down at night, and when you wake in the middle of the night."

When Moses instructed the Israelites to follow the Lord, they were to take His commands and "impress them on your children. Talk about them when you…lie down and when you get up" (Deuteronomy 6:7).

Who Chooses Whom
Aslan: "You would not have called to me unless I had been calling to you."

Jesus: "You did not choose me, but I chose you" (John 15:16).

The Word Works
Puddleglum reminds the children that Aslan's instructions "always work."

God says, "My word…will not return to me empty, but will accomplish what I desire and achieve the purpose for which I sent it" (Isaiah 55:11).

At the Name
Prince Rilian pleads with Jill and Eustace to free him from the Silver Chair, saying, "By the great Lion, by Aslan himself, I charge you."

Paul wrote that Jesus has "the name that is above every name, that at the name of Jesus every knee should bow" (Philippians 2:9–10).

In His Hands
Rilian asserts, "Aslan will be our good lord, whether he means us to live or die. And all's one, for that."

Paul asserted, "If we live, we live to the Lord; and if we die, we die to the Lord. So, whether we live or die, we belong to the Lord" (Romans 14:8).

Hand Yourself Over

Jill is encouraged during battle to "commend [herself] to the Lion."

"And when they had ordained them elders in every church, and had prayed with fasting, they commended them to the Lord, on whom they believed" (Acts 14:23, KJV).

Sin No More

After Aslan prompts Jill Pole to admit her failing, he responds, "Do so no more."

Jesus told the woman caught in adultery, "Go now and leave your life of sin" and the healed blind man, "Stop sinning or something worse may happen to you" (John 8:11; 5:14).

Temporary Anger

Aslan promises he will "not always be scolding."

David wrote in Psalms, "The LORD is compassionate and gracious, slow to anger, abounding in love. He will not always accuse, nor will he harbor his anger forever; he does not treat us as our sins deserve" (103:8–10).

Grieving Savior

When King Caspian dies, Aslan weeps "great lion-tears."

When Lazarus died, Jesus wept such tears that people exclaimed, "See how he loved him!" (John 11:35–36).

Not for Human Eyes

When they travel to Experiment House, Aslan tells Jill and Eustace that the students will see only his back.

God told Moses, "I will cause all my goodness to pass in front of you…. But…you cannot see my face, for no one can see me and live" (Exodus 33:19–20).

THE LAST BATTLE

Fearful Hearts

The Talking Beasts of Narnia begged Shift to approach Aslan for them: "You must always go in and speak to him for us. We daren't, we daren't."

The Israelites begged Moses to "speak to us yourself and we will listen. But do not have God speak to us or we will die" (Exodus 20:19).

Safe in His Arms

Tirian says to Jill, "Courage, child: we are all between the paws of the true Aslan."

Deuteronomy 33:27 says, "The eternal God is your refuge, and underneath are the everlasting arms."

Innocent of Blood

Rishda Tarkaan says of Emeth's decision to enter the stable, "Bear witness all that I am guiltless of this young fool's blood."

Pilate said something similar about Jesus: "I am innocent of this man's blood" (Matthew 27:24).

Water from a Rock

In the midst of heated battle, the children were revived by a trickle of water coming down a rock.

When the Israelites were thirsty in the desert, God gave them water from a rock (Numbers 20:11).

The Lion's Supper

When death seems near, Jewel says the battle "may be for us the door to Aslan's country and we shall sup at his table tonight."

The apostle John wrote, "Blessed are those who are invited to the wedding supper of the Lamb!" (Revelation 19:9). And Jesus told the thief next to Him, "Today you will be with me in paradise" (Luke 23:43).

Taking Sides

The Dwarfs insist that they will not support or join either side. "The Dwarfs are for the Dwarfs."

But there's no such thing as not taking sides in the battle between good and evil. Jesus pointed out, "He who is not with me is against me" (Matthew 12:30).

Goats and Sheep

At the end of Narnia, Aslan faces each creature and they go either through his Door on the right or aside to his left, past the Door.

Jesus said that at the judgment of humankind, He would separate the sheep (true believers) from the goats (the unrighteous); He would put the sheep on His right and the goats on His left (Matthew 25:31–33).

Signs of the End

At the end of Narnia, all the Stars fell from the sky, and the sun and moon turned red as they died.

At the end of the world, John wrote, the sun will turn "black like sackcloth" and the moon "blood red, and the stars in the sky [will fall] to earth" (Revelation 6:12–13).

The Savior's Appearance

When Emeth met Aslan, the "brightness of his eyes [were] like gold that is liquid in the furnace."

John wrote of Jesus, the Rider on the White Horse, "His eyes are like blazing fire" (Revelation 19:12).

Seek and You Shall Find

Aslan says, "For all find what they truly seek."

The writer to the Hebrews said that God "rewards those who earnestly seek him" (11:6). Jesus exhorted

His followers to "seek [my Father's] kingdom," that "he who seeks finds" (Luke 12:31; Matthew 7:8). Proverbs 11:27 says, "He who seeks good finds goodwill, but evil comes to him who searches for it."

Last Days and Judgment

The phony Aslan is like an anti-Christ; people spread untrue rumors about the Lion; Narnians are made slaves; wars come and creatures betray one another.

Jesus warned what events would herald His return and the end of the world: "Don't let anyone fool you. For many will come claiming to be the Messiah, and will lead many astray. When you hear of wars beginning, this does not signal my return; these must come, but the end is not yet. The nations and kingdoms of the earth will rise against each other…you will be tortured and killed and hated all over the world because you are mine, and many of you shall fall back into sin and betray and hate each other. And many false prophets will appear and lead many astray" (Matthew 24:4–11, TLB).

The Stable Door

The children travel through a Door into Aslan's Country.

Jesus said, "I am the door; if any one enters by me, he will be saved, and will go in and out and find pasture" (John 10:9, RSV).

Confirmation of His Coming

"The sky would have foretold [Aslan's coming]," asserts Roonwit.

"Surely the Sovereign LORD does nothing without revealing his plan to his servants the prophets" (Amos 3:7).

The Blood That Saves

Tirian remarked on "the good Lion by whose blood all Narnia was saved."

"For God was pleased to…reconcile to himself all things…by making peace through his blood, shed on the cross" (Colossians 1:19–20).

Rebel Restored

When Tirian delivers the Dwarfs from a hideous fate in the salt-mines, Poggin alone returns to acknowledge/follow Aslan.

Jesus healed ten men from leprosy, but only one returned to thank Him (Luke 17:15).

A Good Death

Roonwit says, "Noble death is a treasure which no one is too poor to buy."

Psalm 116:15 says, "Precious in the sight of the LORD is the death of his saints."

Persecuted for Faithfulness

Jewel is sentenced to die for refusing to acknowledge the false Aslan.

In the end times, all who refuse to worship the anti-Christ will be executed (Revelation 13:15).

A Fearful Result

Ginger is struck dumb for telling lies about Aslan.

Paul said to the lying Elymas, "Now the hand of the Lord is against you. You are going to be blind" (Acts 13:11).

Blind and Deaf by Choice

The Dwarfs refuse to believe they can leave the Stable and enter Aslan's country.

Jesus spoke of the Jews' refusal to see the Messiah in their midst: "Though seeing, they do not see; though hearing, they do not hear or understand. For this people's heart has become calloused.... Otherwise they might see with their eyes, hear with their ears, understand with their hearts and turn, and I would heal them" (Matthew 13:13, 15).

Peter Holds the Keys

Aslan tells Peter to close the Door into heaven. He does so and locks it with a golden key.

Jesus told Peter, "I will give you the keys of the kingdom of heaven" (Matthew 16:19).

Just a Hint

The old Narnia, Digory says, is only "a shadow or copy of the real Narnia."

Moses built a sanctuary that was "a copy and shadow of what is in heaven" (Hebrews 8:5).

Friends in a New Country

"Everyone you had ever heard of"—which means "the great heroes of Narnia"—appear in Aslan's country.

Hebrews refers to "a great cloud of witnesses" (12:1)—those who triumphed in the faith and who hope for us to do the same.

All the Answers to All the Questions

(for Part Two Plus the Narniac Final Exams)

Part 2

The Magician's Nephew

Chapter 2
KID TEST
1. rules
2. better
3. facts, want
4. hurt, animals

Chapter 3
NARNIAC ATTACK #1
1. c, 2. b, 3. c, 4. b, 5. a

Chapter 4
EAR EXAM
right

Chapter 7
EAR EXAM
a pearl necklace

KID TEST
h

Chapter 8
NARNIAC ATTACK #2
1. b, 2. a, 3. b, 4. c, 5. b

Chapter 11
KID TEST
1. kindly
2. justice
3. favorites
4. servants
5. evil
6. retreat
7. children, grandchildren

Chapter 13
KID TEST
the Witch

Chapter 14
LET'S TALK ABOUT IT
eyes

NARNIAC ATTACK #3
1. c, 2. a, 3. c, 4. c, 5. b, 6. c

Chapter 15
LET'S TALK ABOUT IT
sea, gold, floating

ONE-SENTENCE EDITION
Polly, Andrew, magic, Charn, bell, Jadis, horse, lion, animals, pet, apple, garden, tempts, apple, Digory, mother, Polly, rings, lesson

EAR EXAM
a Wardrobe

THE LION, THE WITCH AND THE WARDROBE

Chapter 3
NARNIAC ATTACK #4
1. b, 2. a, 3. c, 4. c, 5. a

Chapter 4
LET'S TALK ABOUT IT
dwarf, idiot

EAR EXAM
having lunch

Chapter 7
NARNIAC ATTACK #5
1. c, 2. c, 3. b, 4. c, 5. c

Chapter 8
LET'S TALK ABOUT IT
Lion, King, Lord, good, shakes

EAR EXAM
at the Stone Table

Chapter 11
NARNIAC ATTACK #6
1. b, 2. c, 3. a, 4. c

Chapter 13
KID TEST
4

Chapter 14
EAR EXAM
lay their hands on his mane

Chapter 16
LET'S TALK ABOUT IT
Silence, roarings, brayings, yelpings, barkings, squealings, cooings, neighings, stampings, shouts, hurrahs, songs, laughter.

EAR EXAM
Mr. Tumnus

Chapter 17
NARNIAC ATTACK #7
1. c, 2. b, 3. c, 4. c, 5. c

THE HORSE AND HIS BOY

Chapter 1
KID TEST
d. The four Pevensie children reign in Narnia at the same time. And while they are gone from England, almost no earth time passes at the Professor's house!

EAR EXAM
Breehy-hinny-brinny-hoohy-hah

Chapter 3
EAR EXAM
raiding

Chapter 4
NARNIAC ATTACK #8
1. a, 2. b, 3. c, 4. c, 5. b

Chapter 5

LET'S TALK ABOUT IT

Archenland, Lune, friend

Chapter 6

KID TEST

1. F, 2. T, 3. F, 4. T

Chapter 7

LET'S TALK ABOUT IT

death, burned, six weeks

LOOK IT UP

1. skilled

2. pure, gracious

3. truth

4. wise

Chapter 9

LET'S TALK ABOUT IT

trots, walks

NARNIAC ATTACK #9

1. b, 2. a, 3. a, 4. c, 5. c

EAR EXAM

the nightingale

Chapter 12

LET'S TALK ABOUT IT

Duffle, Rogin, Bricklethumb

KID TEST

1. neighbor

2. Breakfast

3. Lion

4. -body, -one, -thing

EAR EXAM

red, green

Chapter 15

NARNIAC ATTACK #10

1. c, 2. c, 3. b, 4. b, 5. c

PRINCE CASPIAN

Chapter 1

LET'S TALK ABOUT IT

seagull

KID TEST

2

EAR EXAM

yellowish-golden

Chapter 2

LET'S TALK ABOUT IT

Rhindon, Wolf

Chapter 4

LET'S TALK ABOUT IT

Man, dwarf

Chapter 5

NARNIAC ATTACK #11

1. b, 2. c, 3. a, 4. c, 5. b

EAR EXAM

seven

Chapter 6

LET'S TALK ABOUT IT

bigger, terrier, stop talking; watch, remember

Chapter 8

LET'S TALK ABOUT IT
Dear Little Friend

KID TEST
1. Lantern Waste
2. boat
3. Aslan's How

Chapter 9

KID TEST (*Dwarf Challenge #2*)
1. red, black, 2. four, 3. whiskers, 4. metal,
5. archers, 6. drums

EAR EXAM
Ship, Hammer, Leopard

Chapter 10

NARNIAC ATTACK #12
1. a, 2. b, 3. b, 4. c, 5. c

Chapter 12

EAR EXAM
the Hag

KID TEST
They're all False.

Chapter 13

KID TEST
Wimbleweather, Glenstorm, Bulgy Bear,
Reepicheep, afraid, noon, two hours after noon

Chapter 14

EAR EXAM
Miss Prizzle

Chapter 15

NARNIAC ATTACK #13
1. c, 2. b, 3. a, 4. a, 5. b

THE VOYAGE OF THE
DAWN TREADER

Chapter 2

EAR EXAM
three years

Chapter 5

NARNIAC ATTACK #14
1. c, 2. a, 3. b, 4. b, 5. b

EAR EXAM
the mast

Chapter 7

KID TEST
1. a, 2. c, 3. b, 4. b

EAR EXAM
Reepicheep

Chapter 9

NARNIAC ATTACK #15
1. c, 2. c, 3. a, 4. b, 5. c

Chapter 10

LOOK IT UP
Esther

EAR EXAM
Anne and Marjorie

Chapter 12

EAR EXAM

"Courage, dear heart."

Chapter 13

EAR EXAM

whether to return to Narnia, stay on the island, or sail on

Chapter 14

NARNIAC ATTACK #16

1. c, 2. a, 3. b, 4. b, 5. c

THE SILVER CHAIR

Chapter 4

KID TEST #1

1 and 3

KID TEST #2

2

Chapter 5

LET'S TALK ABOUT IT

Thin, sunken, sharp, beard, ears, gray, solemn, complexion, serious

NARNIAC ATTACK #17

1. c, 2. b, 3. a, 4. c, 5. b

Chapter 6

KID TEST

1. b, 2. Goliath, 3. King Kong, 4. Jolly Green Giant, 5. Jack

EAR EXAM

necks, drowned

Chapter 8

EAR EXAM

a wooden horse on wheels

Chapter 9

LET'S TALK ABOUT IT

steady, back, quickly, run

LOOK IT UP

1. nine
2. boy
3. stone
4. cut it off

Chapter 10

NARNIAC ATTACK #18

1. b, 2. b, 3. c, 4. c, 5. c

Chapter 11

EAR EXAM

She was at the diggings.

Chapter 13

LET'S TALK ABOUT IT

chewed

KID TEST

1. wiggle, Puddleglum
2. dungeon, slavery
3. lady, lord

LOOK IT UP

All of the above! See 2 Corinthians 11:24-25.

EAR EXAM

Coalblack

Chapter 14
Let's Talk About It
good, funeral

Chapter 15
Narniac Attack #19
1. b, 2. c, 3. b, 4. a, 5. c, 6. a

Chapter 16
One-Sentence Edition
wall, Narnia, quest, signs, Puddleglum, giants, eaten, gnomes, Queen, castle, Knight, silver, Rilian, enchant, serpent, head, Underland, Jill, Narnia, King, Aslan, bullies, House

The Last Battle

Chapter 1
Kid Test
3 and 4

Chapter 2
Let's Talk About it
squirrels, Stag, Calormen, Badger

Ear Exam
beech

Chapter 4
Narniac Attack #20
1. b, 2. c, 3. c, 4. c, 5. b

Chapter 6
Ear Exam
Spear

Chapter 7
Look It Up
gold

Chapter 9
Narniac Attack #21
1. b, 2. c, 3. c, 4. a, 5. c

Chapter 12
Ear Exam
saw his horn off and make him draw a cart

Chapter 13
Narniac Attack #22
1. b, 2. c, 3. a, 4. b, 5. c

Chapter 15
Let's Talk About It
boys, girls

Kid Test
ostrich, elephant's, gold, gold, furnace

Narniac Final Exam
(Each answer is followed by the book title and chapter number where you can look it up.)

Part 1. Who Said That?
1. Puddleglum, *Silver Chair* 8
2. Jill, *Silver Chair* 11
3. Mr. Beaver, *Lion* 8
4. Trufflehunter, *Prince Caspian* 12
5. Aslan, *Prince Caspian* 15
6. Trumpkin, *Prince Caspian* 3
7. Caspian, *Voyage* 15

8. Queen Jadis, *Magician* 5

9. Eustace, *Voyage* 3

10. King Tirian, *Last Battle* 6

11. Lasaraleen, *Horse* 7

12. Digory, *Magician* 13

13. Lucy, *Voyage* 16

14. Peter, *Prince Caspian* 13

15. Jill, *Last Battle* 9

16. Jewel, *Last Battle* 12

17. Edmund, *Lion* 9

18. Reepicheep, *Voyage* 12

19. Hwin, *Horse* 14

20. Prince Rilian, *Silver Chair* 13

Part 2. Can You Ruminate in Riddles?

1. Uncle Andrew, *Magician* 1, 11, 7, 2

2. White Witch, *Lion* 3, 3, 4, 2 and 16

3. Lasaraleen, *Horse* 7

4. Reepicheep, *Prince Caspian* 14, 15, 15, *Voyage* 16 and *Last Battle* 16

5. Dufflepuds, *Voyage* 11, 11, 9, 11

6. Puddleglum, *Silver Chair* 5–16

7. Jewel, *Last Battle* 2 and 11, 6, 2, 2

8. Eustace, *Silver Chair* 10, *Voyage* 2, *Voyage* 6, *Voyage* 3

9. Shift, *Last Battle* 3, 3, 7, 1 and 3

10. Queen Jadis, *Magician* 7, 5 and 7–9, 5, 6 and 15

Part 3. The Honest Truth About Girls and Boys

1. c, *Prince Caspian* 9

2. a, *Horse* 14, *Last Battle* 16

3. d, *Horse* 3

4. a, *Last Battle* 5

5. b, *Lion* 7

6. d, *Horse* 15

7. c, *Prince Caspian* 14

8. c, *Magician* 4

9. a, *Voyage* 13

10. b, *Last Battle* 12

Part 4. Details, Details

1. Pittencream, *Voyage* 14

2. Corin Thunder-Fist, *Horse* 15

3. Mabel, *Magician* 7, 15

4. Three, *Prince Caspian* 6

5. Gold, *Prince Caspian* 2

6. Tumnus's father's, *Lion* 6

7. Arm, *Prince Caspian* 3

8. Sixteen, *Prince Caspian* 2

9. Purple, *Voyage* 1

10. Square, *Voyage* 1

Part 5. Animals, Creatures, & Vegetables

1. a, *Prince Caspian* 8

2. b, *Prince Caspian* 11

3. d, *Prince Caspian* 13

4. a, *Magician* 9

5. c, *Prince Caspian* 5 and 7

6. c, *Silver Chair* 10

7. d, *Prince Caspian* 9

8. d, *Prince Caspian* 7

9. b, *Prince Caspian* 9

10. c, *Magician* 13

Part 6. Stumpers for Smarty-Pants

1. Maugrim the Wolf, *Lion* 6
2. Digory, *Magician* 12
3. Lucy, *Prince Caspian* 10
4. Uncle Andrew, *Magician* 14
5. Caspian's nurse, *Prince Caspian* 14, and Reepicheep, *Prince Caspian* 15
6. Mr. Beaver got home (dam) improvements; Mrs. Beaver got a new sewing machine, *Lion* 10
7. Queen Susan, *Lion* 17
8. Puddleglum's, *Silver Chair* 15
9. Mrs. Beaver, *Lion* 7, and Shift the Ape, *Last Battle* 1
10. Hwin and Bree, *Horse* 15
11. Lucy (for tending too long to Edmund, *Lion* 17; for blaming her siblings, *Prince Caspian* 10; for eavesdropping, *Voyage* 10)
12. Talking to Digory about his mom, *Magician* 12, and when Caspian died, *Silver Chair* 16
13. Never
14. Caspian's nurse, *Prince Caspian* 14
15. Reepicheep and Trufflehunter, *Prince Caspian* 15

Part 7. The Profile of Evil

1. F, *Magician* 5
2. F, *Lion* 4 and *Magician* 13
3. T, *Magician* 2
4. F, *Silver Chair* 11
5. F, *Magician* 13
6. F, *Last Battle* 1, 3, 6
7. T, *Horse* 13
8. F, *Last Battle* 7–8
9. T, *Lion* 13
10. T, *Lion* 15

Part 8. What Aslan Said

1. evil, myself, *Magician* 11
2. soon, *Voyage* 11
3. same, twice, *Prince Caspian* 10
4. scolding, *Silver Chair* 16
5. in, up, *Last Battle* 14
6. stream, *Silver Chair* 2
7. belief, *Last Battle* 13
8. courage, *Voyage* 12
9. good, *Magician* 12
10. lonely, mane, walk, *Lion* 14
11. way, *Magician* 12
12. like, *Magician* 14
13. called, *Silver Chair* 2
14. proof, *Prince Caspian* 15
15. holidays, *Last Battle* 16

Part 9. What the Storyteller Said

1. b, *Magician* 10
2. c, *Magician* 10
3. a, *Lion* 9
4. c, *Horse* 6
5. b, *Horse* 9
6. a, *Lion* 16
7. c, *Voyage* 1
8. a, *Silver Chair* 2
9. c, *Silver Chair* 12
10. b, *Last Battle* 8

Part 10. Big Ideas for Narniacs

1. b, *Prince Caspian* 10
2. b, *Voyage* 16
3. a, *Prince Caspian* 2
4. c, *Lion* 14–15
5. b, *Magician* 6–8, 11
6. c, *Voyage* 12
7. c, *Prince Caspian* 10 and *Voyage* 10
8. a, *Horse* 10
9. c, *Horse* 11, 14
10. a, *Last Battle* 16

NARNIAC FINAL EXAM FOR LITTLE ONES

Part 1. Animal Alphabet

1. Reepicheep, *Prince Caspian* 6
2. Puddleglum, *Silver Chair* 5
3. Jewel, *Last Battle* 2
4. Puzzle, *Last Battle* 1
5. Maugrim, *Lion* 9
6. Trumpkin, *Prince Caspian* 5
7. Bree, *Horse* 1
8. Fledge, *Magician* 12
9. Rumblebuffin, *Lion* 16
10. Glimfeather, *Silver Chair* 3

Part 2. Beautiful but Very Bad

1. c, *Magician* 7
2. b, *Magician* 5
3. c, *Silver Chair* 6, 12

4. b, *Lion* 4
5. b, *Silver Chair* 11, 15

Part 3. What's Wrong with This Story?

1. c, *Voyage* 6–7
2. b, *Lion* 2
3. a, *Silver Chair* 5
4. c, *Horse* 2
5. b, *Magician* 2

Part 4. Bravo for the Brave!

1. Reepicheep, *Prince Caspian* 15
2. Jill, *Last Battle* 6
3. Digory, *Magician* 2
4. Puddleglum, *Silver Chair* 12
5. Jewel, *Last Battle* 2
6. Peter, *Prince Caspian* 13
7. Shasta, *Horse* 1
8. Lucy, *Prince Caspian* 10–11
9. Digory, *Magician* 12–13
10. Aslan, *Lion* 14

Part 5. All About Aslan

1. a, *Magician* 8–9
2. b, *Lion* 8
3. c, *Lion* 15, *Prince Caspian* 10, 14
4. a, *Lion* 15
5. b, *Last Battle* 16

Sources for Part 4 Essays

Seeing Through the Mist

Kilby, Clyde S. "The Aesthetic Poverty of Evangelicalism," from *The Christian Imagination*. Colorado Springs: Shaw, 2002.

Lewis, C. S. *Letters to Children*. Edited by Lyle W. Dorsett and Marjorie Lamp Mead. New York: MacMillan Publishing Co., 1985.

Lewis, C. S. *On Stories*. New York: Harcourt, 1982.

Manlove, Colin. *Christian Fantasy*. Notre Dame: University of Notre Dame Press, 1992.

Unicorns, Myth & Mystery

Giblin, James Cross. *The Truth About Unicorns*. New York: HarperCollins, 1991.

Shepard, Odell. *The Lore of the Unicorn*. New York: Avenel Books, 1982.

Williamson, John. *The Oak King, The Holly King, and the Unicorn: The Myths and Symbolism of the Unicorn Tapestries*. New York: Harper & Row, 1986.

Just Say "Boo!"

Miller, Laura. "Oz vs. Narnia." Salon.com, December 28, 2000. http://archive.salon.com/books/feature/2000/12/28/baum/index.html (accessed July 26, 2005).

Color & Culture in Narnia

Lewis, C. S. *The Four Loves*. New York: Harcourt Brace Jovanovich, 1960.

Resources for Narniacs

We relied on a number of excellent resources in the writing of *Roar!* Where possible, these have been cited in the text, but because we were creating a family resource, we chose not to use footnotes. Of the many resources available, we especially recommend the following:

Ditchfield, Christin. *A Family Guide to Narnia*. Wheaton IL: Crossway Books, 2003.

Duriez, Colin. *A Field Guide to Narnia*. Downers Grove, IL: InterVarsity Press, 2004.

Ford, Paul. *Companion to Narnia*. San Francisco, CA: HarperSanFrancisco, 1980.

Karkainen, Paul A. *Narnia Explored*. Old Tappan, NJ: Revell, 1979.

Lindskoog, Kathryn. *Journey into Narnia*. Pasadena, CA: Hope Publishing House, 1998.

Sammons, Martha C. *A Guide Through Narnia, Revised and Expanded Edition*. Vancouver, BC: Regent College Publishing, 2004.

Sayer, George. *Jack*. San Fransisco: Harper & Row, 1988.

Sibley, Brian. *Through the Shadowlands*. Old Tappan, NJ: Revell, 1985.

Sibley, Brian. *The Land of Narnia*. San Francisco, CA: Harper Collins, 1989.

About Our Contributors

Marcus Brotherton is a journalist, writing collaborator, and ordained minister. He holds an M.A. in theology from Talbot Seminary at Biola University. He has written thousands of articles including investigative news, features, and profiles. Marcus was born in Canada. He lives with his wife, Mary Margaret, and two-year-old daughter, Addy, in Washington.

Mark Buchanan is a pastor and award-winning author who lives with his wife, Cheryl, and three children on the west coast of Canada. Educated at the University of British Columbia and Regent College, he has been published in numerous periodicals, including *Christianity Today* and *Books and Culture*. His books include *Your God Is Too Safe*, *Things Unseen*, *The Holy Wild*, and the upcoming, *The Rest of God* (W Publishing).

Erin Healy is the owner of WordWright Editorial Services and is a full-time wife, mom, editor, writer, and wannabe film editor from Colorado. She edits novels and works regularly with fantasy writers such as Ted Dekker, Shane Johnson, and L. B. Graham. She is the former editor of *Christian Parenting Today* and thinks a lot about writing her own novel...tomorrow. *The Silver Chair* is her favorite of the Chronicles, maybe because Puddleglum is her doppelganger, but he was fit for Aslan's service anyway.

Kristen Johnson Ingram is the author of thousands of articles and twenty-two nonfiction books, including *Revealed: Spiritual Reality in a Makeover World* (Revell); *Wine at the End of the Feast* (Loyola, 2003); *Beyond Words: 15 Ways of Doing Prayer* (Morehouse, 2004); and the gift book *I'll Ask My Grandmother: She's Very Wise* (Barbour, 1999). She has also published two murder mysteries. When she isn't writing or teaching writing, Kristen enjoys travel, photography, cooking, and spending time with her husband, Ron, her five grandsons and great-granddaughter, and her eighteen-pound criminal cat, Grendel.

J. I. PACKER is Board of Governors Professor of Theology at Regent College in Vancouver, British Columbia. He also serves as a contributing editor to *Christianity Today.* Packer's writings include books such as *A Quest for Godliness* (Crossway), *Growing in Christ* (Crossway), and *Rediscovering Holiness* (Servant) and numerous articles published in journals such as *Churchman, SouthWestern Journal, Christianity Today, Reformation & Revival Journal,* and *Touchstone.*

LAURIE WINSLOW SARGENT is the author of *Delight in Your Child's Design: How to Better Understand, Nurture, and Enjoy Your Child's Unique Traits and Temperament* (Tyndale, 2005) and *The Power of Parent-Child Play* (2003), and a contributor to numerous other books and magazines. Laurie speaks frequently to parent groups nationwide to inspire more joyful, purposeful parenting. For tips and event information, visit www.ParentChildPlay.com.

BRIAN THOMASSON is the dad of Elliot, Emmae, Cambria, and Will and the husband of his beloved Jennifer Lynn. Sometimes he runs up the stairs shouting, "Further up and further in!"

ACKNOWLEDGMENTS

This book could not have happened without the help of a lot of people. First among them, we thank Don Jacobson, publisher, for jump-starting our thinking on a Multnomah Narnia project for families. Also for the trust he extended to the creative team as *Roar!* began to take shape, and for his good advice along the way.

For their support and excellent ideas, we are grateful to many other Multnomah folk: Kristina Coulter, Eric Weber, Kimberly Brock, Jason Myhre, Brian Thomasson, Jay Echternach, Darren Henry, David Sheets, Kim Shurley, Kristin Paul, Steffany Woolsey, Tiffany Lauer, and Brian Flagler, among many others.

We appreciate and respect our contributing writers, whose work has greatly enhanced the book: J. I. Packer, Marcus Brotherton, Laurie Winslow Sargent, Erin Healy, Brian Thomasson, Kristen Johnson Ingram, and Mark Buchanan. Special thanks to Holly Halverson for her assistance in compiling our indexes.

On the visual side, we have been privileged to work with illustrator Martin French. His amazing talents and personal passion for *Roar!* have blessed us immensely. Same goes for our gifted designer, David Carlson of Gearbox, who proved to be a perfect match for the project. Special thanks also to Katherine Lloyd, typesetter, for her enthusiasm and hard work.

And finally we are profoundly grateful for our copyeditor, the truly remarkable Lisa Bowden. Without her knowledge, good judgment, and persistence, errors and embarrassment would have abounded.

AUTHORS AND ILLUSTRATOR

Heather Kopp is an editor, bestselling author, and a Narnia fan since childhood. Her dozens of books include the God's Little Book of Guarantees series and the bestselling *The Dieter's Prayer Book*. She also coauthored *Because I Said Forever*. Kopp and her writer/editor husband, David, have five adult children and live in Central Oregon.

David Kopp is the founding editor of *Christian Parenting Today* magazine and worked with Bruce Wilkinson as his writing partner and editor on the bestselling *The Prayer of Jabez, Secrets of the Vine,* and other books. David grew up in a missionary family in Africa (where, as a proper British school-boy, he sang "God Save the Queen!" every school-day morning).

Martin French grew up in the San Francisco Bay Area and graduated from ArtCenter College of Design in Pasadena, California. His clients include *The Atlantic Monthly*, Apple Computers, Inc., ESPN, the Grammy national music awards, and Scholastic. Martin has received awards of excellence from *Communication Arts, Graphis, 3x3,* and the Society of Illustrators which granted him the Gold Medal in 1999. He has illustrated five books including the award-winning *The Song Shoots Out of My Mouth* by Jamie Adoff. Martin lives with his family in the Pacific Northwest.

ALL ABOUT RoarofNarnia.com

If you are enjoying Roar! *you'll also want to visit our website, RoarofNarnia.com. There you can:*

- Talk to other Narniacs in our forum about everything Narnian
- Ask our online "Professor Narniac (DLF)" important questions about the Chronicles
- Download the Narniac Final Exam and the Narniac Final Exam for Little Ones
- Learn more about illustrator Martin French and his artwork
- Win free copies of *Roar!* artwork
- Find links to other popular Chronicles of Narnia sites, especially for Christian families
- Learn the latest news on upcoming Chronicles of Narnia films
- Find crossword puzzles and other fun quizzes, tests, and activities that aren't included in *Roar!*
- Find *Roar!*-related materials created especially for homeschoolers